Foreign Trade Regimes
and Economic Development:
GHANA

Foreign Trade Regimes and Economic Development:

A Special Conference Series on Foreign Trade Regimes and Economic Development

VOLUME II

NATIONAL BUREAU OF ECONOMIC RESEARCH

New York   1974

GHANA

by **J. Clark Leith**

UNIVERSITY OF WESTERN ONTARIO

DISTRIBUTED BY Columbia University Press
New York and London

NATIONAL BUREAU OF ECONOMIC RESEARCH

A Special Conference Series on Foreign Trade Regimes and Economic Development

Library of Congress Card Number: 74–77690
ISBN for the series: 0–87014–500–2
ISBN for this volume: 0–87014–502–9

Printed in the United States of America

Relation of the Directors of the National Bureau to Publication of the Country Studies in the Series on Foreign Trade Regimes and Economic Development

Contents

Tables

Figures

Charts

Co-Directors' Foreword

This volume is one of a series resulting from the research project on Exchange Control, Liberalization, and Economic Development sponsored by the National Bureau of Economic Research, the name of the project having been subsequently broadened to Foreign Trade Regimes and Economic Development. Underlying the project was the belief by all participants that the phenomena of exchange control and liberalization in less developed countries require careful and detailed analysis within a sound theoretical framework, and that the effects of individual policies and restrictions cannot be analyzed without consideration of both the nature of their administration and the economic environment within which they are adopted as determined by the domestic economic policy and structure of the particular country.

The research has thus had three aspects: (1) development of an analytical framework for handling exchange control and liberalization; (2) within that framework, research on individual countries, undertaken independently by senior scholars; and (3) analysis of the results of these independent efforts with a view to identifying those empirical generalizations that appear to emerge from the experience of the countries studied.

The analytical framework developed in the first stage was extensively commented upon by those responsible for the research on individual countries, and was then revised to the satisfaction of all participants. That framework, serving as the common basis upon which the country studies were undertaken, is further reflected in the syntheses reporting on the third aspect of the research.

The analytical framework pinpointed these three principal areas of research which all participants undertook to analyze for their own countries.

Subject to a common focus on these three areas, each participant enjoyed maximum latitude to develop the analysis of his country's experience in the way he deemed appropriate. Comparison of the country volumes will indicate that this freedom was indeed utilized, and we believe that it has paid handsome dividends. The three areas singled out for in-depth analysis in the country studies are:

1. *The anatomy of exchange control:* The economic efficiency and distributional implications of alternative methods of exchange control in each country were to be examined and analyzed. Every method of exchange control differs analytically in its effects from every other. In each country study care has been taken to bring out the implications of the particular methods of control used. We consider it to be one of the major results of the project that these effects have been brought out systematically and clearly in analysis of the individual countries' experience.

2. *The liberalization episode:* Another major area for research was to be a detailed analysis of attempts to liberalize the payments regime. In the analytical framework, devaluation and liberalization were carefully distinguished, and concepts for quantifying the extent of devaluation and of liberalization were developed. It was hoped that careful analysis of individual devaluation and liberalization attempts, both successful and unsuccessful, would permit identification of the political and economic ingredients of an effective effort in that direction.

3. *Growth relationships:* Finally, the relationship of the exchange control regime to growth via static-efficiency and other factors was to be investigated. In this regard, the possible effects on savings, investment allocation, research and development, and entrepreneurship were to be highlighted.

In addition to identifying the three principal areas to be investigated, the analytical framework provided a common set of concepts to be used in the studies and distinguished various phases regarded as useful in tracing the experience of the individual countries and in assuring comparability of the analyses. The concepts are defined and the phases delineated in Appendix F.

The country studies undertaken within this project and their authors are as follows:

Brazil	Albert Fishlow, University of California, Berkeley
Chile	Jere R. Behrman, University of Pennsylvania
Colombia	Carlos F. Diaz-Alejandro, Yale University
Egypt	Bent Hansen, University of California, Berkeley, and Karim Nashashibi, International Monetary Fund
Ghana	J. Clark Leith, University of Western Ontario

India	Jagdish N. Bhagwati, Massachusetts Institute of Technology, and T. N. Srinivasan, Indian Statistical Institute
Israel	Michael Michaely, The Hebrew University of Jerusalem
Philippines	Robert E. Baldwin, University of Wisconsin
South Korea	Charles R. Frank, Jr., Princeton University and The Brookings Institution; Kwang Suk Kim, Korea Development Institute, Republic of Korea; and Larry E. Westphal, Northwestern University
Turkey	Anne O. Krueger, University of Minnesota

The principal results of the different country studies are brought together in our overall syntheses. Each of the country studies, however, has been made self-contained, so that readers interested in only certain of these studies will not be handicapped.

In undertaking this project and bringing it to successful completion, the authors of the individual country studies have contributed substantially to the progress of the whole endeavor, over and above their individual research. Each has commented upon the research findings of other participants, and has made numerous suggestions which have improved the overall design and execution of the project. The country authors who have collaborated with us constitute an exceptionally able group of development economists, and we wish to thank all of them for their cooperation and participation in the project.

We must also thank the National Bureau of Economic Research for its sponsorship of the project and its assistance with many of the arrangements necessary in an undertaking of this magnitude. Hal B. Lary, Vice President-Research, has most energetically and efficiently provided both intellectual and administrative input into the project over a three-year period. We would also like to express our gratitude to the Agency for International Development for having financed the National Bureau in undertaking this project. Michael Roemer and Constantine Michalopoulos particularly deserve our sincere thanks.

JAGDISH N. BHAGWATI
Massachusetts Institute of Technology

ANNE O. KRUEGER
University of Minnesota

Preface

In 1969 the University of Ghana invited the University of Western Ontario to join in a twinning arrangement between their two Departments of Economics, sponsored by the Canadian International Development Agency. The details were quickly worked out, and a team of Western Ontario faculty members including myself were seconded to the University of Ghana starting with the 1969–70 academic year. My family and I spent two delightful years in Ghana: we affectionately remember the kind hospitality of our hosts.

My research interests focused on the foreign sector of the Ghanaian economy. Issues such as the failure of the import-substitution strategy as an engine of growth, the deteriorating export performance, and the effect of the exchange control and licencing system attracted my attention. I had barely begun to investigate these issues when I was asked to join the National Bureau of Economic Research project on Exchange Control, Liberalization and Economic Development, and in particular to contribute a study on Ghana. This monograph is the result.

In the process of completing this study I have incurred numerous intellectual debts. The other participants in the project all contributed a great deal to a sharpening of my own thoughts on the issues tackled, and their specific criticisms forced me to rethink and attempt to clarify many parts. Hal Lary of the National Bureau provided leadership and organization for us all. The co-directors of the project, Anne Krueger and Jagdish Bhagwati, deserve thanks for their sustained efforts to improve my work. Yet each of the authors in this project was given great scope to pursue issues and interpretations his own way.

As a result, the approach I have taken and the conclusions I have reached are clearly my own.

Numerous people in Ghana contributed to this study. My principal research assistant in Ghana was S. M. Ntim who handled the task of collecting, organizing and analyzing a considerable amount of the material contained in this study. His unstinting efforts are greatly appreciated. In addition, for shorter periods J. K. Afful and J. A. Sackey helped out as research assistants.

At the University of Ghana many of my colleagues and students were generous in the time and patience they devoted to educating me about Ghana and its economic problems. I also benefited from the thoughtful comments made at various sessions of the Economic Research Workshop Seminars of the Economics Department in Legon where I presented early drafts of several parts of this study. At the risk of singling out one particular colleague, I would like to thank J. B. Abban whose role in discussions and in assisting in obtaining the data for Chapter III was a great help. Typing of early drafts of some sections was cheerfully done by G. T. Adjabeng, B. K. Freeman, and E. M. Qudozia.

At the Ministry of Finance, Ministry of Trade and Industries, Bank of Ghana, Customs and Excise, and the Central Bureau of Statistics I was received with great courtesy and provided with considerable cooperation. The data made available and background information contributed by officials of these agencies have been crucial in completing this study.

Economist friends from various parts of the world contributed very helpful comments on several parts of the study. Peter O'Brien commented extensively on drafts of most chapters. Tony Killick, John Odling-Smee, Michael Roemer, Joseph Stern, and Max Steuer, as well as my colleagues on the Western Ontario Team in Legon—Ake Blomqvist, Merritt Brown and Edward Vickery—all commented on various sections.

In the summer of 1971 I returned to the University of Western Ontario to complete this study. In doing so I benefited greatly from the facilities provided by the Ghana Development Workshop which is funded by the Canadian International Development Agency as part of the twinning arrangement with the University of Ghana. Mrs. Ellen Hall, the Workshop Research Assistant cheerfully and energetically carried a substantial load in collecting and organizing material for me. The members of the Ghana Development Workshop, and also the Trade Workshop, deserve my thanks for their insightful comments on several sections. Typing of numerous drafts and of the final manuscript was very competently and willingly handled by Mrs. M. Gower along with Miss Y. Bowman, Mrs. J. Dewar, Mrs. F. Scott, and Mrs. S. Webster.

Finally, Carole Ann, my wife, and the children, who so enthusiastically accepted Ghana and patiently put up with my preoccupation with this study, deserve a very special mention.

All of those named must share the credit. Yet in the end, the responsibility for the study as a whole rests with me. Shortcomings, and perhaps errors, inevitably remain: for these I accept full blame.

J. Clark Leith

Principal Dates

1844	Signing of "The Bond" by coastal chiefs, in which they acknowledged British jurisdiction (March 6 to December 2).
1874	Gold Coast declared a British colony.
1896	Ashanti forced to submit to British "protection."
1902	Ashanti becomes a British colony and the Northern Territories Protectorate established.
1916	Six Africans included in Legislative Council.
1922	British Togoland mandate from League of Nations, to be administered as part of the Gold Coast Colony.
1946	African majority in Legislative Council.
1948	Political agitation against 1946 constitution.
1951	Internal self-government granted in new constitution. Election landslide by Convention Peoples Party (C P P), led by Nkrumah who was then released from jail to lead government.
1954, 1956	Further elections won by CPP under Nkrumah as Prime Minister.
1957	Independence, with Nkrumah as Prime Minister (March 6, exactly one hundred and thirteen years after signing of first Bond).
1960	Ghana becomes a republic within the Commonwealth and Nkrumah becomes President (Chief of State and head of government).
1961	Exchange control and import licencing severely tightened (July and December).

1964   CPP becomes sole party.

1966   Military *coup d'état* overthrows Nkrumah and establishes the government of the National Liberation Council (February).

1967   Devaluation from N₵ .71 per dollar to N₵ 1.02 per dollar (July). Liberalization of imports begun and continued for next four and one-half years.

1969   Elections under new constitution won by Progress Party, government led by Busia, who became Prime Minister (August and October).

1971   Devaluation from N₵ 1.02 per dollar to N₵ 1.82 per dollar (December).

1972   Military *coup d'état* overthrows Busia government and establishes National Redemption Council. Revaluation from N₵ 1.82 per dollar to N₵ 1.28 per dollar and controls reimposed (January and February).

CHAPTER I

Introduction

"At long last the battle has ended!...
Ghana is Free Forever!"
Kwame Nkrumah, 6 March, 1957.[1]

Ghana was independent. A society whose roots lay in the powerful Negro empires of the Sudanic civilization that had flourished from the time of Europe's Dark Ages through the early twentieth century, was now launched as a modern state, the first black African country to do so. In terms of modern Western criteria, Ghana had a promising start as one of the richest, most successful and politically mature regions of black Africa. Per capita income was reportedly the highest, real growth was satisfactory, sterling reserves substantial, and development plans were well formulated.

The new Ghana was again an empire with sovereignty over many traditionall kingdoms.[2] But the new state retained the European socioeconomic institutions and system of organization that had been built up over the previous decades as a colony. The colonial system was well designed to facilitate intervention by the central political state in social and economic affairs for the further transformation of society. And it was put to work to achieve that end. Prime Minister Nkrumah became President (1960), and his party became the sole party (1964). Economic planning, state enterprises, foreign exchange licencing and control, and internal price controls were employed. However, a national consensus about the rules of the game, both politically and economically, was not reached. President Nkrumah's system was rejected by a military *coup* in early 1966.

The National Liberation Council (NLC) government formed by the military was committed to the re-establishment of a relatively free political and

1. From his speech on the moment of independence, quoted in his *I Speak of Freedom*, Praeger, New York, 1961, pp. 106-107.
2. The ancient empire of Ghana was one of the early Sudanic empires, physically located in present-day Mali. J.B. Danquah was largely responsible for the hypothesis of a connection between the largest present-day language group in Ghana, the Akans, and the ancient Ghana. His work on this began in the late 1920's and 1930's, and when the time came to choose a name for the independent Gold Coast colony, his choice was adopted. He sets out his views in "The Akan Claim to Origin from Ghana," *West African Review*, Vol. XXVI, Nov. and Dec., 1955, pp. 963-70 and 1107-11.

economic system. In 1969, at the end of a brief period of three years, it turned the reins of government over to a freely elected civilian Parliament led by Prime Minister Busia. In the meantime the NLC had begun to relax the economic controls. The Busia government pushed forward with the liberalization of the economic system, but failed to solve a serious balance of payments problem that accompanied it. In a little over two years, on January 13, 1972, the experiments of civilian government and economic liberalization ended in another military coup.

Now, some fifteen years after the self-confident declarations of independence day, there was a sense of uncertainty about just what the political and economic system of Ghana should be. While the system was open to question, the capacity of Ghana to find its own way was not. Most observers would argue, as Danquah had elegantly asserted a decade earlier,

> 'All my life I have pinned my faith in the Ghanaian, that he is sensible and is capable of thinking as a human being. I do not wish to lose my faith in Ghana! May God help my faith ' [3]

This book concerns an important part of the economic experimentation undertaken during those first fifteen years of independence — the system of exchange control and the attempted liberalization. To illuminate in as much detail as possible its workings and effects, we confine our attention almost entirely to the control system.[4] We begin with a review of the evolution of the restrictive system (Chapter II) in which we examine the workings of the instruments brought to bear on the foreign sector. The restrictive regime affected the Ghanaian economy in two major ways: resource allocation and growth. In Chapter III we consider the allocative effects, using a variety of indicators, including our detailed estimates of effective rates of protection for the industrial sector. Then, in Chapter IV we consider the growth effects, paying particular attention to the capital market and input intensities. In the short span of five years the control system was discredited, and Ghana attempted to extricate herself from it with a gradual liberalization. Chapter V

---

3. J.B. Danquah, January 1, 1963, quoted in *Danquah — An Immortal of Ghana*, compiled by the Danquah Funeral Committee, Geo. Boakie Publishing Co., Accra, 1968. Danquah, "The Doyen of Ghanaian Politics," spoke these words six months after his release from his penultimate detention, only two years before his death while under Nkrumah's detention again.
4. We do so at the cost of providing too much detail and too narrow a focus for the reader interested in a broader survey of the Ghanaian economy. One such survey already exists, in W. Birmingham, I. Neustadt, and E.N. Omaboe, eds., *A Study of Contemporary Ghana*, Vol. 1, *The Economy of Ghana*, Northwestern University Press, Evanston, 1966, largely containing the careful research of Tony Killick and Robert Szresczewski; some more up-to-date surveys are in preparation.

deals with the attempted liberalization, beginning with a detailed consideration of the first step, devaluation, and followed by a review of the nature, timing, and magnitude of the steps taken to liberalize the system. Finally, in Chapter VI we bring together the major conclusions we have drawn from the study.

CHAPTER II

Evolution of the restrictive system

1. Introduction[1]

The early 1960's marked a major change in the direction of Ghanaian external economic policy. A relatively free system of international trade and payments was replaced by a restrictive foreign-exchange regime involving licencing and exchange control. The consequences for the structure and performance of the Ghanaian economy were profound. In this chapter we set the stage by examining the evolution of the system.

The history of the restrictive exchange regime is one of hasty introduction, difficult implementation, frequent change, organized corruption, serious shortages, and finally an attempted liberalization. To provide an overview of the history we begin in section 2 by characterizing the system as a series of phases (see also Appendix F-2). Given the outline provided by the phases, we analyze in subsequent sections the various instruments used to influence the foreign-exchange market, reporting several indicators of restrictiveness. There has been a great variety of instruments available and used; some consciously adopted to achieve foreign-exchange objectives, others only inadvertently brought to bear on the situation. First, there are those such as taxes and subsidies on trade which introduce an explicit price differential and leave quantities to adjust. These are treated in section 3. Second, some instruments operate by affecting the financing available for foreign transactions. These we deal with in section 4. Third, there are instruments such as licences which restrict quantities and leave the corresponding domestic prices to adjust. We discuss these in section 5. Finally, there are instruments such as fiscal and monetary policies which affect the levels of aggregate demand and overall domestic prices. We consider these instruments in section 6, not so much because they were heavily relied upon but more because they were frequently

---

1. This chapter draws heavily on both the documentary record and interviews with Ghanaian officials past and present. While exonerating the latter from any responsibility for what is contained here, I wish to acknowledge their generous assistance. In particular, I would like to single out for special thanks S.K. Botchway, R.K.O. Djang, H.P. Nelson, J. Phillips, and Dr. J. Ofori-Atta. Valuable research assistance for this chapter was provided at various stages by M. Behkish, E. Hall, and S.M. Ntim.

forgotten in the proliferation of approaches to the foreign exchange problem. [2]

It is important to keep in mind that all instruments will affect the exchange regime's restrictiveness. Hence in the following delineation of phases based on varying degrees of restrictiveness we have attempted to take an overview of the entire set, even though most of our quantitative indicators refer only to taxes on trade.

2. Delineation of phases

The Ghanaian experience with a restrictive foreign-exchange regime has been one of both sudden and gradual changes, making a precise delineation of phases subject to a necessarily arbitrary selection of dates. [3] With this qualification in mind, the following sequence represents a brief survey of the restrictive regime. An overview of the phases set against several key economic variables is contained in Chart II-1.

(a) Liberal regime, 1950–1961 (Phase V)

Ghana, as a member of the sterling area, was subject to the general prescription of currency requirements of the area as a whole. Payments to and from other countries of the area were relatively free while payments to and from countries outside the area were subject to the sterling restrictions. Within this framework Ghana experienced a fairly liberal regime.

The most interesting feature of this period was the rapid buildup of foreign exchange reserves in the boom years of the Korean war, followed by a gradual drawing down of the large reserve accumulation. After independence in 1957 the drawing down of reserves accelerated, still largely within a permissive liberal system (see Table A-3b). The acceleration of reserve loss continued, to the point that in 1961 the payments pressure had become untenable and controls were rapidly imposed.

(b) Imposition of controls, 1961–1963 (Phase I)

A variety of instruments were brought to bear on the rapidly growing balance-of-payments deficit. Initially exchange control was extended to in-

---

2. We do not wish to overdraw the distinctions among the various instruments. For example, stiff new indirect taxes on trade will dampen aggregate demand while implementation of fiscal policy may require changes in taxes on trade. Our distinctions are made largely as a means of organizing the discussion.
3. The phase numbers refer to those set out below, Appendix F-2. Detailed description will be found in J.N. Bhagwati and A.O. Krueger, *Exchange Control, Liberalization, and Development: Experience and Analysis,* forthcoming.

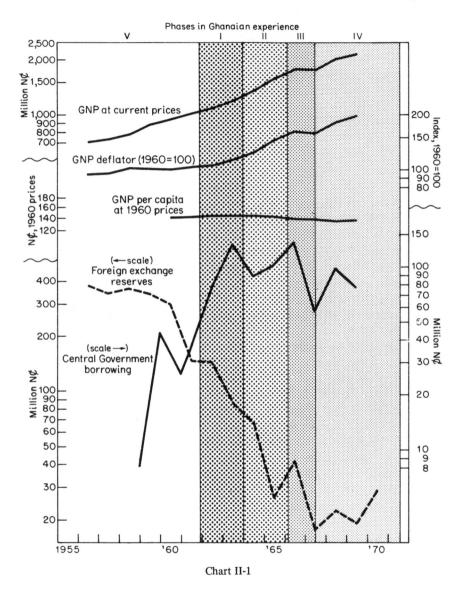

Chart II-1

clude the sterling area, several bilateral trade and payments pacts were launched, and an attempt was made to employ conventional methods to suppress aggregate demand in general and demand for imports in particular. On current account any effect these might have had was swamped by speculative demand for imports in anticipation of licencing. The apparently inevitable application of import licencing came on December 1, 1961.

During 1962 the new restrictive system was sorted out, and was reasonably settled by year end. It continued with a few minor changes during most of 1963. The level and distribution of exchange allocations were based on estimated foreign-exchange availability and perceived national needs (e.g., import-substitution, industrialization, and diversification of trade toward East Bloc countries).

(c) Breakdown of system, 1964–1966 (Phase II)

Beginning in late 1963 the system experienced a variety of changes, the most notable of which was the introduction of substantial corruption in the issue of import licences. Changes in regulations were frequent in a frantic attempt to patch up a system that had one big hole in it: the corrupt and erratic issue of import licences. This culminated in a splurge of imports and massive assumption of short-term debt for 1965. The country was left with a foreign debt amounting to about one-half of Gross Domestic Product (GDP), and no substantial new lines of credit at the time of the *coup d'état* overthrowing President Nkrumah in early 1966.

(d) Austerity and devaluation, 1966–1967 (Phase III)

The military-civilian National Liberation Council (NLC) government that replaced Nkrumah chose to follow a "stabilization" program in which *de jure* the system changed little, but *de facto* involved a resumption of the type of controls employed in 1962 and 1963 (prior to the massive corruption of 1964–1966) combined with the imposition of a substantial expenditure reduction. Temporary relief of payments pressure was also achieved by a major rescheduling of short-term external debt.

It soon became evident to both the government and to outside official agencies supporting its efforts that these policies were not enough to contain the payments pressure. In July 1967 Ghana resorted to major devaluation.

(e) Import liberalization, 1967–1970 (Phase IV)

The devaluation was a turning point in the direction of gradual liberalization of the trade and payments regime. Beginning with a few moves at the time of devaluation and continuing for over three years, both the NLC government and the government of Prime Minister Busia (elected in 1969) gradually reduced the specific import-licence list to the point that by the end of 1970 about 60 per cent of all imports had been removed from the specific licence list. The task of dismantling the complex import-control syster proved difficult, and because many controls still remained in place the ex pected benefits were slow to emerge. Further, a number of strategic error: were made which in the end proved fatal to the import liberalization. Taxes on freed imports were relatively low. Aggregate demand pressure was not contained. And a huge windfall of cocoa export earnings was not treated as such.

(f) Collapse of import liberalization, 1971–1972 (return to Phase I)

When cocoa export revenues resumed more normal levels in 1971 it became evident that external payments were at an unsustainable level. The open deficit would somehow have to be closed. Despite this, imports were further liberalized in mid-1971, and no substantial moves to dampen the demand for imports were taken. As the payments pressure accelerated during late 1971 the need for a quick solution became pressing. Still fully committed to the import liberalization approach they had adopted, only two options appeared feasible to the government: debt relief and devaluation. Very little debt relief was obtained, and the government chose not to repudiate any of the debts. Instead, it settled on a huge devaluation of nearly 80 per cent. The jolt of the sudden reduction in real income implied by the devaluation was too much for the fragile political situation. The military stepped in, with evident popular support, to end both the experiment in democratic government and the import liberalization.

The remainder of this chapter is devoted to a detailed discussion of Phases I, II and III. Phase IV and the return to Phase I are taken up in Chapter V.

3. Taxes on foreign trade

By far the most important and extensively used instruments have been taxes on trade. Initially employed primarily as a source of government revenue, trade taxes came subsequently to be used as a balance-of-payments instrument. Because they have been so significant in the Ghanaian experience they merit extended consideration. We begin by reviewing the mechanisms whereby trade taxes affect the foreign-exchange market, and then examine the magnitudes of taxes employed.

Underlying the generation and use of foreign exchange are the domestic markets in which exporters are paid and importers pay in local currency for the goods and services that are sold on or purchased from international markets. If there are taxes on these transactions the rates at which domestic offers and demands of local currency (new cedis or "N¢") for dollars rise will differ from the rates at which national offers and demands are made. On the export side a tax means that exporters receive fewer new cedis per dollar than the nation does. And on the import side tariffs mean that the importers pay more new cedis per dollar of imports than the nation does. The rates of tax indicate the degree of divergence or "distortion"[4] facing the sellers of exports and purchasers of imports *vis-à-vis* the international market in one way: as rates with respect to the international prices of the goods. These rates can be converted into rates in terms of the foreign-exchange market and subtracted from (export tax) or added to (import tariff) the official exchange rate to yield effective exchange rates: the new cedis earned by an exporter per dollar's worth of exports and the new cedis paid by importers per dollar's worth of imports.

Algebraically, for each of the export and import sides a rate of new cedis per dollar facing the exporter or importer can be expressed in the following manner. For the exporter the new cedi receipts are less than in national export values by proportion of the *ad valorem* export tax rate (t_x). Converting this at the official new cedis per dollar exchange rate (r) yields the effective exchange rate on exports (EER_x):

$$EER_x = 1 - t_x)r. \tag{II.1}$$

Similarly, on the import side where t_m is the *ad valorem* tariff rate on imports, the effective exchange rate on imports (EER_m) is:

$$EER_m = (1 + t_m)r. \tag{II.2}$$

For a number of reasons the effective exchange rate may change without a change in the official exchange rate. Anything that alters the new cedis that purchasers of imports pay for a dollar's worth of imports or exporters receive for a dollar's worth of exports will alter the relevant effective exchange rate. Changes in the rate of export tax or import tariff will clearly change the effective exchange rate. So also will the introduction of some new levy or transfer that is a function of exporting or importing.

Examples of this type of change include the introduction of a compulsory 180-day deferred payment or credit for imports[5] and a 1 percent import licence fee, which add to the degree of distortion and hence increase the effective exchange rate on imports. Further, a change in the *ad valorem* equivalent rate of tax or tariff may come about even in the absence of explicit action. Such is the case of cocoa where the divergence between

---

4. "Distortion" in this sense carries no normative connotation. Rather, it is a concept used in theory to refer to the existence of some change in a relationship. In this case the one to one relationship between domestic and international prices of a tradeable is altered or "distorted" by a trade tax.
5. Payment in foreign exchange to suppliers of imports is deferred 180 days from the time of local currency payment by the importer.

producer receipts and national export receipts is a residual that depends on the arbitrarily fixed producer price[6] and the constantly moving export price. On the import side most tariffs are scheduled at *ad valorem* rates, but exemptions are numerous and arbitrary, yielding constant changes in the average effective import exchange rates even at the most disaggregated level. Putting all these together, we have calculated the rates of trade taxes facing importers and exporters over the period since 1955, and in turn the corresponding effective exchange rates.

(a) Import effective exchange rate

The data for the import side are contained in Table II-1. Note first the gradual proliferation of instruments.[7] For many years only the tariff was used, but in the 1960's the authorities resorted first to a purchase tax,[8] followed by a sales tax,[9] a 180-day compulsory credit scheme,[10] the small import licence fee,[11] and finally surcharges.[12] The overall sum of these instruments traced out a fairly constant path of the effective import-exchange rate from 1955 through 1960, an accelerated rise through 1965, and a decline

6. The producer price at the buying stations scattered throughout the country is fixed without direct reference to the world price and is kept constant for periods ranging up to several years.

7. Omitted from these calculations are the effects of various instruments used to control the financing of foreign trade set out in section 4 below. Their omission is due to their small and generally non-quantifiable effects.

8. Instituted July 1961 and applied almost entirely to imported manufactured goods. Abolished January 1965 on all but motor vehicles in conjunction with increased tariff rates.

9. Applied to both imported and domestic goods, but dampening demand for imports. It is administered as a manufacturer's sales tax. Act dated 21 January, 1965.

10. Instituted March 1965. M.J. Sharpston in his forthcoming study "The Costs of Trade and Tariff Policy: The Case of Ghana," Cambridge University Dept. of Applied Economics, *Occasional Paper*, Chap. 3, develops estimates of the import-cost inflation due to this scheme. His estimates range from 6 percent to 20 percent of the invoice value, depending on the nature of the goods and size of the importer. This is made up of the allowed 6 percent per annum interest cost plus higher prices of goods due to export credit cover, loss of cash discount, and the cost of using confirming houses. As a conservative estimate of the average effect we have assumed an 8 percent of c.i.f. value cost inflation due to this scheme. This is made up of 5 percent higher price charged by suppliers and a 3 percent allowance for interest (at 6 percent per annum). Aid-financed imports and bilateral trade pact imports are not subject to this compulsory credit. However, because of the impossibility of separating out such imports, in our calculations we applied the average minimum inflation of import cost to total imports.

11. Applicable in 1966, 1967 and 1968 only.

12. Begun February 1969; National Liberation Council, *Decree 325*, 11 February, 1969.

TABLE II-1

Price distortions facing total imports and corresponding effective exchange rates, 1955 through 1969 (percentages of c.i.f. value, and new cedis per dollar)

Year	Tariffs	Purchase tax	Sales tax	Surcharge	180-day credit	Import licence fee	Total rate	Absolute change from 1955	Effective exchange rate (N¢/$1)	Percent change in EER from 1955
1955	17.07	—	—	—	—	—	17.07	—	0.8362	—
1956	17.14	—	—	—	—	—	17.14	0.07	0.8367	0.06
1957	17.46	—	—	—	—	—	17.46	0.39	0.8390	0.33
1958	17.61	—	—	—	—	—	17.61	0.54	0.8401	0.47
1959	15.38	—	—	—	—	—	15.38	-1.69	0.8241	-1.45
1960	17.03	—	—	—	—	—	17.03	-0.04	0.8359	-0.04
1961	21.45	0.78	—	—	—	—	22.23	5.16	0.8730	4.40
1962	25.92	1.77	—	—	—	—	27.69	10.62	0.9120	9.06
1963	26.78	1.86	—	—	—	—	28.64	11.57	0.9189	9.89
1964	27.90	2.26	—	—	—	—	30.16	13.09	0.9297	11.18
1965	26.47	0.7	10.89	—	9.87	—	47.93	30.86	1.0566	26.36
1966	30.83	1.11	12.33	—	10.21	1.00	55.48	38.41	1.1105	32.80
1967 A	28.98	1.27	10.57	—	10.04	1.00	51.86	34.79	1.0847	29.71
1967 B	25.89	0.91	9.67	—	9.82	1.00	47.29	30.22	1.5029	79.72
1968	20.10	0.79	5.38	—	9.31	1.00	36.58	19.51	1.3937	66.67
1969	17.07	0.83	4.59	0.82	9.15	—	32.46	15.39	1.3516	61.64
1970	17.02	0.91	7.82	2.56	9.42	—	37.73	20.66	1.4054	68.07
1971	18.57	1.39	7.41	5.71	9.65	—	42.73	25.66	1.4564	74.17

Notes and Sources: See next page.

Notes to Table II-1

Notes: 1. See Appendix B for details at the 1-digit SITC level.
          2. Entry of [−] indicates instrument not operative for year.
          3. 1967A is January through June; 1967B is July through December. Devaluation July 8, 1967.
          4. Exchange rate to July 8, 1967 was N₵ 0.714286/$1, and after was N₵ 1.020408/$1.
          5. The average effective exchange rate for 1967 (weighted by dollar value of imports) is, 1.2717 $1/N₵.
          6. 1971, provisional.
Sources: 1. Import tariff rates calculated from imports and collections data found in CBS, *Quarterly Digest of Statistics,* 1956−1969.
          2. Collections data for purchase tax, sales tax, surcharge, and 1970 and 1971 tariffs supplied by Ghana Customs and Excise. Special thanks for extracting these data are due to Mr. Quaye of the Statistics Section.
          3. The 180-day credit scheme effect calculated on assumption that it increased the c.i.f. price by 5 percent (and hence included in the base for the duty and other collections) plus the allowable 6 percent per annum (*i.e.,* 3 percent of value) interest cost.

from 1965 through 1969: which, however, was more than offset by the 1967 official devaluation. These direct price divergences accounted for a 22 percent devaluation of the import effective exchange rate 1955 through 1971. Taking into account the 43 percent official devaluation in 1967, the effective price of foreign exchange facing importers increased by 75 percent over the period 1955 to 1971.[13]

(b) Export effective exchange rate

     Turning to the export side, trade taxes have been levied in various forms on cocoa, wood and timber, and diamonds.[14] For cocoa, we have included the tax implicit in the Cocoa Marketing Board (CMB) surplus of sales value over purchase and operating costs, while for wood and diamonds we have used simply the government tax receipts. The results (Table II-2) clearly indicate that the major export tax is on cocoa, while wood and diamonds have been subject to very low rates. This, of course, is due to the fact that Ghana has employed the cocoa export tax as a device to obtain monopoly

13. These data are in nominal terms only. We adjust for the price level in Table II-8 below. Note that the effective exchange rate is the product of the import taxes and the exchange rate.
14. Other minerals (bauxite and manganese) were subject to an export tax in earlier years, but in 1952 this was changed to an internal mineral duty, and revised again in 1962. As it now stands the minerals tax is implicitly a royalty payment on a sliding scale, depending on operating costs.

TABLE II-2

Price distortions facing taxed exports and total exports, and corresponding effective exchange rates, 1955 through 1969 (percentages of f.o.b. value and new cedis per dollar)

Year	Cocoa		Wood and timber		Diamonds		Total exports		Total excl. cocoa	
	Tax rate	EER$_x$	Tax rate	EER$_x$	Tax rate	EER$_x$	Tax rate	EER$_x$	Tax rate	EER$_x$
1955	44.74	0.3946	1.67	0.7024	4.89	0.6794	31.26	0.4910	1.4	0.7043
1956	13.22	0.6198	1.99	0.7001	4.93	0.6791	8.55	0.6532	1.74	0.7019
1957	33.79	0.4728	1.72	0.7020	5.04	0.6783	19.61	0.5742	1.58	0.7030
1958	49.55	0.3603	1.93	0.7005	5.20	0.6771	30.86	0.4939	1.65	0.7026
1959	37.07	0.4495	2.26	0.6981	5.04	0.6783	24.00	0.5429	1.76	0.7017
1960	19.68	0.5737	2.94	0.6933	3.87	0.6866	12.36	0.6260	1.90	0.7007
1961	39.70	0.4307	2.88	0.6937	4.34	0.6833	25.68	0.5309	1.85	0.7011
1962	4.04	0.6854	2.95	0.6932	2.69	0.6951	3.07	0.6924	1.45	0.7040
1963	22.73	0.5519	2.98	0.6930	2.98	0.6930	15.80	0.6014	1.52	0.7034
1964	-3.02	0.7358	2.42	0.6970	1.83	0.7012	-1.46	0.7247	1.41	0.7042
1965	54.25	0.3267	3.10	0.6921	0.14	0.7133	51.26	0.3481	1.13	0.7062
1966	40.59	0.4243	3.39	0.6901	0.02	0.7142	35.78	0.4587	1.08	0.7066
1967 A	27.95	0.5146	3.15	0.6918			17.94	0.5861	0.87	0.7081
B		0.7352		0.9883				0.8374		1.012
1968	40.66	0.6055	2.22	0.9977			25.93	0.7558	0.63	1.014
1969	46.87	0.5422	1.92	1.008			30.95	0.7046	0.55	1.015

Note: Total includes taxes on kola nuts (1955 through 1969) and pepper (1968 only).

Sources: 1. For cocoa, our own calculations are employed; using CMB *Annual Reports*, we converted from crop year to calendar year, estimated CMB costs (included in producer costs), and estimated local sales (included in base of exports tax). Details of these calculations are available from the author, on request.

2. All other tax collections and export values from CBS, *Quarterly Digest of Statistics*, 1956 through 1969.

profits from cocoa, while for the other exports such a strategy is not possible because of Ghana's insignificant shares of the world market.

The implicit cocoa export tax exhibits considerable instability, due largely to the policy of fixed producer prices in the face of variable supply and stable cocoa export earnings. Consequently, the changes in implicit tax revenue that emerge are in large part due to the changes in the volume produced and shipped by Ghana.[15] The bumper crop of 1964 is the clearest example of a low tax due to high volume, while in the later 1960's the lower volume meant an increased tax rate. For wood and timber the tax rate rose up to the time of the 1967 devaluation and declined thereafter, due in part to the specific nature of the tax, but mostly to reduced levies that accompanied devaluation. The tax on diamond exports before 1962 was on all diamond exports, but from that date applied only to diamonds won (dug) by African diggers and not to commercial mines which paid instead the internal mineral duty.[16] The officially recorded output of African diggers virtually disappeared in the 1960's, and as a consequence the export tax rate on diamonds on the whole declined to near zero. The tax was eventually abandoned at the time of the devaluation.

Looking at the export and import sides together we see a widening gap between the effective exchange rates facing average importers and average (total) exporters. The upward trend in the import rate since 1960, due to both higher import taxes and the devaluation (which was only slightly offset by lower import taxes), together with the relative constancy of the total export tax rate, meant that the excess of the effective exchange rate on imports over that on total exports rose by about 0.30 N¢ per dollar from 1955 to 1969. If, however, we exclude cocoa from our export calculations, it is clear that the major widening of the gap between the import and export rates took place between 1960 and 1965, with a slight reduction subsequently. Thus in broad terms the discrimination in favor of import-competing production and relatively against non-cocoa export production developed during the period in which quantitative restrictions emerged.

15. On the stability of earnings see J.C. Leith, "Export Concentration and Instability: The Case of Ghana," *Economic Bulletin of Ghana,* Second Series, Vol. 1, No. 1, 1971. The average annual deviation of earnings from trend for cocoa was about 4.4 percent in the period 1957 through 1965. A good crop, for example, leaves total cocoa earnings virtually unchanged as the price falls. Yet producers' incomes rise due to the fixed price they receive, while the tax (which is the residual between producer and total receipts) falls.

16. See note 14 concerning the internal mineral duty.

4. Financing of foreign trade

A further approach used by the Ghanaian government to influence the foreign exchange market consisted of various devices to affect the financing of foreign trade. These differ from taxes on trade in that no measurable explicit commodity price differential is introduced. They are, however, fundamentally similar in that they work through the price system in the commodity market, and do not involve a suspension of the commodity market as licences and controls do.[17]

Three instruments of this type were used: (1) regulation of payment terms, (2) regulation of the credit available for foreign trade, and (3) prior deposits on imports. The first was begun by Exchange Control in early 1962, while the other two were not introduced until April 1964, when the Bank of Ghana assumed an expanded role in the regulation of credit.

(a) Regulation of payment terms

With the institution of exchange control and licencing in 1961 it very quickly became evident to the authorities that improved payment terms on the part of the Ghanaian importer could be used as a method of offsetting suppliers' concern over the new restrictions. This had the unwanted effect of speeding up foreign-exchange payments. Exchange control regulations dealing with payment for imports were therefore issued (February 1962) and subsequently revised from time to time. These regulations required Authorized Dealers in foreign exchange (i.e., the commercial banks) to ensure that payment terms conformed with those specified in the import licence and to obtain a number of supporting documents: manufacturers' and suppliers' invoices, bill of lading, and customs entry form. In general, payment for imports could be authorized only against documents (i.e., goods already shipped) or evidence of importation. Remittances prior to dispatch of goods could not be made without specific prior approval, and were seldom allowed.[18] Regulations further specified details and/or limits of commission payments, freight charges, insurance on goods, interest on acceptance bills, normal bank charges, and rebates on acceptance bills paid before maturity.[19]

---

17. The compulsory 180-day credit scheme perhaps falls within this definition, but because it is translated, virtually automatically, into an implicit price differential we included it in our discussion of direct price divergences.
18. The stipulation that imports could only be financed by sight or acceptance documents was repeated in the *Commercial and Industrial Bulletin* at least twice: 20 March, 1964 and 24 December, 1964.
19. *Commercial and Industrial Bulletin,* 20 December, 1963, quoting from Bank of Ghana Exchange Control Committee notice of 28 September, 1963.

TABLE II-3

Commercial bank loans (excluding cocoa financing) at mid-year (in millions of new cedis)

Year	For imports	Total	Percent for imports
1963*	16.9	77.4	21.8
1964*	9.2	75.8	12.1
1965	10.3	68.4	15.1
1966	24.4	66.1	36.9
1967	17.8	58.3	30.5
1968	15.0	55.5	27.0
1969	12.3	67.9	18.1
1970	25.1	80.3	31.3

Note: * Year end.

Sources: Bank of Ghana, *Report of the Board for the Financial Year Ended 30 June,*
          1965 (for 1963–1965); 1968 (for 1966–1968); and 1970 (for 1969 and
          1970).

(b) Regulation of credit

The major measures relating to the finance of foreign trade were contained in the credit control regulations introduced on April 1, 1964. The general move to establish credit regulations was clearly part of the evolution of the Bank of Ghana into a full-fledged central bank, so the major thrust of these new regulations was to set out reserve ratios for the commercial banks and to detail their reporting requirements. In addition, however, two features of the regulations were of potentially considerable importance for foreign trade.

The first set out a requirement that credit facilities over N₵ 10,000 for purposes other than agriculture and industry could be made only with the prior approval of the Bank of Ghana.[20] This provided a mechanism for restricting imports by limiting the credit available to those engaged exclusively in the import trade, but could not prevent multi-activity firms such as the big trading companies from shifting funds internally. On the surface the policy appears to have had some initial effect in redirecting credit. Commercial bank loans for the import trade dropped absolutely and relatively in 1964 and maintained a fairly low level in 1965 (see Table II-3). This occurred despite the general lament by the bank of Ghana that "the effectiveness of the quantitative credit control regulations might have been greater if the commercial banks had complied fully with regulations."[21] It is doubtful, however, that the excess demand for imports was substantially reduced by this device.

20. *Commercial and Industrial Bulletin,* 17 April, 1964.
21. Bank of Ghana, *Report of the Board for the Financial Year Ended 30 June,* 1965,
    p. 82.

(c) Prior deposits

The further device concerning the import trade contained in the 1964 credit control regulations was the establishment of a minor prior-deposit system. The scheme for prior deposits on imports, although relatively insignificant as an element in the array of restrictive instruments, is in many ways typical of a proliferation of instruments bearing on the foreign sector. Further, its history is indicative of the rapidity of change that is often encountered at the height of restrictiveness.

Initially, the system announced in April 1964 was one in which commercial banks were required to obtain and hold a 15 percent minimum down payment before opening a letter of credit for imports of consumer goods, including consumer durables.[22] In June 1964 this was revised by requiring that the margin be deposited with the Bank of Ghana. A further tightening took place in December of the same year; the margin was extended to all imports of consumer goods, regardless of the method of finance, and the deposit had to be made before the specific licence would be issued.[23] This apparently was not fully enforced, for in June 1965 a request appeared, addressed to holders of 1965 specific licences for consumer goods, "to pay forthwith to the Bank of Ghana the mandatory 15 percent cash margin of the value of the licences."[24] And in July 1965 a repeat request appeared, combined with a modification of the procedures — which apparently permitted payment of the deposit after the licence was issued but before the opening of a letter of credit, or within fourteen days of confirmation of an order to be paid by documentary credit.[25] This system continued throughout 1966 and was set out as part of the 1967 licencing procedures announced in July 1966, but was finally scrapped following the devaluation of July 1967.[26]

An assessment of the effect of the prior deposits is difficult because of their constant changes and relatively short duration. What is clear is that they were probably little more than a nuisance for the large importers, as the cost was considerably less than one percent of the c.i.f. value and hence provided little price deterrent to importation.[27]

22. *Commercial and Industrial Bulletin,* 17 April, 1964.
23. *Ibid.,* 24 December, 1964.
24. *Ibid.,* 25 June, 1965.
25. *Ibid.,* 30 July, 1965.
26. The above description is based on the record appearing in the *Commercial and Industrial Bulletin.* However, we have been told that some additional changes and complications took place: for part of 1965 the margin was set at 30 percent, but only one-half of the margin deposited with the Bank of Ghana; for 1966 some small margins were established for raw materials (5 percent) and capital goods (1 percent), but within a few months abolished.
27. Assuming the importer had to borrow the 15 percent margin at 8 percent per annum for three months, the prior deposit adds 2 percent of 15 percent, i.e., 0.3 percent, to his c.i.f. cost of goods.

5. Quantitative restrictions

(a) The setting

Another major set of instruments used to affect the foreign-exchange market consists of direct quantitative restrictions. Such restrictions are designed to place controls on the level and composition of foreign-exchange use. During 1961 three instruments of this type were applied with substantially greater restrictiveness than previously: control of foreign-exchange transactions, licensing of trade in goods, and bilateral trade and payments agreements. While all these instruments had been in use before 1961, they had generally been applied in a liberal manner. Hence, the 1961 move to tighten the quantitative controls on international transactions represented a major shift in Ghanaian economic policy.

Underlying this change was a predilection on the part of President Nkrumah to controls as an allocative device in bringing about the desired structural transformation of the colonial economy. A belief in the efficiency of direct intervention as a solution to all-important economic problems, together with a desire to re-orient the trade pattern, particularly the geographic and commodity composition, resulted in a strong push towards controls by the national leadership. For those in the governing circles with a less interventionist approach, no substitute for controls seemed available. Traditional macro methods had allegedly not worked to dampen the level of foreign-exchange expenditure, and nothing short of controls was apparently available to achieve the generally accepted objective of transforming the existing structure into an unspecified "modern" structure. Hence, a broad temporary coalition developed ranging from those who favored a permanent interventionist role through those who viewed controls as a temporary expedient to be used while the structural transformation of the economy took place, to those who regarded controls as an interim measure until more orthodox methods could be made to work.

In resorting to controls, however, few members of the governing circles distinguished between their capacity to achieve broad allocative objectives and their capacity to allocate in the small. The subsequent proliferation of detailed regulations and the difficulties encountered point up the failure to appreciate this distinction. The assumption made by most was that controls could be implemented: that an objective stated and corresponding instruments announced would ensure the achievement of the objective.

The substantial tightening of controls was precipitated, not so much by a conscious decision to move in that direction, but more in response to a rapidly deteriorating balance-of-payments situation. Export revenues were

stagnant.[28] A sharp increase in expenditures on imports of goods and services, due initially to a rapid expansion of aggregate demand,[29] and fed by the
dual expectations that the level of foreign-exchange expenditures would be
sharply curtailed by controls and that the geographic and commodity composition of trade would be altered by bilateral agreements, produced an
intolerably rapid decline in reserves. And, as the inevitability of some form of
drastic remedial action became more obvious, the rise in both merchandise
and non-merchandise payments accelerated[30] — to the point that during the
six months preceding the imposition of stricter exchange control in July 1961
external reserves reportedly fell by more than N₵ 69 million,[31] compared
with the December 31, 1960 level of N₵ 297 million. And the decline continued for the rest of the year: reserves dropped by N₵ 150 million in
calendar 1961 (Table II-4).

The sequence of events in 1961 also suggests that government officials had
done little to prepare a comprehensive set of controls. For example, the initial
moves involved the signing of bilateral trade and payments agreements with
several socialist and a few African countries, a process which continued
throughout the year. Recognizing that the only way to engage in significant
trade with socialist countries would be via trade pacts, 16 bilateral pacts were
signed in the period May 1961 through January 1962.[32] However, most were
not immediately implemented, and complementary policies to ensure that
imports obtained under such agreements would be marketed competitively
with imports from existing sources were not immediately instituted. The
result was a speculative demand for imports from traditional sources which
fed the growing speculative demand arising from the expectation of overall

28. However, the contention that the price deterioration in cocoa produced a decline in
    export revenue is not borne out by an examination of the data for 1961. For an
    example of this conventional view, cf. Naseem Ahmad, *Deficit Financing, Inflation
    and Capital Formation, The Ghanaian Experience 1960-1965,* Weltforum Verlag,
    Munich, 1970, p. 73.
29. See section 6 below.
30. See Table A-3a. Payments for imports, non-factor services, earnings on investments,
    and transfer payments on current account all increased rapidly in 1960 and 1961.
31. Cited by Ahmad, op. cit., p. 74, from Bank of Ghana, *Report,* June 1962, p. 17.
32. The only previous bilateral trade and payments agreement was signed with Israel in
    1958. The agreements were: Israel (5 July, 1958), United Arab Republic (31 May,
    1961), Upper Volta (18 June, 1961), Guinea (6 July, 1961), Mali (8 July, 1961),
    Peoples' Republic of China (18 August, 1961), Rumania (30 September, 1961),
    Bulgaria (5 October, 1961), Albania (7 October, 1961), Yugoslavia (11 October,
    1961), Czechoslovakia (16 October, 1961), German Democratic Republic (19 Octo-
    ber, 1961), Hungary (23 October, 1961), Holland (26 October, 1961), USSR (4
    November, 1961), Dahomey (20 December, 1961), Cuba (27 January, 1962).
    Source: IMF, *Annual Report on Exchange Restrictions,* 1959 and 1962.

controls. And the authorities were not immediately in a position to control this demand.

In mid-year, exchange control plus budgetary measures were introduced, apparently in a belated effort to stem the non-merchandise flow via exchange control while relying on internal deflation and slightly higher tariffs to dampen the net outflow on merchandise account. Virtually simultaneously, in July 1961 application of the exchange-control system was widened from non-sterling accounts to include the sterling area, and an allegedly deflationary budget introduced.

The budgetary moves emphasized orthodox measures designed to deal with the payments pressure: emphasis was placed on increased government revenue to contain private demand in general and for imports in particular. The personal income tax net was widened and personal exemptions abolished, rates increased and a withholding system instituted. A compulsory savings plan was also introduced. Finally, a purchase tax and increases in import duty rates were announced.[33]

(b) Exchange control

The widening of the exchange-control net to include the rest of the world may be seen by comparing the nature of exchange restrictions before and after July 1961. Prior to the instigation of universal exchange control, the Ghanaian regulations were not unlike those of other sterling area countries. Visible current account items were subject to licencing and payment restrictions designed primarily to discriminate in favor of the area and protect its overall balance-of-payments position. Imports were subject to licencing, but Open General Import Licences (OGL), which permitted importation without prior authorization, covered virtually all commodities from the sterling area and most other nondollar countries, but only wheat flour from Canada and the United States.[34] Exchange cover for all permitted imports was provided automatically on application. Exports were also subject to licencing, but again with a wide range of items covered by Open General Export Licences. The usual exchange-control requirement to collect (within 6 months of shipment)

33. While the increased duty rates on individual items were substantial, the increase in total collections as a percentage of total imports was not large, yielding only an effective devaluation of the import-exchange rate of less than 4 percent. (See Table II-1.)
34. In March 1960 OGL was extended to cover almost all imports from the dollar area. The previous special treatment accorded wheat flour was apparently designed to maintain a low price for bread, a procedure typical of many West African countries. See, for example, Peter Kilby, *African Enterprise: The Nigerian Bread Industry*, Stanford University Press, Stanford, 1965.

and surrender export proceeds applied only to sales to some non-sterling area countries.

Invisibles transactions were similarly relatively free within the sterling area. Payments to other territories of the area were not subject to exchange control, whereas payments outside required approval, and receipts in specified non-sterling currency were subject to surrender requirements.

On capital account, again no restrictions were placed on movements within the area, but payments to outside and foreign investment from outside the area required Exchange Control approval.[35]

With the institution of universal exchange control in 1961 the discrimination between the sterling area and the rest of the world was largely dropped by extending controls to cover the whole world. Exchange cover for licenced imports was still provided automatically, but exporters to all countries were now subject to the six-month collection and surrender requirements. All invisible payments were subject to specific individual approval, while the magnitudes of those normally approved were limited. All proceeds from invisibles had to be surrendered. All capital movements, both in and out, also required approval. Further, to ensure adequate control over foreign-held balances, Exchange Control began to centralize all foreign exchange balances into the hands of the Bank of Ghana. The results, which in 3 years involved a doubling of the proportion held by the Bank of Ghana, are outlined in Table II-4. In sum, Ghana, rather than the sterling area as a whole, became the unit around which the exchange-control wall was built.

The exchange-control system underwent a variety of changes in the period 1961-1965. Most were the product of a general sorting out of regulations,[36] with occasional reversals of policy evident.[37]

35. Although the official title of the exchange control authorities changed from time to time, we use the current official designation of Exchange Control throughout this book.

36. For example, regulations were introduced to require presentation of manufacturers' and suppliers' invoices (*Commercial and Industrial Bulletin,* 6 September, 1963); and refunds on air tickets outside Ghana were prohibited (*ibid.,* 22 July 1965).

37. Two cases illustrate this point. In 1962 a requirement was introduced that foreign investors must reinvest at least 60 percent of net profits in Ghana, but this was repealed the following year (IMF, *Annual Report on Exchange Restrictions,* 1963 and 1964). A second case involved the surrender of foreign-held balances by Ghanaian residents as specified in the 1961 Exchange Control Act. A reminder appeared in 1962 (*Commercial and Industrial Bulletin,* 4 May, 1962), but in 1963 a "Special Unnumbered Licence" (SUL) category for imports was introduced, permitting individuals to use foreign-held balances to import goods. See Bank of Ghana notice of 28 September, 1963, appearing in *ibid.,* 20 December, 1963. SUL imports did not become a significant portion of total imports, and are therefore omitted from our discussion here.

TABLE II-4

Ghana's foreign-exchange reserves by holder, 1957 through 1964, year end

Year	Bank of Ghana (1) (in millions of N¢)	Other (2) (in millions of N¢)	Total (3) (in millions of N¢)	Percent in Bank of Ghana (1)/(3) (percent)
1957	76.3	270.6	346.9	22.0
1958	78.5	288.0	366.5	21.4
1959	92.6	246.6	339.2	27.3
1960	107.7	189.6	297.3	36.2
1961	86.2	65.2	147.4	58.5
1962	94.5	50.3	144.8	65.3
1963	69.6	17.4	87.0	80.0
1964	65.7	18.1	83.8	78.4

Note: The category marked "Other" includes: Treasury, Cocoa Marketing Board (to 1962), Commercial Banks (negative from 1962), Local Authorities (to 1962), Higher Educational Institutions (to 1962); plus a small additional "miscellaneous" factor.

Source: Bank of Ghana, *Report of the Board for the Financial Year Ended 30 June,* 1965.

Once the sorting out was completed, the system remained virtually static until 1965 when, faced with an out-of-control situation, Exchange Control introduced two new and more restrictive regulations. The time permitted to exporters to collect and surrender their proceeds was reduced from 6 months to 60 days from the date of shipment. Also, in an apparent attempt to squeeze foreign-owned firms for more foreign exchange, a regulation was introduced which required prior Exchange Control approval of domestic loans and overdrafts to resident companies controlled by non-residents. These regulations have remained in force since.

(c) Import licencing

Returning to the situation of 1961, one will recall that budgetary measures and exchange control were introduced in mid-year in an attempt to contain the balance-of-payments pressure. Despite the budgetary measures the central government deficit continued to enlarge (see Table A-5), and aggregate demand pressure on imports was not abated. Further, and probably more importantly, expectations that the net of controls would be expanded to include restrictive licencing of merchandise imports generated substantial speculative demand, particularly for consumer durables, resulting in an increase rather than a decrease in merchandise imports.

By November 1961, the government felt it had only one instrument left to deal with the situation: stringent im, ort licencing. On November 24 the existing licencing system was hurriedly altered, with a switch from a system in which virtually everything was on (GL to one in which the general rule was a specific licence for everything v ith a very few exceptions placed on OGL.

The new Open General Import Licei ce list published at the time allowed for importation of only: (1) single copi s of books and periodicals addressed to individuals and (2) non-merchandise articles — trade samples, personal effects, and small gifts.[38] All other imports required specific licences.

The licencing authorities then set out to consider the current import needs. Due to the large stocks of imports built up in anticipation of licencing, a highly restrictive policy could be and was followed over the first year of licencing (1962). The overall objective was one of keeping imports to the barest minimum possible. Initially this was pursued on an *ad hoc* basis. As their capabilities to handle applications expanded, the authorities developed procedures for handling various categories and invited applications for specific licences in each category. Beginning with manufacturers' materials and then vehicles, equipment, building materials, textiles, chemicals, consumer non-durables, and so on, dates and procedures for applications were announced. At the same time a few items were added to the OGL list to provide for specific needs (education, sports, water works, agricultural feeds, and seeds), for traditional border trade in livestock and food, for spare parts, and temporarily for essential food items.

The hurried way in which licencing had been introduced and the *ad hoc* nature of the procedures inevitably generated dissatisfaction with the working of the system. Shortages of specific items, together with persistent rumors of corruption in the licencing administration brought the situation to a head, and in late 1962 a commission of enquiry was appointed. While it took over a year to complete its work,[39] the licencing authorities immediately attempted to streamline the day-to-day administration of the system. They also turned their attention to the development of a longer-run system containing the following elements: (a) Expected foreign exchange available for specifically licenced imports was estimated. (b) An import program was drawn up in which available foreign exchange was provisionally allocated among various categories of specifically licenced imports. (c) Importers were registered and classified. Allocations among the categories of specifically licenced imports were based initially on historical shares, with the shares of "non-essentials"

38. A tabulation of annual OGL lists is available from the author on request.
39. The final report is contained in: Republic of Ghana, *Report of Commission of Enquiry into Alleged Irregularities and Malpractices in Connection with the Issue of Import Licences,* Accra, February 1964.

(i.e., items that in the licencing authorities' view could be reduced) scaled down. Importers (but not licences) were of two general types: manufacturers importing for own use, and importers buying for resale. Within each general type importers were assessed on the basis of their historical shares, current size of their operations, payments of taxes, and employment. Licences were then allocated to importers which were specific to that importer and specific in the commodities that could be imported.[40]

Given the relatively small manufacturing sector, the licencing authorities appeared to be able to develop a reasonably clear understanding of local manufacturers' requirements for materials and spare parts, and attempted to meet those requirements. The importers of goods for resale proved to be more of a problem for the licencing authorities. A system involving grades for importers was introduced, with grades ranging from A (large trading firms) through D, based on historical shares of turnover, taxes paid, and employment. Within each grade (except A) firms were allocated approximately equal amounts of foreign exchange. Very soon a fifth grade, E, had to be introduced as the number of "importers" began to grow, arising from both new entrants and a multiplication of old firms. Further, although resale of licences was prohibited, it was impossible to deal with petty instances of the equivalent resale of goods. A common device was for a small recipient of a licence to arrange for a larger experienced firm to handle all aspects of the importation on behalf of the smaller importer — with profits, of course, split between them.

During the early part of the second year of licencing (1963) administration of the system appeared to work reasonably smoothly. Stocks depleted during the previous year were gradually rebuilt, and the OGL list was adjusted to meet apparent difficulties and slightly expanded. Some attempt was also made to limit imports of goods in which import-substitution appeared possible. For example, it was announced in October 1963 that imports of certain kinds of footwear, matches, toilet paper, nails, and plastic utensils were prohibited.[41]

The licencing authority was organized internally with a system of control and records designed to permit efficient handling of applications and at the same time prevent irregularities in the granting of licences. The set of records permitted easy reference to the details concerning an applicant, and the system of controls involved a four-stage procedure in which (1) the allocation

40. Trading in licences and resale of manufacturers' materials were prohibited. Undoubtedly some trading and resale did take place, but a large organized continuing market for licences and materials never developed.
41. See: *Commercial and Industrial Bulletin,* 4 October, 1963. In practice, however, published prohibited and restricted lists were seldom adhered to.

was decided, (2) the allocation approved, (3) the licence issued, and (4) the licence checked against the approved allocation and recorded. In preparation for the 1964 licence year, the procedures outlined above were well underway in the final quarter of 1963.

In late 1963, however, a new Minister of Trade was appointed, Mr. A.Y.K. Djin. He quickly saw the potentialities for corruption inherent in a restrictive licencing system. As the investigative commision appointed after the overthrow of the Nkrumah regime found:

> ...He assumed direct responsibility for the issue of import licences, and no such licences could be issued without his express direction...: licences were issued solely at his discretion, capriciously exercised with the consequent development of a crisis in the import trade and attendant trade malpractices... [He] also embarked on irregularities in the issue of licences and fraudulently exploited the situation created by himself for his own benefit, to the advantage of members of his family and personal friends....[42]

The Commission also found instances of "fraudulent exploitation, corruption and malpractices."[43] For example, a small trading firm under Mr. Djin's direction had received a licence valued at £G 35,000 for 1963, but in 1965 was awarded a licence worth over £G 700,000.[44] Apparently to facilitate the manipulation of the licencing system, the expanded OGL list of 1963 was restricted in 1964. The rest of the government bureaucracy viewed these developments with disfavor. The careful administrative procedures that had been designed to meet the apparent national needs and to minimize capricious discrimination among importers was frequently set aside in favor of Mr. Djin and his associates.

In the first half of 1965 a number of steps were taken in an attempt to reverse the situation created by Mr. Djin. President Nkrumah replaced Mr. Djin by Mr. Kwesi Armah as Minister of Foreign Trade and appointed a further commission of enquiry, which quickly did its work.[45] In addition, a foreign-exchange budget was published for the first time. The only significant result of these moves was a more systematic form of corruption. Mr. Armah, rather than restricting himself to profiting on some licences, proceeded to

42. Republic of Ghana, *White Paper on the Report of the Commission of Inquiry into Alleged Irregularities and Malpractices in Connection with the Grant of Import Licences,* W.P. No. 4/67, Accra, 1967, p. 3.
43. *Ibid.,* p. 3.
44. *Ibid.,* p. 3.
45. Republic of Ghana, Office of the President, *Report of the Commission of Enquiry into Trade Malpractices in Ghana,* Accra, January 1966.

develop a system that would permit him to share in the profit on all licences. As the post-Nkrumah commission reported:

> He [Mr. Armah] introduced the system whereby all applications for import licences had to be addressed to him personally under registered cover and he alone was responsible for processing the said applications... [T]here was open corruption and malpractices in the matter of grant of import licences during this period. Import licences were issued on the basis of a commission corruptly demanded and payable by importers on the face value of the import licences issued. The commission was fixed at 10%, but was in special cases reduced to 7½ or 5%.[46]

The result was that licences were refused for essential commodities in short supply while at the same time Armah "was issuing huge licences to importers for non-essential goods."[47] Again the stated priorities for rationing foreign exchange were being thwarted.

The restriction of the OGL list begun by Mr. Djin was continued. At the end of July 1965 a new OGL list was announced which apparently limited OGL to about the level prevailing when licencing was first introduced in late 1961. And in October 1965 OGL was further restricted in significance with the introduction of a requirement that OGL importers had to apply to Exchange Control before entering into a contract.[48] This system continued until the ouster of President Nkrumah in late February 1966.

(d) Bilateral trade pacts

The licencing system during 1962 and part of 1963 was not well designed to induce importers to purchase from bilateral-pact countries. Licences were valid for importation of the specified items from any country.[49] While official entities were redirecting their purchases, for private importers the only apparent advantage that might be achieved by purchasing from trade-pact countries revolved around payment in local currency to the bilateral account in the Bank of Ghana and the consequent reduction in problems associated with arranging payment to suppliers. This was seldom enough to offset the traditional ties with West European and U.S. suppliers. The result of this situation was a substantial undersubscribing of the bilateral accounts in 1962, yielding a positive net balance in bilateral clearing accounts of nearly N₵ 6 million (see Table II-5). This phenomenon and its meaning were not unno-

---

46. *White Paper*, 1967, *op. cit.*, p. 4.
47. *Ibid.*, p. 5.
48. *Commercial and Industrial Bulletin*, 1 October, 1965.
49. See, for example, invitation for applications for specific import licences, *Commercial and Industrial Bulletin*, 26 October, 1962: "Items originating in any country except [South Africa and the Portuguese monetary area]," p. 847.

TABLE II-5

Net balances on clearing accounts, 1961 through 1969 at year end (in millions of new cedis).

Year	Net balance	Change over year
1961	0.5	
1962	6.0	+5.4
1963	2.5	−3.5
1964	−1.0	−3.5
1965	−36.2	−35.2
1966	−30.0	+6.2
1967	−8.9	+21.1
1968	−9.9	−1.0
1969	−22.6	−12.7

Source: Bank of Ghana, *Report of the Board for the Financial Year Ended 30 June,* 1965 (for 1961–1963); 1968 (for 1964–1967); 1970 (for 1968–1969).

ticed,[50] and in 1963 specific licences distinguished between trade-pact sources and other areas. In addition imports of certain goods (8 commodities) could be obtained only from those countries, and 20 percent of other specified imports (28 commodities) were to come from trade-pact countries. For 1964 the redirection of licences to bilateral trade-pact countries was strengthened. A special exchange allocation was provided, and a list of 35 commodities developed which permitted purchases only in bilateral-pact countries. Further, in order to discriminate among the various bilateral partners the system of simply distinguishing between bilateral partners as a group and all others was abandoned in favor of specifying the bilateral partner country from which the licenced commodity had to be imported.

These moves succeeded in turning the balance around, so that at the end of 1964 there was a small negative balance, and by the end of 1965 Ghana had succeeded in becoming a net borrower to the extent of over N₵ 36 million. Moreover, the methods employed in 1964 succeeded in redirecting imports from some large negative-balance countries to countries with positive balances. This reduced absolutely the large negative balances with the Peoples' Republic of China (from − N₵ 2.2 million to − N₵ 1.8 million) and the negative balance with Mali (from − N₵ 1.0 million to − N₵ 0.4 million). At the same time the large positive balance with the USSR was substantially

50. *The Economic Survey,* published by the Central Bureau of Statistics (CBS), for 1962, p. 112, noted that "this [credit balance] amounted to the almost ridiculous position of Ghana offering interest-free loans to certain industrialized countries." And *The Economic Survey* for 1963 noted problems with delivery dates and unknown products in the Ghanaian market.

reduced (from N₵ 4 million to N₵ 2.6 million).[51] The discrimination between bilateral-pact countries and others, as well as among bilateral-pact
countries, continued until well after the coup.[52]

(e) Consequences of the system under the Nkrumah government

The tight application of quantitative restrictions during the last four years
of the Nkrumah government (1962 through 1965) failed to achieve what
must be regarded as its primary objective — reducing the substantial negative
balance of payments on goods and services. Although highly variable, the net
balance of payments on goods and services remained strongly negative over
the period (see Table A-3a). On the import side, the share from bilateral
trade-pact countries had increased by over ten percentage points (see Table
A-4b). Shares of imports by end-use had been redistributed away from consumer goods and to increases in the shares of materials and capital equipment
(see Table A-4a). On the export side, the overall dependence on staple primary exports continued, with commodity concentration rising slightly. New
markets, particularly for cocoa, were opened in the trade-pact countries,
resulting in a minor reduction in geographic concentration.[53] It did, however,
have the advantage of permitting Ghana to expand the output of cocoa
without seriously weakening the price obtained. Financing of the current
account deficit was done largely via contracting external debt. While small
amounts of private foreign capital were received over the period and reserves
were further depleted, the great bulk of the funds which permitted the large
current deficits were obtained by entering into debt. By the time of the coup
in February 1966, the external debt totalled N₵ 805.3 million, of which only
20 percent was in the form of long-term loans. The remainder was made up in
large part by suppliers' credits (57.9 percent),[54] arrears of current payment
(10.6 percent), and bank loans (6.5 percent) (Table II-6). This legacy was to
create serious problems for subsequent governments.

The system was also generating considerable internal dissatisfaction. Again
a commission of enquiry was appointed (April 1965), although on this occasion the focus was more broadly defined to include a variety of trade "mal-

51. See Bank of Ghana, *Report of the Board for the Financial Year Ended 30 June,*
    1965.
52. Unfortunately no careful assessment of the relative benefits and costs of the trade-
    pact experience has yet been published.
53. See J.C. Leith, "Export Concentration and Instability: The Case of Ghana," *op. cit,*;
    and J.C. Leith, "The Competitive Performance of Ghanaian Exports in the Nkrumah
    Period," *Ghana Social Sciences Journal,* Vol. 1, No. 1, May 1971.
54. The unfortunate experience Ghana had with suppliers' credits is described in L.E.
    Grayson, "The Role of Suppliers' Credits in the Industrialization of Ghana," *Eco-
    nomic Development and Cultural Change*, Vol. 21, No. 3, April 1973.

TABLE II-6

External debt (other than private) as of February 23, 1966 (in millions of new cedis, postdevaluation)

Type	Value	Percent
Long-term loans	161.4	20.0
Suppliers' credit	466.1	57.9
Arrears	85.3	10.6
Banking loans	52.7	6.5
IMF	8.9	1.1
Other	30.9	3.8
Total	805.3	100.0

Source: Republic of Ghana, Statement by E.N. Omaboe, Commissioner for Economic Affairs, *Developments in the Ghanaian Economy between 1960 and 1968*, Ghana Publishing Corporation, Accra, undated (published for the election campaign period in mid-1969).

practices," such as the internal distribution system. The report,[55] presented shortly before Nkrumah's overthrow, found a variety of cases in which shortages of imports created difficulties. The State Paints Corporation closed between May and July 1965. Agricultural inputs (fertilizers and machetes) were frequently in short supply. A factory under construction was unnecessarily delayed because of import delays. And considerable corruption was exposed.[56]

Criticism was not confined to the official enquiry. The annual *Economic Surveys* issued by the Central Bureau of Statistics contained strong indictments, couched in diplomatic language, of the undesirable consequences of inadequate supplies of raw materials and of shortages of essential food items.[57] Similarly, the Planning Commission expressed open concern about the consequences of spare parts and raw material shortages.[58] Further, an unpublished study cited by Killick estimated that in 1964 manufacturing capacity utilization was at about 60 percent of single-shift capacity.[59]

---

55. Republic of Ghana, Office of the President, *Report of the Commission of Enquiry into Trade Malpractices in Ghana, op. cit.*
56. For a review of the Commission's report, emphasizing the internal trading aspects, see Rowena M. Lawson, "Inflation in the Consumer Market in Ghana: Report of the Commission of Enquiry into Trade Malpractices in Ghana," *Economic Bulletin of Ghana,* No. 1, 1966, pp. 36-51.
57. See CBS, *Economic Survey,* 1964, p. 77; 1965, p. 75.
58. Office of the Planning Commission, *Annual Plan for 1965,* Accra, 1965.
59. Tony Killick, "The Purposes and Consequences of Import Controls in Ghana," mimeograph, Accra, 1972.

By 1965, faced with growing criticism of the system at home, the government turned to the International Monetary Fund (IMF) and the International Bank for Reconstruction and Development (IBRD), but received little more than affirmation of the apparent. As the commentator in the *Economic Survey* for 1965 noted:

> The Fund Mission's Report confirmed what has been obvious to most observers all along. The Report stated that "the Ghana economy is severely overstrained, the balance of payments is in serious deficit, and the country's foreign exchange reserves are at a precariously low level. Foreign debt repayments are increasing, putting added pressure on the balance of payments."[60]

In a similar vein, the response of the IBRD called for strong medicine.

> The World Bank Mission recommended "a restoration of the balance between government revenue and expenditure" stating that "such action would hopefully be regarded by all sectors of the world financial community as constituting a determined effort on your part and deserving of their assistance in complementing the efforts of your government."[61]

The situation was serious. Heavy borrowing by Nkrumah plus a further depletion of foreign-exchange reserves had been used to finance the import binge of 1965. Predictably, these sources were quickly drying up. With a short- and medium-term external debt totalling N¢ 645 million (Table II-6) — nearly two times annual export earnings — and reserves of only N¢ 26 million (Table A-3b), Ghana's credit was nearly exhausted. The prospect for 1966 was not good, for even with a reliance on normal export earnings, current account expenditures would have to be cut by about 35 percent from the 1965 level if further borrowing and reserve depletion were to be avoided. In itself this was a very serious situation. Compounding the difficulties was a glut on the cocoa market, and total merchandise export earnings were falling. The 1966 returns eventually showed a 13 percent decline in merchandise exports from 1965 to 1966. A drastic cutback of imports, and hence real income, was required. Licencing was again tightened.

(f) Stabilization

The difficulties experienced in the economic sphere contributed in no small way to the political events of early 1966. February 24, 1966 marked a major change in the political, social and economic life of Ghana. A military coup replaced the regime of President Nkrumah with a National Liberation

60. *Economic Survey,* 1965, p. 50.
61. *Ibid.*, p. 51.

Council (NLC). The new government set itself the task of national reconstruction which, in the economic field, involved an austerity or "stabilization" program designed to bring both the foreign and government sector accounts into balance again.

In dealing with the foreign sector, the NLC government severely restricted the overall level of foreign exchange available for imports and attempted to allocate foreign exchange among competing demands on a basis that it regarded as systematic and rational. The former was relatively easily accomplished once the licencing system was reorganized to resemble the system developed in the earlier years. The latter objective, faced with the inevitable conflict among competing "rational" uses of a rationed item, together with the delays inherent in a system designed to prevent abuse, was not as readily achieved.

The system that emerged during 1966 emphasized fair and open treatment of applicants while at the same time attempting to meet the objective of mobilizing domestic resources and ensuring an adequate and cheap supply of essential commodities for consumers.

The overall foreign-exchange budget was struck by the Bank of Ghana, and in turn allocations were made to the various ministries responsible for specific allocations of licenses:

Ministry of Trade — commercial imports,
Ministry of Industries — imports for private industrial use,
State Enterprises Secretariat — state industrial enterprises,
Ministry of Economic Affairs — government imports.

The final issuance of licences remained with the Ministry of Trade, and the resulting allocations were published in the *Commercial and Industrial Bulletin* for all to see.[62] Of major interest and importance are the procedures adopted for private commercial and for private industrial imports.

The system of grading commercial importers established in the early days of import licencing was retained. However, a complete revision of the register of commercial importers was undertaken. Grades were assigned according to past volume.[63] Importers with N¢ 2 million annual volume over the period 1961 to 1965 were assigned the top grade. The remaining grades ranged from importers with an annual volume of N¢ 100,000 to those with N¢ 20,000

---

62. The allocations were published in such a way, however, that it is impossible to distinguish among allocations for commercial, industrial or governmental use.
63. This, of course, tended to perpetuate inequities that had developed over the years, excepting only the extreme cases that were the subject of the official post-coup inquiry.

volume. Within each grade commercial importers were assigned approximately equal foreign-exchange allocations. The objective in this approach was to "obtain goods on competitive terms and at reasonable prices to the consumers,"[64] hence the reliance on larger firms with proven trade and financial contacts and facilities to ensure that the country had adequate supplies of essential commodities.

Private industries' requirements for imported materials new equipment and spare parts were assessed by the Ministry of Industries. Again, a system of various categories was employed which reflected the conflicting objectives of protection of the consumer (hence a high priority given to imports for use by producers of essential consumer goods), of export promotion (with consequent high priority for export industries), and of import-substitution (also a high-priority category). From the given allocation of foreign exchange assigned it, the Ministry of Industries first divided the available foreign exchange among the categories and then attempted to make *pro rata* allocations among firms within a category based approximately on previous market shares but taking into account their assessment of the firms' "performance" in such things as employment, taxes paid, and what was called general efficiency of operation. While there is no evidence of corruption during this period, the bureaucrats' assessment of performance inevitably resulted in some arbitrary allocations.

The import-licence system, since it had virtual life and death powers over most industries, came to be used as an industrial licencing system as well. The Ministry of Industries saw a conflict between the need for competition among domestic producers and the wasteful expenditure involved in duplicating underutilized domestic facilities, but generally resolved it during the NLC period in favor of "rationalization" of industries and against new entrants.

The post-coup review of the licencing machinery also brought an attempt to alleviate the very serious shortages that had developed in the later Nkrumah era and which had resulted in empty shops, as well as idle factories due to the lack of imports. The OGL list for 1967 was expanded a little over that of 1965 and 1966, and the administrative system was designed to permit the issuance of licences in advance of the year for which they would be valid — in contrast with the 1964 and 1965 experience of licences often being issued very late in the year for which they were valid. A schedule for submission of applications for 1967 licences was set up, with applications for essentials (flour, sugar, rice, milk, butter, tinned fish and meat, and other meat) being called for in August, spare parts and raw materials in September, etc., with the objective of having licences for virtually all foreseeable imports

64. *Commercial and Industrial Bulletin,* 7 October, 1966, p. 778.

issued before the beginning of the calendar year in which they would be used. In practice, however, it was difficult to achieve this, for there was typically some delay in striking the overall foreign-exchange budget and, in turn, delay in sifting through the multi-staged allocational process which preceded the specific firm allocations.

The system as it emerged and was applied in 1967 was substantially more open and less corrupt than the chaotic state of affairs which had prevailed in 1964 and 1965. Within the tight foreign-exchange budget, the licencing authorities did attempt to allocate licences in a way that reflected their perception of national needs and, subject to this constraint, avoided serious discrimination between individuals. It does not follow, however, that the system was necessarily any less arbitrary than in the late Nkrumah period.

(g) Liberalization

The worst abuses of the late Nkrumah period apparently had been removed. Yet the interventionist approach to allocation remained, and this too was being called into question. A growing belief developed among policy-makers that import licencing was not a long-run solution to the Ghanaian foreign-exchange problem.[65] Pressure to pursue a liberalization of licencing was also brought to bear on the government from both outside the country by bilateral donors and international agencies, and by internal dissatisfaction with licencing. As a consequence, a tentative commitment to long-range liberalization developed.

The first major steps toward a liberalized trade and payments regime were taken in the third quarter of 1967. A substantial devaluation of nearly 43 percent was introduced in July, together with some import duty and export tax reductions. Accompanying the devaluation was an announcement of an expanded OGL list. The net result was that 3 percent of all imports came under OGL for calendar year 1967, and over 18 percent of all imports in 1968.[66] Progress was also made in mopping up the massive foreign-exchange payments arrears that had accumulated prior to the coup (Table II-6 above), so that by the end of 1967 foreign-exchange cover had been provided or special arrangements had been made for virtually all arrears that had been pending in early 1966.

The import-liberalization process is considered in more detail below (Chapter V). In terms of the present narrative, the important point to note is that the process of import liberalization was a gradual one in which the licencing system was retained intact, albeit somewhat shrunken in magnitude. While by

65. The evident dissatisfaction in official circles is illustrated by the sniping at the system during the late Nkrumah period cited in article (e) above.
66. See Table V-11 below.

the end of 1970 the OGL system had expanded to cover 60 percent of all imports and a much higher proportion of essential consumer and producer goods, the system governing import licencing remained much the same as the system that had developed in the early years. The foreign-exchange budget was struck, an import program drawn up taking into account recent shares of imports by end-use plus expected OGL imports, and a block of foreign exchange assigned to each of the Trade and Industries divisions for allocation to commercial and industrial importers respectively.[67]

Commercial imports subject to specific licencing, which now constituted nearly all the specifically licenced imports, were allocated by the Trade division first among 56 classes of goods and second among registered importers. The detail of the commodity classification varied from the SITC three-digit to the six-digit level. Some items, such as fuels and lubricants and essential consumer goods not yet assigned to the OGL list, would be automatically allocated sufficient foreign exchange to meet expected demand, while the remaining foreign exchange was divided among the residual items. The allocation to firms continued to be based on the grading system with the top-grade firms handling about 60 percent and virtually the entire range of licenced commercial imports.[68] It was on these firms that the government continued to rely to keep imports flowing smoothly. A major limit on the share of licences going to grade-A firms appears to have been the extent of their financial capacity to handle imports. In the lower grades firms were allocated licences for only those few commodities in which they specialized. Typically, all firms within a grade would receive about equal allocations, although some attempt was made to distinguish among the medium-sized firms on the basis of their overall turnover, local commodity sales, employment and tax payments. However, to minimize suspicion of favoritism on their part, the licencing authorities clearly preferred to assign a flat rate to each importer within a grade and departed from that only when there was clear evidence of superior "performance," such as employment.

While the administrative apparatus remained essentially unchanged in its procedures and intent from the original system developed in the early part of the decade, a number of other elements of the system had changed. First, there was now a continuing process of foreign-exchange budgeting, involving

---

67. Commercial imports covered nondurable consumer goods, durable consumer goods, fuels and lubricants. Industrial imports covered nondurable producers' goods, durable producers' goods, and producers' equipment.

68. Ghana National Trading Corporation, the large state-owned trading company continued to receive a somewhat larger share than the other grade-A firms because of its obligation to carry larger stocks and broader ranges of imported goods. However, it continued to experience a decline in its share of total imports.

the preparation of forecast receipts and programmed imports. While attempts to develop a foreign-exchange budgeting system had begun in the late Nkrumah period, the budgets prepared for 1965 and 1966 were little more than scraps of paper.[69] Only after the coup was any serious attempt made to implement a foreign-exchange budget. Prompted by the need to present a coherent case for aid to donor countries, foreign-exchange budgets were drawn up and published beginning in 1967.[70] However, even these attempts were far from successful. Tony Killick has provided some interesting comparisons of programmed and actual imports for the years 1968 and 1969.[71] The budgets were regarded as targets, both for the level and the composition of foreign-exchange use. In both years, non-durable consumer goods imports exceeded programmed imports by substantial margins, while actual producers' materials imports fell short of the programmed values. And, in looking at specific items he found typically wide differences between actual and programmed values. He concluded that "the import programmes were only very loosely implemented when it came to details and this and other factors resulted in an actual detailed composition of imports that bore only the most approximate relationship to the intentions of the planners."[72] The allocation of licences was not, apparently, closely geared to the target budgets.

Second, promotion of small Ghanaian businesses became one of the objectives of a variety of government policy instruments, including the import-licencing system. As early as October 1966, in the exercise of reviewing the register of importers following the coup, special consideration was given to small Ghanaian importers. Some 763 Ghanaian importers were initially struck from the register because their volume fell below the N₵ 20,000 per annum minimum required for the lowest grade, but they were quickly reinstated.[73] Similarly, in the post-coup period the transfer of licences between firms and between commodities remained illegal under the threat of fines and deregistration. However, a licence once issued could now be returned for endorsement to another importer, thus permitting small firms to import via a larger firm with established buying and credit connections. The endoresment procedure, however, was open only to small Ghanaian firms. In other words, the licencing system was also being used to promote the Ghanaianization of small

---

69. The 1965 central government budget contains the first published foreign-exchange budget, and a similar document was prepared for 1966 (prior to the coup).
70. Republic of Ghana, *Ghana's Economy and Aid Requirements in 1967,* Accra, 1967. Similar titles were used for the 1968 (Accra, 1968) and the January 1969–June 1970 documents (Accra, 1969).
71. "The Purposes and Consequences of Import Controls in Ghana," *op. cit.,* Accra, 1972.
72. *Ibid.,* pp. 22-23.
73. See *Commercial and Industrial Bulletin,* 7 October, 1966.

businesses, thus adding a further objective to an already overburdened instrument.

Third, as the OGL list expanded to include most producer materials and equipment it became evident that import licencing could no longer be used as an industrial licencing instrument. The Minister of Trade and Industries responded with the Manufacturing Industries Act, which came into force in April 1971. The Act provided for licencing of new or expanding manufacturing activities, and enabled the Minister to issue instructions and regulations for any manufacturing industry "relating to the quality, quantity and prices of products."[74]

Fourth, the extent to which the licencing system effectively discriminated between luxury "inessentials" and less luxurious "essential" commodities was impaired by the liberalization of licence allocations. Licence categories were broadened and the number reduced to the point that in 1971 non-OGL commercial import licences were allocated among only 56 categories. Without a corresponding adjustment of the tariff (which discriminates between commodities at a much finer level of detail) or of the sales tax system, the result of these developments was a substantial increase in imports of more luxurious consumer goods.

Finally, the rapid expansion of the OGL list from 1968 was not generally used to reduce protection of domestic producers. On the contrary, accompanying the expanded OGL list, which emphasized liberalization of materials, equipment and spare parts imports, was a list of restricted/prohibited imports amounting to some 80 or more customs items. Without a corresponding increase in excise tax rates (applicable to domestically produced goods only), the net protection of many domestic producers was probably increased.[75] While this approach represents an import-substitution orientation of the licencing system, there is little evidence that it constituted a major justification of licencing. Rather, given the existence of licencing, the development of a restricted/prohibited list was primarily an *ad hoc* response to pressure by domestic manufacturers already engaged in production.[76]

---

74. *Manufacturing Industries Act,* Act 356, 1971, paragraph 8.
75. Prior to 1965 individual announcements of restricted/prohibited items had been made from time to time, but for 1966 a list published in October 1965 pulled together previous prohibitions, including various kinds of textiles and footwear. A similar list for 1967 consisted of 81 items. (See *Commercial and Industrial Bulletin,* 19 July, 1966.) Subsequent lists were all of approximately the same magnitude.
76. The theme of protection for import-substitution is taken up again in Chapter III.

6. Aggregate demand, domestic prices, and trade

We consider now a different set of instruments, those affecting aggregate demand in the domestic economy. In contrast with the instruments discussed so far, the aggregate instruments are not designed to single out particular activities in the domestic economy, but rather to act on the total level of domestic activity. This is not to say that given other policies the effects are likely to be neutral between sectors. Rather, the focus is on the total balance in the economy.

(a) Aggregate demand and domestic prices

The process of achieving aggregate balance of national income and expenditure may be described as the way in which the economy moves towards the equilibrium:

$$Y \equiv C + I + X - M \tag{II.3}$$

The variables in this well-known identity are net output (Y), consumption expenditure (C), net investment expenditure (I), exports (X) and imports (M). They are all value flows of goods and services per period in current prices.

In general, the potential supply of output depends on the productive resources available to the economy. Expenditures on output are determined by a great variety of factors, including the instruments of fiscal and monetary policies. Unless there is a significant gap between actual and potential output, the real level of output is unaffected by the magnitudes of the variables on the right-hand side of equation (II.3). Hence the response to increased expenditure must involve some adjustment via an increase in imports and in the price of domestic output or a reduction in the value of expenditure components.

The nature of the adjustment depends largely on the country's trade and payments system. If the system permits a free flow of trade and payments without quantitative restrictions, then for a small country the domestic price level of tradeables is linked directly with international prices of the same goods. Under these circumstances aggregate demand pressure, *ceteris paribus*, is vented largely on the external balance with increased imports and decreased exports: the domestic price level of tradeables is given by international prices. If, however, adjustment via the external balance is blocked by some mechanism such as controls over imports, the link with international prices is cut. Aggregate demand pressure is vented on the domestic price level to bring about the adjustment, leaving an unsatisfied excess demand for imports. As the domestic price level moves out of line with the international price level, the unsatisfied excess demand for imports is exacerbated and, to the extent that export supply depends on relative prices, exports fall off.

Ghana has experienced both of these types of adjustments to aggregate demand pressure.[77] In 1959, responding to the desire to speed development, the government incurred a substantial deficit (see Table A-5), creating an excess of total expenditure over output. With a fixed exchange rate and a relatively free system of international trade and payments, the adjustment came about largely in the form of increased imports of goods and services, which jumped by more that one-third in 1959. The excess demand for real resources in general was thus turned into a demand for foreign goods and services. This demand was met via a current account deficit, which was accomodated by drawing on foreign-exchange reserves and external capital account borrowing, largely on the part of the government. At this stage, then, the pressure was largely vented on the external balance and not on domestic prices.

The capital account balance turned strongly negative in 1961, while the current account balance moved into an even larger deficit position. In that year reserves dropped from N₵ 297 million to N₵ 147 million. Such a reserve loss was clearly not sustainable. At some point the home excess demand for real resources at the fixed exchange rate would be resisted by foreigners. In the absence of any action by the home government, the foreigners' response would ultimately have been to charge a higher price for foreign exchange, either directly by not accepting the official exchange rate, or indirectly adjusting the prices of tradeables and refusing credit on capital account. The result for domestic residents would have been a movement up along the domestic excess demand curve for foreign exchange.

For the home government, if it were to avoid allowing the foreigners to make the adjustment for them — and failing a change in the official exchange rate — some device had to be found to close the deficit. The options included: (a) a reduction in the overall excess demand for resources in general and hence for external resources in particular; (b) an increase in the effective domestic price for foreign exchange; or (c) a system of non-price rationing of foreign exchange. Initially, a combination of all three was chosen. One recalls from section 3 above that in 1961 an attempt was made to institute deflationary policies, taxes on imports were increased, and the non-price rationing of foreign exchange via exchange control and import licencing were drastically tightened.

---

77. We are not here considering the implementation of fiscal and monetary policies. The reader is referred to W. Birmingham *et al., op. cit.*, and to N. Ahmad, *op. cit.*, for detailed discussions of the workings of the fiscal and monetary system.

By choosing to employ non-price rationing as one of the devices to close the external deficit, the policymakers instituted an important change that was not perhaps fully understood at the time. Pressure of domestic excess demand would now be vented largely on the domestic price level, permitting it to get out of line with international prices. Failure to control aggregate demand would now show up as higher domestic prices rather than as a loss of reserves.

TABLE II-7

Price deflators of national accounts components (1960 = 100).

Year	GDP minus exports of goods & non-factor services	Exports of goods and non-factor services	Imports of goods and non-factor services	GDP
1956	93.23	93.58	96.73	91.97
1957	97.50	89.45	97.69	92.32
1958	97.22	123.85	96.73	101.11
1959	96.87	110.09	99.60	100.11
1960	100.00	100.00	100.00	100.00
1961	108.96	88.41	101.24	103.20
1962	119.60	74.07	95.74	105.40
1963	127.15	75.97	92.95	112.48
1964	134.38	91.14	104.04	123.70
1965	174.29	75.45	107.43	144.60
1966	195.04	71.57	102.89	161.10
1967	179.05	92.01	128.76	156.93
1968	197.21	128.12	141.04	179.90
1969	208.43	153.43	147.02	195.63

Sources: 1. Current prices: GDP
        1956 through 1959, *Economic Survey, 1967*;
        1960 through 1962, *Economic Survey, 1968*;
        1963 through 1969, *Economic Survey, 1969*.
      Exports of goods and non-factor services
        1956 through 1959, *Economic Survey, 1967*;
        1961, *Economic Survey, 1968*;
        1960, 1962 through 1969, *Economic Survey, 1969*.
    2. Constant prices: GDP
        1959 through 1969, *Economic Survey, 1967* and 1969;
        1956 through 1958, Birmingham *et al., The Economy of Ghana,* Vol. I,
        p. 50.
      Exports of goods and non-factor services
        1956 through 1958, Birmingham *et al., The Economy of Ghana,* Vol. I,
        p. 50.
        1959, *Economic Survey, 1967*;
        1961, *Economic Survey, 1968*;
        1960, 1962 through 1969, *Economic Survey, 1969*.

In the absence of compensatory increases in the nominal effective exchange rates facing exporters and importers, the prices of tradeables relative to non-tradeables would become cheaper and cheaper. This, in fact, is what did happen (from 1960 onwards). Looking at the domestic component of the GDP deflator (GDP–X), we find that by 1966 it had reached an index of 195, compared with an f.o.b. export index of 75, and a c.i.f.-plus-duty import index of 102 (Table II-7, 1960 = 100).

There was little explicit recognition of the problems created by this approach for either exports or imports. With the rising domestic price level, offsetting action on both the export and import sides was required to maintain relative prices at the pre-1960 situation. When such action was either not forthcoming (exports) or inadequate (imports), the already serious aggregate imbalance on external account was exacerbated by increasingly inappropriate relative prices in the domestic economy. The remainder of this section is thus devoted to a discussion of the consequences of aggregate imbalance and domestic price inflation for exports and imports. Our discussion is confined to the pre-devaluation period, as the response to a major shock such as the 1967 devaluation may well be different. These latter issues are taken up in Chapter V below. For an overview of major trends of imports, non-cocoa and cocoa exports, together with the corresponding price-level-deflated effective exchange rates, see Chart II-2.

(b) Exports

We consider first non-cocoa exports, which typically account for 35 to 40 percent of total merchandise export earnings. We have computed the price-level-deflated effective exchange rate facing these exports (Table II-8). It is clear that the nominal effective exchange rate facing non-cocoa exports was not kept in line with the domestic price level.[78] At the same time there was the continuous[79] decline in non-cocoa exports valued in constant prices detailed in Table II-9. These data, together with the price-level-deflated effective exchange rate series from Table II-8, permit us to examine explicitly the response of non-cocoa exports to the relative price facing them. To do so, we estimated the equation:

$$\ln N\mathcal{C}X_t = \alpha + \beta \ln (EERX/P)_{t-\frac{1}{2}} + u_t \qquad (II.4)$$

---

78. A minor attempt was made to introduce an export incentive scheme for manufactured goods. It was announced that, effective January 1, 1966, exporters of manufactured commodities would be provided with additional import licences. This scheme was abolished shortly after the coup of February 1966. See IMF, *Annual Report on Exchange Restrictions*, 1966 and 1967.

79. Prior to 1961 there had been a continuous rise, averaging about 7.0 percent per annum (compound) over the period 1955 through 1960.

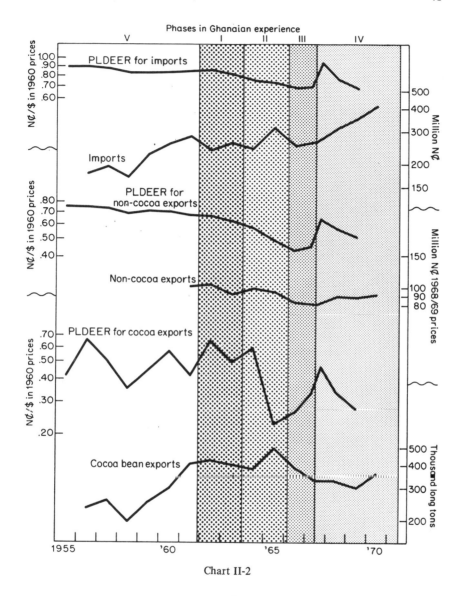

Chart II-2

where N₵X = the value of non-cocoa domestic exports in constant 1968–1969
prices, millions of N₵, from Table II-9, and EERX/P = the price-level-deflated
effective exchange rate facing non-cocoa exports, N₵/$ from Table II-8. The
results, using ordinary least squares, for t = 1961–1962 through 1966–1967

TABLE II-8

Price-level-deflated effective exchange rates facing imports and exports (new cedis per dollar in constant 1960 prices)

Year	For imports	For non-cocoa exports	For cocoa exports
1955	0.8888	0.7486	0.4194
1956	0.8912	0.7477	0.6602
1957	0.8798	0.7372	0.4958
1958	0.8229	0.6882	0.3529
1959	0.8232	0.7009	0.4490
1960	0.8359	0.7007	0.5737
1961	0.8457	0.6791	0.4172
1962	0.8653	0.6679	0.6503
1963	0.8169	0.6254	0.4907
1964	0.7516	0.5693	0.5948
1965	0.7307	0.4884	0.2259
1966	0.6893	0.4386	0.2634
1967A	0.6910	0.4512	0.3279
1967B	0.9590	0.6449	0.4685
1968	0.7747	0.5636	0.3366
1969	0.6909	0.5188	0.2712

Sources: Computed from effective exchange rates of Tables II-1 and II-2, and the GDP deflator of Table II-7.

$$\ln N\text{\textcent}X_t = 2.778 + 0.4359 \ln (EERX/P)_{t-\frac{1}{2}}$$
$$\quad\quad\quad (9.89)\quad (6.28)$$

Observations = 6
$R^2 = 0.908$
D.W. = 1.91, t-values in parentheses.

Even this limited number of observations permits us to see that there was indeed a close relationship. The estimated equation explains over 90 percent of the variance. The coefficient for the price-level-deflated effective exchange rate, significant at the 0.005 level, shows the elasticity to be sufficiently large to merit attention: the response to a 10 percent decline in the price-level-deflated effective exchange rate was a 4.36 percent decline in non-cocoa export earnings valued in constant prices.[80] Clearly, the continuing neglect of

80. A regression of current non-cocoa exports on current price-level-deflated effective exchange rate yielded a lower elasticity and a lower R^2. A regression on the price-level-deflated effective exchange rate lagged one year also had a lower R^2, but a slightly higher elasticity. We have deliberately excluded the pre-1961 period from our regression because we are concerned about the response within the context of the control system.

TABLE II-9

Non-cocoa domestic exports, constant 1968–1969 prices, 1961–1970 (in millions of new cedis)

Calendar years (January through December)		Fiscal years (July through June)	
1961	100.1		
1962	103.6	1961/62	100.2
1963	91.8	1962/63	97.6
1964	99.8	1963/64	99.7
1965	94.3	1064/65	96.5
1966	83.3	1965/66	88.8
1967	80.4	1966/67	81.6
1968	89.5	1967/68	86.1
1969	88.0	1968/69	85.3
1970	90.6	1969/70	87.4

Notes: The data consist of all the traditional non-cocoa exports including timber, gold, bauxite, manganese, and diamonds, plus a number of minor exports, but exclude Valco aluminum exports. Some few minor items, such as lime juice, amounting to about 10 percent of non-cocoa exports, are not included because of incomplete quantity data.

Source: Computed by J.J. Stern, mimeograph, Accra, March 1972.

the relative price facing this large segment of exports resulted in a serious deterioration of export earnings.

Cocoa exports are more complex to explain. They have long provided the major share of Ghana's foreign-exchange revenues. Since the mid-1950's cocoa has accounted for about 60 percent of merchandise export receipts and has been a major source of stability in those receipts.[81] However, because of Ghana's major position in the world cocoa market and because of the long gestation period for new plantings, the policy options for cocoa are considerably more complex.

Ghana's substantial share of the world output has a number of implications. Ghana cannot take the world price as given: she has a significant effect on it, and hence the cocoa export tax is intended to move the price in Ghana's favor. Recent econometric estimates suggest that the demand elasticity facing Ghana is (absolutely) greater than minus-one in the long run. For example, the work by Blomqvist and Haessel, using a distributed lag model, suggests that the long-run demand elasticity facing Ghana is on the order of −1.4.[82] Thus a long-run expansion of output would increase Ghana's revenue

81. See J.C. Leith, "Export Concentration and Instability: 'The case of Ghana,"*op. cit.*
82. A.G. Blomqvist and Walter Haessel, "The Price Elasticity of Demand for Ghana's Cocoa," *Economic Bulletin of Ghana*, Second Series, Vol. 2, No. 3, 1972. The estimate of −1.4 is based on a market share of 30 percent.

from cocoa exports. However, in the shorter run the demand elasticity facing Ghana is somewhat less (absolutely) than −1; consequently, a sudden expansion of quantity sold would lead to a decline in revenue. This is a problem, particularly in bumper crop years, as was the case in 1965; while the immediate price decline is ameliorated by purchaser stock piling, prices are depressed in subsequent years until the excess inventories are worked off.

Several factors enter into the supply side. Since the late 1930's the prices paid to producers have been set by the Cocoa Marketing Board, which also has legal monopsony powers. This price is usually set and held for a year or more at a time, but has historically moved in response to the broad trends of the world cocoa price.[83] Estimates of the short-run response to the real producer price have yielded elasticities of the order of + 0.15 to + 0.20.[84] These represent the response of harvesting and maintenance and do not take into account the effect of additional planting. The gestation period to full bearing for cocoa trees is currently 7 or 8 years, and hence the long-run response involves adjustment of the stock of trees. The estimates of long-run price elasticity of supply range from + 0.71 to about 1.0.[85] The long-run response relationship, however, is further complicated by the fact that there is a minimum real producer price below which no new plantings take place.

Other factors also have major effects on supply. In the short run, excessive rainfall and humidity during the late maturing stage of the pods can damage the crop, while later rainfall builds up more moisture reserve to carry the growth through the harmattan (dry season). In the longer run, the capacity is favorably affected by insecticide use, which keeps young trees healthy.[86]

A further complicating element in the cocoa policy determination is the implicit conflict among the producer interests, the government revenue interests, and perhaps the national welfare interest. Thus, given the elasticities cited above, an increase in the real producer price would eventually increase Ghana's export revenues. However, such a producer price increase would raise producer incomes more than the increased export revenues, and would in-

83. See P. Ady, "Supply Functions in Tropical Agriculture," *Bulletin of the Oxford Institute of Statistics*, Vol. 30, No. 2, May 1968, Chart 2, p. 165.

84. See M.J. Bateman, "Supply Relations for Perennial Crops in Less Developed Areas," in C.R. Wharton, ed., *Subsistence Agriculture and Economic Development*, Aldine, Chicago, 1969, p. 251; and Bateman's more recent unpublished work on Ghanaian cocoa: "Cocoa Study," in IBRD, *Economic Report*, Vol. IV, mimeograph, Washington, D.C., March 1972.

85. See Bateman, "Supply Relations for Perennial Crops in Less Developed Areas," *op. cit.*

86. Bateman, in his "Cocoa Study," *op. cit.*, estimates that about one-third of the substantial increase in capacity between the 1950's and the 1960's was due to insecticide use.

crease the Cocoa Marketing Board's handling cost to the extent that output would expand, with the result that the residual for the government would be reduced. [87]

In the circumstances, beyond a general statement that an optimum tariff should be employed, the appropriate first-best set of policies for cocoa is not obvious. And because it is seldom possible to distinguish which distortions must be taken as given, even a second-best optimum may not be possible to specify. We have no unique contribution to make in this regard. Rather, we are interested in the extent, if any, to which the system of the 1960's altered the relative attractiveness of cocoa exporting *vis-à-vis* other activities in the economy.

A simple summary indicator of the relative attractiveness of cocoa exporting is the price-level-deflated effective exchange rate (Table II-8). From the mid-1950's through 1964 a relatively constant level was maintained, with fluctuations around a rate somewhere above N₵ 0.50 per dollar. However, a distinct break occurred in 1965. The domestic inflation permitted by the exchange control system resulted in a drastic drop in the price-level-deflated effective exchange rate facing cocoa exports. Some recovery followed in 1966 and early 1967, but the level was nevertheless substantially below the average of previous years. The emergence of domestic inflation, together with the low nominal fixed producer prices, thus led to a relative decline in the attractiveness of growing cocoa for export.

This pattern, given the approximately unitary long-run supply elasticity cited above, resulted in a withdrawal of resources from the cocoa sector. In 1964/65 new plantings ceased, and have apparently not been resumed since. For the long run this suggests a potentially serious stagnation of cocoa export earnings.

(c) Imports

On the import side a limited policy response to rising relative domestic prices was attempted. In an effort to mop up the excess demand spilling over on imports during the first half of the 1960's, higher taxes on imports were imposed, with an increase in the effective exchange rates facing imports of almost 33 percent by 1966 over 1960 (see Table II-1). This, however, was not nearly enough to keep the relative price of imports in line with the domestic

87. For example, if the demand elasticity were −1.4 and the producer supply elasticity were 1.0, a 10 percent increase in producer price would result in 10 percent additional output, a fall in the export price of about 7 percent, and a rise in export receipts by about 2.3 percent. For the absolute size of the residual between export receipts and producer payments to increase (rather than decrease) in these circumstances, the producers' share would have to be less than 2.3 percent/21 percent = 11 percent of export receipts.

price level: the domestic component of the GDP deflator rose by about 95 percent in the same period (Table II-7).

Instead, the government assumed that licencing could be used to contain imports. Yet the licencing system was far from adequate to cope with the pressure on imports. While the pressure was initially vented on domestic prices, this in turn shifted the demand for imports outward, resulting in an unsatisfied demand for imports at the tariff inclusive price which was even greater than the initial excess demand. The result was rising pressure on the licencing system. By 1965 as we noted above (section II-5) the licencing system had almost completely broken down. The reason for this failure of the licencing system goes beyond mere corruption on the part of administrators: the relative price difference had grown so large that major internal forces were clamoring for a relaxation of licencing.[88] Had reduced aggregate demand policies and/or a realistic effective exchange rate facing imports been used to dampen the demand for imports, the licencing system would not have had to bear the pressure which it ultimately proved it could not withstand. Put another way, licencing could be used to limit imports for an extended period only when apparently redundant instruments such as tariffs and reduced aggregate demand are also employed.

Thus, our hypothesis is that the import system worked in a way that the level of aggregate demand in current prices was the major determinant of the level of imports. Licencing may have had some negative effect on imports, but was not the sole determinant. Rather, the import system generally responded to increased aggregate demand by increasing imports in much the same way as before the introduction of licencing. To test this we expressed the relationship in the following linear form:[89]

$$M_t = \alpha + \beta_1 \, GDP_t + \beta_2 \, DLIC_t + u_t \tag{II.5}$$

where M = c.i.f. value of imports of goods at current prices, millions of N¢

88. See Tony Killick, "The Purposes and Consequences of Import Controls in Ghana," *op. cit.*
89. Because we are considering total merchandise imports rather than some subset, we chose to use a highly aggregated indicator of demand pressure (GDP in current prices) as an explanatory variable. Real and price components, private and public components, consumption and investment components, are all lumped together in the one explanatory variable. The overall relationship masks changing composition of imports and of GDP. Work by J.L.S. Abbey and C.S. Clark is currently underway at the University of Western Ontario on a macroeconomic model of Ghana which, among other things, will provide disaggregated import functions. Our purpose here is far more limited: to give a descriptive first approximation of how the import system worked.

(Table A-4a), GDP = gross domestic product at current prices, millions of N¢ (Table IV-2), DLIC = 1 for all years licencing enforced (1962, 1963, 1964, 1966) and zero for all other years. Ideally we would want a constant price series for imports. Since such a series is not available for the entire period we are interested in, we have specified the value of imports in current c.i.f. prices on the grounds that there has not been any major variation in the foreign prices of imports facing Ghana.[90]

For the period 1955 through 1966 the ordinary least squares regression yielded:

$$M_t = 114.9 + 0.1205 \, \text{GDP}_t - 32.10 \, \text{DLIC}_t$$
$$\quad (3.456) \ (3.560) \qquad (-1.287)$$

Observations = 12
$R^2 = 0.605$
D.W. = 1.367

The coefficient for GDP is significant at the 1-percent level, while that of DLIC only at the 15-percent level. The Durbin-Watson test is inconclusive. This result suggests that the system permitted imports to respond significantly to GDP in current prices, and somewhat less precisely to licencing. It is important to note that this estimated relationship does not represent an import demand function, but rather is simply a description of the behavior of the import system which operated prior to 1967.

To sum up, the strategic choice made in 1961 to opt for direct controls of both exports and imports resulted in the venting of aggregate demand pressure on domestic prices. This, in the absence of compensatory policies, led to an immediate deterioration of non-cocoa exports and eventually to a cessation of new cocoa plantings. At the same time the system of direct controls proved inadequate to contain the pressure of domestic demand, which without a sufficiently high effective exchange rate facing imports resulted in a continuing high level of imports.

Aggregate demand and hence, in a world of controls, relative prices in the domestic economy proved to be powerful forces affecting the performance of exports and the level of imports. Neglect of these forces to concentrate on symptomatic treatment by attempting direct control resulted in unsustainable balance-of-payments deficits. By the end of 1966 it was clear that something drastic had to be done, and done soon.

90. Note that the exchange rate remained unchanged during the period considered in the regression.

CHAPTER III

Allocation of resources

The balance-of-payment difficulties of the 1960's called into play a wide range of instruments designed primarily to control the external balance. Yet these instruments inevitably created incentives which could, if allowed full play, profoundly alter the allocation of resources in the Ghanaian economy. The general direction of the incentives was largely one which favored the already existing import-substitution and industrialization strategy. Hence, the allocational effects of the exchange control and licencing system did not counter, but usually reinforced, protectionist policies. The overall effect of the combined policies was a substantial transformation of the composition of economic activity within a brief period of 15 years.

The purpose of this chapter is to consider the general reallocation of resources in the Ghanaian economy and to examine in more detail the allocative forces bearing on the favored industrial sector. We begin with an overview of the changing composition of economic activity (section 1) and then turn to an examination of the structure of industrial activities (section 2). The remainder of the chapter is devoted to detailed consideration of industrial protection (sections 3 and 4).

1. The changing structure of production, 1955–1969

Kwame Nkrumah had led Ghana to political independence in 1957, but a major objective which remained unfulfilled at that time was "economic independence, without which our political independence would be valueless."[1] Hence, a "constant, fundamental guide is the need for economic independence.... An important essential is to reduce our colonial-produced economic vulnerability...."[2] This was to be done in large part by promoting import-substituting industrialization for, he argued, "Every time we import goods that we could manufacture...we are continuing our economic dependence and delaying our industrial growth."[3]

A series of development plans, formulated in the 1950's, had been designed

---

1. Kwame Nkrumah, *Africa Must Unite,* first published 1963; new edition, International Publishers, New York, 1970, p. 107.
2. *Ibid.,* p. 108.
3. *Ibid.,* p. 112.

to provide infrastructure and social services to lay the foundation and to begin the process of industrialization.[4] By the time of the Seven Year Development Plan (1963), the commitment to an import-substitution strategy of industrialization was strong.

> To the largest degree possible domestic substitutes should be produced for those manufactured staples of consumer demand for whose supply Ghana is now entirely dependent upon foreign sources and expends large sums in foreign exchange each year.[5]

To a remarkable extent the actual results, in terms of the composition of economic activity, corresponded to the plans. Within a relatively short period there was a major shift in the composition of economic activity. The available national income estimates suggest that the turning point was in the early 1960's. The groundwork for this was laid in the last half of the 1950's, with the economy growing at a satisfactory real rate, and gradual shifts in the industrial origin of GDP.

To illustrate the changing composition of economic activity, let us consider the contrast between 1955 and 1960, as contained in Table III-1. Despite some difficulties with the data (discussed below) one can discern a number of major characteristics of the 1955-60 period. There was a relative shift from cocoa and local foods, whose shares declined by about 3 percentage points each, and a shift to the activities of forestry and sawmilling, manufacturing, other industries (mostly organized commercial transport, distribution and services), government enterprises and general government. In other words, the shift was from traditional agriculture towards "modern" activities. Nevertheless, many of these modern activities were still relatively small in 1960. Manufactures and government enterprises (including electricity), which were to grow substantially in the 1960's, together still accounted for less than 4 percent of GDP.

Turning to the 1960's, we are not as fortunate in the availability of national accounts estimates by industrial origin.[6] Table III-2 is a very rough attempt to put together some of the available statistics to give an indication of the approximate proportions of GNP originating in a few of the important sectors. In these rough terms, what emerges is a continuing decline in the share of cocoa producer incomes to the point that by 1969 value-added at producer prices in manufacturing exceeded that in cocoa. Also declining relatively in the 1960's were the other two traditional export sectors, logging and sawmilling, and mining — the latter very rapidly. Construction's share also declined.

4. The plans of the 1950's were: First Development Plan (1951–1957), Consolidation Development Plan (1957–1959), and Second Development Plan (1959–1964).
5. Republic of Ghana, *Seven Year Development Plan,* Accra, 1963, p. 93.
6. Work on gathering GDP by industrial origin for the period 1965–1968 is in progress within the Central Bureau of Statistics. At the time of writing these were not yet publicly available.

Table III-1
Industrial origin of GDP, 1955 and 1960 at current market prices
(in millions of new cedis)

Sector	1955		1960		Annl. Comp. Gr. Rate (percent)
	Value	Percent	Value	Percent	
Cocoa - production	84	12.6	90	9.6	1.4
- marketing	46	6.9	60	6.4	5.5
Other agricultural exports	2	0.3	6	0.6	24.6
Local food prodn. and distribution	220	32.9	278	29.6	4.8
Forestry and sawmilling	28	4.2	52	5.5	13.2
Mining	30	4.5	42	4.5	7.0
Manufacturing	4	0.6	18	1.9	35.1
Construction, private	24	3.6	36	3.8	8.4
Industries, other private	60	9.0	114	12.2	13.7
Rent (net), pers. and hsld. serv.	56	8.4	86	9.2	9.0
Govt. enterprise and public corp.	6	0.9	18	1.9	24.6
General government	26	3.9	48	5.1	13.0
Residual	82	12.3	90	9.6	1.9
(1) GDP at mkt. prices (=expenditure)	668	100	938	100	7.0
(2) Indirect taxes	90		92		
(3) GDP at factor cost	578		846		
(4) Net factor income from abroad	−4		−10		
(5) Expenditure on GNP at market prices	664		928		

Note: The GDP estimate is derived from the expenditure side. These estimates of
         industrial origin, which do not cover the entire range of activities, are equated
         with GDP by inclusion of the residual item.
Source: Dorothy Walters, *Report on the National Accounts of Ghana,* 1955–1961,
         mimeograph, CBS, Accra, 1962, Tables I and II, pp. 2-3.

We should emphasize that the data of Tables III-1 and III-2 are subject to
some severe limitations. First, there is the usual problem of double counting
— value-added for a particular activity included in more than one sector —
which limits our confidence in any absolute size comparison between sectors.
Second, the components of Tables III-1 and III-2 are based on 1960 benchmark ratios of value-added to gross output. To the extent that substantial
structural change occurred between, say, 1955 and 1969, comparisons of
relative sectoral growth are open to doubt. Further, the total GDP estimates
— which are made from the expenditure side — are also based on 1960
benchmarks. The most serious shortcoming of this approach is undoubtedly
in the largest single element of consumption expenditure — local foods. This

Table III-2

GNP and rough estimates of value-added at current producer prices in selected activities, 1955, 1960, 1965, 1969

	Values, millions of N¢				Percentage of GNP				Average compound growth rates			
	1955	1960	1965	1969	1955	1960	1965	1969	1955–1960	1960–1965	1965–1969	1955–1969
GNP	664	946	1,589	2,284	100	100	100	100	7.3	10.9	9.5	9.2
Electricity	N.A.	2.2	6.4	21.1	N.A.	0.2	0.4	0.9	N.A.	23.8	34.8	N.A.
Timber and saw-milling exports	16	20.6	25.4	39.4	2.4	2.2	1.6	1.7	5.2	4.3	11.6	6.6
Manufacturing	4	16.4	54.7	121.1	0.6	1.7	3.4	5.3	32.6	27.0	22.0	27.6
Mining	29	41.2	32.5	39.3	4.4	4.4	2.1	1.7	7.3	-3.9	4.8	2.2
Cocoa	67	91.8	78.4	112.1	10.1	9.7	4.9	4.9	6.5	-2.8	9.4	4.3
Construction	50	85.2	112.4	104.1	7.5	9.0	7.1	4.6	11.2	5.7	-1.8	5.4
Public consumption	27	47.8	106.3	117.2	4.1	5.1	6.7	5.1	5.3	17.3	2.5	8.6
Total of activities listed	193	305.2	416.2	554.3	29.1	32.3	26.2	24.3	9.6	6.4	7.4	7.8

Sources: See next page.

Sources to Table III-2

Sources: 1. GNP at market prices, computed from expenditure side only. Sources: 1955, D. Walters, *op. cit.*; others, *Economic Survey,* 1969.
2. Value-added in electricity generation and distribution. Sources: 1960, R. Szereszewski, "The Inter-sectoral Accounts," Table 3.1., in Birmingham *et al.*; 1965 and 1969, *Economic Survey,* 1969.
3. Timber and sawmilling exports includes exports of logs, lumber and plywood, less export duties on logs and lumber. Sources: 1955 and 1960, CBS, *Annual Report on External Trade of Chana*, 1958, and 1959–1960; 1965 and 1969, CBS, *Quarterly Digest of Statistics,* June 1968 and December 1969.
4. Manufacturing value-added excluding sawmilling and plywood. Sources: 1955, Walters; 1960, Szereszewski; 1965 and 1969, *Economic Survey,* 1969.
5. Mining value-added. Sources: 1955 and 1960, Walters — less mineral export duties from *Annual Report on External Trade of Ghana*, 1958, and 1959–1960; 1965 and 1969, *Economic Survey,* 1969. The mines' own production of electricity is included in the value-added computation for 1955 and 1960, excluded in 1965 and 1969. This accounted for 36.3 percent of total national killowatt hours in 1965 and 0.8 percent in 1969.
6. Cocoa value-added consists of purchases by the Marketing Board at the cash price received by producers less purchases of insecticides. Sources: 1960, Szereszewski; for 1955 and 1965, producer receipts recorded in CMB *Annual Report,* 1962/63 and 1964/65 provided figures on weekly purchases, which were converted to calendar-year figures, and producer prices. 1969 data obtained directly from CMB. The Szereszewski ratio of value-added to gross output of 99.35 percent is applied to yield the results in our table.
7. Construction value-added. 1960 from Szereszewski; gross output for 1955 from Walters, "Gross Domestic Fixed Capital Formation in Buildings and Other Construction and Works"; and 1965 and 1969 from *Economic Survey,* 1969, "Gross Domestic Fixed Capital Formation in Building and Construction." The Szereszewski ratio of value-added to gross output of 64.64 percent applied to 1955, 1965 and 1969 data to yield the results in our table.
8. Public consumption value-added. 1960 from Szereszewski; 1955, from Walters, "General Government Consumption Expenditure"; 1965 and 1969, "General Government Consumption Expenditure," in *Economic Survey,* 1969. The Szereszewski ratio of value-added to total expenditure of 51.84 percent is applied to 1955, 1965 and 1969 data to yield the results in our table.
9. Total probably overstates extent of coverage due to possibilities of double counting between activities listed.

is assumed to grow at the same real rate as estimated population growth, and is converted to current values by the local foods price index. Third, the data of Tables III-1 and III-2 are in current prices because constant price data for the details are unavailable. Thus, the changing sectoral shares of national income we observe involve both changes in volume and changes in prices. The data do tell us how the distribution of income between sectors has changed, but they do not tell us the extent to which quantities of factors have shifted between sectors. This is particularly important in the largely import-substituting manufacturing sector, whose growth in the 1960's was due to substantial protection.

Despite these limitations of the data, a strong impression remains that the distribution of economic activity was substantially altered in the 1960's. The favored modern sectors, particularly manufacturing, now received important shares of national income. In this redistributive sense the objective of industrialization was being successfully attained. Yet when we recognize that a substantial price element was contained in the growth of manufacturing (see section 2, following) and, as we shall see in Chapter IV, that the economy as a whole failed to provide significant overall growth of per capita incomes in the 1960's, the strategy of industrialization to induce real growth was clearly far less than a success.

2. Growth of the industrial sector

We turn now to a more detailed examination of the industrial sector, considering first a variety of aggregate indicators for the whole sector (mining, manufacturing, electricity), as contained in Table III-3. Unfortunately, our period of coverage is limited. Industrial surveys were conducted for 1958 and 1959, but not resumed until 1962. Further, the detailed reports beyond 1968 are not yet published. As a result, much of the important detail, such as constant price data and value-added per person engaged, is available for less than the full period of this study. Despite these limitations, a number of important aspects of Ghanaian industrial development are clear.

The price element in the growth of industrial output and value-added was substantial. In current prices, value-added grew by about 143 percent between 1962 and 1969, while at constant prices the growth was 50 percent. One will further note that the constant price series probably overstates real values because of the major structural change over this brief period. New entrants typically required greater protection than was enjoyed by the early entrants. However, the higher prices for the former have a low or negligible weight in the price index used to deflate the current price data.

Growth of employment in industry was markedly slower than growth of

Table III-3

Selected industrial statistics, 1958, 1962, and 1966–1969

	1958	1962	1966	1967	1968	1969
1. Gross output (in millions of NȻ)						
1a. current prices	86.6	122.3	208.3	241.1	295.8	337.0
1b. constant (1962) prices	N.A.	122.3	173.0	179.9	204.0	217.6
2. Value-added (in millions of NȻ)						
2a. current prices	57.0	81.2	142.1	158.4	176.7	197.7
2b. constant (1962) prices	N.A.	81.2	120.1	119.7	124.4	121.7
3. Persons engaged (thousands)	N.A.	60.9	69.9	69.5	77.6	N.A.
4. V.-a. per person engaged (in thousands of NȻ)						
4a. current prices	N.A.	1.33	2.03	2.28	2.28	N.A.
4b. constant (1962) prices		1.33	1.72	1.72	1.61	N.A.
5. Wages and salaries (in millions of NȻ)	N.A.	24.3	34.4	36.6	44.3	N.A.
6. Wages and salaries per person engaged (NȻ)						
6a. current prices	N.A.	399.2	492.1	526.8	570.3	N.A.
6b. constant (1962) consumer prices	N.A.	399.2	287.1	335.8	336.1	N.A.
7. Distribution of v.-a. by nationality						
of ownership (percent)- Ghanaian	N.A.	26.8	26.9	27.5	29.3	N.A.
- Non-Ghanaian	N.A.	67.0	59.2	58.5	51.5	N.A.
- Mixed	N.A.	6.2	13.2	14.0	19.2	N.A.
8. Distribution of v.-a. by type						
of ownership (percent)- State	N.A.	22.9	22.1	23.5	24.7	N.A.
- Joint-State-Priv.	N.A.	4.2	8.1	9.0	11.7	N.A.
- Co-op	N.A.	0.1	0.1	0.1	0.0	N.A.
- Private	N.A.	72.9	69.7	67.4	63.6	N.A.
9. Distribution of v.-a. by region						
manufg. only (percent)- Western	N.A.	42.3	33.2	30.8	25.9	N.A.
- Accra Cap. Dist.	N.A.	31.0	45.8	51.5	53.3	N.A.
- Ashanti	N.A.	17.1	17.6	13.5	16.9	N.A.
- Other	N.A.	9.6	3.4	4.3	3.9	N.A.

Notes: 1. 1958 entry under gross output refers to sales, not gross output.

2. The deflator used to obtain the constant price wage and salary series is the consumer price index.

3. Regional distribution of value-added refers to manufacturing only.

Sources: 1969, CBS, *Economic Survey,* 1969; 1966–1968, CBS, *Industrial Statistics,* 1966–1968; 1962, CBS *Industrial Statistics,* 1962–1964; 1958, CBS, *Industrial Statistics,* 1958–1959.

output or value-added. The rate of growth of constant price value-added between 1962 and 1968 was twice the rate of growth of employment. At the same time, employees do not appear to have captured a larger share of value-added. Looking at current price data, the share of wages and salaries in value-added fell from 30 percent in 1962 to 25 percent in 1968. To put it another way, value-added grew at a rate two-thirds greater than the rate of growth of wages and salaries. And, the wages and salaries per employee, when deflated by the consumer price index, declined by about 16 percent between 1962 and 1968. The industrial sector thus does not appear to have proven a dynamic source of growth for either employment or income of employees over the period.

The distribution of ownership of the industrial sector indicates the dominance of private foreign owners followed by Ghanaian state-owned activity. Since by definition state-owned enterprises are Ghanaian, we can see that the privately-owned Ghanaian enterprises account for a small portion of value-added. The foreign private owners have had a decreasing share, but this is largely due to increasing use of the joint state-foreign private form of enterprise, and is not the result of growth by private Ghanaian firms.

The distribution of manufacturing value-added by region series indicates a shift of the center of manufacturing activity from the Western Region to the Accra Capital District. (We cite only the manufacturing data, because the location of mining activity is determined largely by deposits, while electricity is, from 1966, almost entirely from the Volta Dam.) A variety of reasons is undoubtedly responsible for the increasing dominance of the Accra district in manufacturing activity. Since nearly all of the sector produces for the domestic market, location in the largest single high money income market is undoubtedly important. Added to this are the advantages of the modern port of Tema for imports of materials and equipment, and the network of transport and communication facilities that radiate from Accra. Finally, Accra has the major advantage of being located close to the grantors of import licences and other discretionary favors.

Turning from the aggregate picture of the industrial sector, consider now the growth of output and value-added in individual activities outlined in Table III-4. The patterns of growth were far from uniform. In 1958 the strong dominance of the traditional activities of mining and sawmilling, plus the "easy" import-substitution activities of beverages and tobacco, are clearly evident. Only one "modern" activity, transport equipment, had a value-added exceeding N¢ 1 million. In 1962 the picture is much the same, except for the emergence of a significant edible oils and chemicals manufacturing activity. It is at this point that the beginning of major change in the structural shares of industrial production becomes evident. By 1965 two new industries, metal products and petroleum refining, emerged as important contributors to indus-

Table III-4
Industrial sector, value-added and gross output, 1958, 1959, and 1962–1968 at current
prices (in millions of new cedis)

ISIC Digit Code	Description	Value-added					
		1958	1959	1962	1963	1964	1965
Div. 1, Mining							
12	Metal mining	29.3	24.3	25.4	24.7	23.3	22.4
19	Other mining	5.9	6.1	9.1	8.4	10.1	10.8
Div. 2, 3, Manufacturing							
20	Food manufacturing	0.9	0.8	1.6	1.7	2.1	3.1
21	Beverages	} 7.3	8.2	{ 6.5	8.3	8.7	11.1
22	Tobacco manufactures			9.9	11.7	13.1	14.6
23	Textile manufactures	0.1	0.1	0.1	0.9	0.6	2.0
24	Footwear, apparel and textile goods	–	–	0.5	1.4	2.0	1.8
25	Sawmilling and plywood	8.0	9.5	12.3	12.1	13.0	14.9
26	Furniture manufactures	0.2	0.4	1.6	1.6	0.9	1.6
27	Paper and paper production	–	–	0.1	0.5	0.6	0.7
28	Printing and publishing	1.3	0.9	1.5	2.8	2.2	2.0
29	Travel goods manufactures	–	–	0.3	0.2	0.2	0.2
30	Manufactures of raw rubber	0.2	0.2	0.3	0.4	0.6	1.2
31	Chemicals and oils manufactures	0.5	0.9	2.9	4.2	5.5	5.4
32	Petroleum refining	–	–	–	1.9	4.5	4.2
33	Non-metal mineral production	0.3	0.4	0.5	0.6	0.5	0.8
34	Iron and steel manufactures	–	–	0.3	0.3	0.1	0.1
35	Metal products	0.1	0.2	1.6	1.8	2.5	2.5
37	Electrical appliances and appar.	–	–	–	–	–	–
38	Transport equipment manufactures	1.4	2.0	0.9	1.2	1.1	2.4
39	Miscellaneous manufacturing	–	–	0.1	0.5	0.9	0.8
Div. 5, Electr. and gas							
51	Electricity	1.5	2.1	5.8	7.3	8.8	13.1
	Total	56.9	56.1	81.2	92.4	101.4	116.0

Notes: 1. Entries may not add to total due to rounding.
          2. [–] = no value recorded.
          3. Coverage includes only those establishments with 30 or more employees.
          4. Major items contained in broadly-defined 2-digit groups are:

Group	Major subgroups included
12	gold, bauxite, and manganese
19	salt, diamonds
20	meat, fruit squash, fruit and vegetable processing, flour, biscuits, bread, cocoa butter, misc. foor preparations
21	spirits, beer, soft drinks
23	spinning, weaving and knitting
24	shoes, apparel, jute bags, mattresses, sheets, blankets

1966	1967	1968	1969	Gross output									
				1958	1959	1962	1963	1964	1965	1966	1967	1968	1969
23.8	26.9	30.0 } 39.3		{39.5	36.2	33.5	32.6	31.0	31.3	30.8	35.5	39.4	37.2
17.2	18.0	13.5		{ 7.4	7.5	10.3	9.7	11.8	12.4	18.0	18.8	14.9	15.3
2.3	4.1	6.6	12.9	2.9	3.3	4.2	4.3	4.7	9.6	10.8	18.5	23.3	33.9
15.3	13.7	18.1	17.9 }	11.5	13.2 {	10.3	13.9	14.3	17.7	21.5	18.5	24.4	25.3
18.0	17.7	21.6	21.7 }		{	12.7	14.6	16.5	18.0	20.5	21.0	25.9	25.7
3.8	9.0	11.9	13.2	0.3	0.5	0.3	1.7	2.6	4.0	7.0	15.3	25.9	33.9
3.2	6.7	10.7	9.1	–	–	1.7	3.3	4.4	5.8	8.3	12.7	21.6	19.5
14.7	13.0	8.9	16.1	14.6	15.9	20.4	20.2	21.6	23.4	22.7	23.7	24.1	30.5
1.7	1.3	1.3	1.3	0.5	0.7	2.5	2.8	3.5	3.1	2.9	2.3	2.4	2.4
1.4	2.7	3.3	4.9	–	–	0.2	0.8	1.0	1.4	2.8	5.0	6.2	9.1
4.0	4.4	5.2	4.2	2.3	1.8	2.4	4.1	3.1	3.4	5.4	5.6	6.7	7.0
0.2	0.2	0.3	0.4	–	–	0.5	0.4	0.5	0.4	0.4	0.5	0.7	0.8
0.2	0.2	0.2	0.4	0.4	0.5	0.5	0.5	1.4	2.0	0.3	0.3	0.3	0.6
7.8	8.5	8.1	11.4	0.8	2.0	5.7	10.1	13.5	11.5	16.5	20.0	21.5	28.0
4.4	5.4	5.3	6.0	–	–	–	2.0	4.9	5.1	5.2	6.1	6.4	6.5
1.5	1.7	3.8	5.5	0.4	0.6	1.0	1.3	1.1	1.4	3.0	3.4	9.8	12.8
0.3	0.9	0.5	0.4	–	–	0.5	0.5	0.2	0.9	0.9	1.5	1.1	1.2
3.0	3.5	4.2	5.0	0.3	0.8	5.7	7.2	8.3	6.5	7.0	8.4	9.9	11.1
0.3	0.6	1.2	1.6	–	–	–	–	–	–	0.7	1.5	3.0	3.5
2.2	3.9	3.2	2.7	3.0	3.8	2.1	4.2	3.8	4.3	4.8	5.4	7.6	7.4
0.7	0.7	1.0	2.6	–	–	0.4	1.0	1.8	1.6	1.4	1.3	2.3	3.8
16.0	15.6	18.0	21.1	2.7	3.8	7.2	9.1	11.0	15.0	17.4	16.0	18.6	21.7
142.2	158.5	176.7	197.7	86.5	90.6	122.4	144.5	160.8	178.8	208.3	241.1	295.8	337.0

31 - industrial chemicals, copra oil, groundnut oil, palm kernel oil, other oil fats, paints, soap, matches, perfume, pharmaceuticals, detergents, candles
33 - bricks and tiles, glass and products, cement, concrete blocks
35 - aluminum ware, nails, misc. other
38 - boat building and repair, railway equipment, motor vehicle assembly
39 - plastics

Sources: Computed from CBS, *Industrial Statistics,* 1958–1959, 1962–1964, 1965–1966, 1966--1968; and from CBS, *Economic Survey*, 1969.

trial value-added. Between 1965 and 1969 a substantial alteration in the industrial structure took place. In the latter year several nontraditional activities, including food manufacturing, footwear and apparel, paper products, non-metal mineral products, and metal products, had also emerged as important segments of the industrial sector. In addition, new activities such as travel goods, iron and steel, electrical appliances and apparatus, and plastics had become smaller, but undoubtedly permanent, parts of the Ghanaian industrial scene.

The growth of some activities was in part due to the "normal" course of events in which they became relatively more profitable due to forces such as larger markets, cheaper inputs (e.g., electricity), and the availability of low-cost specialized factors. Growth of specific activities was also in part due to a set of deliberate import-substitution policies involving a variety of incentives to favored activities. It is to these incentives that we now turn.

3. Protection of industry

A great variety of incentive policies was employed to stimulate domestic production in import-substituting industries. In this section we focus on the protection of domestic production *vis-à-vis* the world market.[7] We begin with a review of the major devices used to protect local industry.

(a) The protective system

The Ghanaian system of protection revolved largely around the system of tariffs and indirect taxes together with import licencing. Our earlier discussion (Chapter II) of these instruments focused attention on their broad application, passing over their detailed use to discriminate between domestic and imported commodities at a very fine level of detail. Yet the issue facing a local producer concerns the extent to which those specific imports that compete directly with his lines are permitted and at what price, together with the availability and price of his required inputs, including importable inputs. The various instruments used in the protective system are generally capable of discriminating in favor of an individual producer at the necessary level of detail.[8]

---

7. In the process of providing protection against foreign products there will also be discrimination among domestic producers. This aspect, together with other devices used specifically to discriminate among domestic activities, is taken up in Chapter IV below.

8. However, because some producers may use inputs produced by others, it is not always possible in practice to provide the desired discrimination in favor of all import-competing producers.

Consider each of the major elements in the protective system which prevailed in the period 1968–1970. First, the Ghanaian customs tariff frequently discriminated at the level of detail corresponding to the SITC 6-digit level, and on occasion at an even finer level of detail. Typically the tariff escalated by "stage" of production, with low rates on materials and higher rates on finished products, particularly those produced locally.[9] In addition to the rate of differentiation by degree of product processing, there were concessionary rates on materials of any type which were specifically destined for use in the manufacture of numerous particular products.[10]

Added to the customs tariff was a set of domestic indirect taxes designed largely to raise revenue. However, because there was rate differentiation between domestic and foreign sources on some commodities, the indirect tax system affected the level of nominal protection. The major indirect taxes were the sales tax, the excise tax, and the purchase tax. The sales tax was administered at the manufacturer and customs house level, and was applied equally to most imported and domestic goods for final use at the standard rate of $11\frac{1}{2}$ percent. Exemptions included producer goods, "essential" consumer goods, corporations enjoying tax concessions,[11] and sales for export. The excise tax was levied on the traditional objects of alcoholic beverages and tobacco, plus a set of specified "luxuries" at rates ranging from 5 percent to 15 percent and a few specific rates. Exemptions in practice were the same as for the sales tax. The excise tax applied only to domestic output, but the sales tax was reduced on excisable items to $7\frac{1}{2}$ percent or 5 percent, depending on the item. Coverage did not yet include a number of recent import-substitution luxuries such as electrical appliances. The purchase tax applied to motor vehicles only, at rates on a rising step scale. Locally assembled commercial vehicles enjoyed a lower rate.

The combined protective effect of the tariffs and domestic indirect tax system was complex and often difficult to evaluate for an individual product line. Further, a change in one element without a compensating change in another often resulted in unintended changes in protection. Despite the complexity and frequent changes in individual rates, there was no continuing and

9. For example, in the BTN Chapters 50 through 56 dealing with fibers and products thereof, cotton, flax, and man-made fibers are subject to a 10 percent duty while woven fabrics are subject to a minimum 75 percent rate (NLC *Decree, 185*, (1967).

10. These are specified in Part B of the import tariff schedule, Republic of Ghana, *Customs and Excise Tariff*, Accra, 1966.

11. While apparently the Volta Aluminum Company (VALCO) is the only firm legally entitled to exemption on its purchases, others employing tax concessions believe themselves to be exempt and do not pay.

systematic evaluation of the protective effects by a "tariff board" type of agency.

In early 1969 an additional tax on imports was introduced in the form of a "temporary surcharge" on OGL imports. Initially the rate was 5 percent of c.i.f. value and applied only to what was at the time a limited list of OGL items. The budget presented in mid-1970 contained a substantial extension of the OGL list together with a differentiated set of surcharges at rates ranging from 5 percent to 150 percent of c.i.f. value on most OGL imports.[12] In one swift stroke the protective structure was greatly altered, yet there is no evidence that the protective consequences of this new complex addition to the protective system received detailed advance consideration.

A second major element in the protective system was import licencing. In principle the licencing system was expected to limit or prevent imports competing with domestic products; it was also expected to ensure that local producers receive adequate supplies of imported materials.[13] In practice the restricted lists for which "no application will be entertained except under special circumstances,"[14] allowed a substantial volume of imports.[15] And as we have noted (Chapter II), in the late Nkrumah period shortages of inputs were frequent. As a source of protection for domestic producers the licencing system was uncertain and erratic.

In addition to the specifically protective devices listed, the Capital Investments Board had at its disposal a variety of concessions which it could grant to foreign investors with substantial protective consequences. Of particular interest in the context of protection, a producer of goods for export or import-substitution could be exempted from the payment of duties and indirect taxes on imported inputs, and apparently from the payment of excise taxes on output, for a period of 5 years.[16] Beyond the number of projects approved, which has averaged about 15 per year since 1965, with a typical investment of about N₵ 2 million,[17] no details on the concessions granted

12. See Chapter V/section 4, for general discussion of the surchages in the context of the liberalization.
13. See Chapter II, section 5.
14. This, the typical phrase used to indicate the meaning of the restricted list, appeared in the *Commercial and Industrial Bulletin,* 18 August, 1967.
15. For example, the restricted items listed in *ibid.* for 1968 were imported during 1968 to a total of at least N₵ 16 million, or 5.1 percent of total imports (our tabulation). This does not include restricted items defined more narrowly than the SITC 6-digit trade data contained in the CBS, *External Trade Statistics,* December, 1968.
16. In addition, the Capital Investments Act, 1963 (Act 172) authorized the Board to guarantee repatriation of funds, grant exemption from company income tax for up to 10 years, grant accelerated depreciation allowances, and grant exemptions from property taxes.
17. Capital Investments Board, *Annual Report and Accounts,* various years.

are publicly available. We understand, however, that there was considerable variation in the concessions granted investors until 1971, largely because an ever-changing Board made decisions on an individual basis.[18] It is thus quite possible for three different domestic producers of the same commodity to face substantially different situations: a domestically-owned enterprise with no concessions, a foreign-owned enterprise with one or two concessions, and a second foreign-owned enterprise with the full basket of concessions.

Altogether, then, several instruments were used to grant protection, with levels of individual instruments for particular establishments and industries determined independently by different agencies.[19] It is important to note that one agency did not play a significant part in the detailed assignment of protection to individual activities. This was the planning agency. While, as we noted above, the development plan charted the general course of import-substituting industrialization, planning was largely divorced from the adminis-tration of the protective system. Thus, the magnitudes of the incentives were not determined by the detailed priorities of the plan, but rather by a hap-hazard system of protection which conferred vastly different stimuli on indi-vidual activities in the industrial sector. To measure these stimuli is our next task. We begin with a brief outline of the method of measurement.

(b) Method of measuring protection

The magnitude of the protective stimuli afforded each domestic industrial activity depends on the structure of price divergencies between domestic and international markets created by the various protective instruments. The sub-sidy effect arising from protection of output and the taxing effect of higher

---

18. Recently an augmented staff has attempted to apply uniform criteria and conces-sions.
19. To illustrate, consider a hypothetical potential foreign investor who in 1968 had been promised a set of CIB concessions involving duty-free entry of machinery and spare parts (but not materials) plus a company tax holiday. He would be the sole producer of the item in the domestic market. He had a great variety of ways open to him to increase the potential protection. He might have tried to convince the Minis-ter (or Commissioner) of Finance to increase the tariff on competing imports, or to establish a special concessionary rate for imports of his inputs. He could have tried to persuade Customs and Excise to reduce the excise tax on domestic production to a lower bracket. He could have attempted to convince the Trade Division of the Ministry of Trade and Industries to limit the licences issued for competing imports, and simultaneously dealt with the Industries Division of the same Ministry to ensure adequate licences for his imported materials. And, he could have attempted to obtain further concessions from the CIB. The degree of protection received thus depended on the policies of several agencies, each capable of acting independently of the others.

input costs are well known.[20] Our purpose here is to apply the general principles, using standard definitions, to the Ghanaian case. We have taken into account the major devices that create a measurable divergence between international and domestic prices.

To illustrate the relationships involved, consider the effect of each instrument. First, import tariffs raise domestic prices above world prices. Second, indirect taxes are sometimes applied to imports and/or domestic production, possibly at different rates.[21] Third, and often most important, licences give rise to quota premia that raise domestic prices above the tariff and tax-laden prices. Finally, various devices such as licence fees and the system of compulsory credit purchasing of imports add to the price of importables. The first three elements are illustrated in Figure III-1. The domestic supply curve at free-trade prices is S, and the domestic demand curve is D, yielding free-trade imports of $Q_0 Q_6$ at the free-trade price of P_w. The effect of a tariff on competing imports of the product at the rate t is to raise the domestic price to $P_w(1 + t)$, assuming infinitely elastic supply of imports. Tariffs on intermediate importable inputs result in a parallel upward shift in the supply curve to S'. The net result of the tariffs alone would be an expansion of output to Q_1 in response to the net stimulus provided by the tariff-protecting output less the higher input costs.

If we add indirect taxes to the set of tariffs, we find that indirect taxes on imports raise the domestic price to $P_w(1+t)(1+sm)$, where sm is the indirect tax rate on imports. At the same time indirect taxes on domestic output shift the supply curve proportionately upward to $S'(1+sd)$, where sd is the indirect tax rate on domestic output. (We have drawn Figure III-1 such that sm exceeds sd.) The net result of the set of tariffs plus the set of indirect taxes is a stimulus to output, yielding an expansion to Q_2.

Finally, if the domestic market is competitive and we impose on this situation a binding quota on imports of the competing product, setting the quota at $Q_3 Q_4$ quantity, which is less than $Q_2 Q_5$, the domestic price rises to P_d. In other words, the domestic price rises above the world price by the rate qr, and domestic output expands to Q_3.

20. The literature on this topic is far too large for a single footnote. Two major seminal pieces are: W.M. Corden, "The Structure of a Tariff System and the Effective Protective Rate," *Journal of Political Economy*, Vol. LXXIV, No. 3, June 1966, pp. 221-37; and H.G. Johnson, "The Theory of Tariff Structure with Special Reference to World Trade and Development," *Trade and Development*, Institut Universitaire de Hautes Etudes Internationales, Geneva, 1965.
21. See J. Clark Leith, "Tariffs, Indirect Taxes and Protection," in H.G. Grubel and H.G. Johnson, eds., *Effective Tariff Protection*, GATT and Graduate Institute of International Studies, Geneva, 1971.

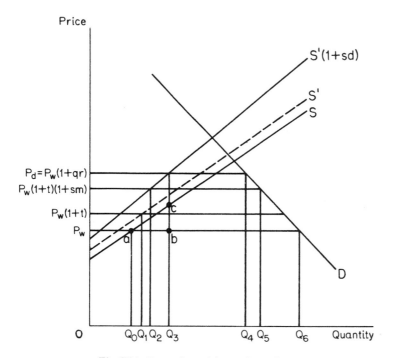

Fig. III-1. Protection of domestic market.

The net effect of the various protective devices illustrated in Figure III-1 is a stimulus to output amounting to bc per unit. This has resulted in an expansion of output along the original supply curve from point a to point c, for a change in output quantity of $Q_0 Q_3$. If our interest is in matters involving the product market such as the extent of import-substitution or restriction of imports, the net stimulus of bc is expressed as a rate with respect to the free trade price P_w: the net rate of protection of output. If however we are interested in the process by which value is added by primary factors, the net stimulus is more appropriately considered with respect to free-trade per unit value-added: the effective rate of protection of value-added.[22]

In cases where the quota is the binding constraint on imports, such as the competitive case illustrated in Figure III-1, it may be important to know how much of the protection is attributable to the quota and how much due to the

22. For further discussion of the net and effective rates of protection, as well as the assumptions underlying the analysis, see J. Clark Leith, "The Effect of Tariffs on Production, Consumption and Trade: A Revised Analysis," *American Economic Review,* Vol. LXI, No. 1, March 1971.

other devices such as tariffs and indirect taxes. For example, if the quota restriction on competing imports were to be lifted by placing an item on OGL, we would want to know what would happen to protection of domestic activities. When there is a monopoly in domestic production (but the quota is not held monopolistically), use of a quota instead of a tariff enables the domestic monopolist to exercise his monopoly power. Hence if the quota is set at the same level of imports as would prevail under a tariff, the quota premium exceeds the tariff and domestic production is less than under a tariff.[23] In either case — monopoly or competition in the domestic market — it is useful to calculate both the premium due to the binding quota restriction and the latent premium due to tariffs and indirect taxes which would pertain in the absence of the quota. The difference then tells us how much premium the licence system provides over and above the tariff and indirect tax system.

Changes in the magnitudes of the various components of the protective structure can also be considered. For example, the introduction of extensive surcharges in 1970, which simultaneously placed many items on OGL, can be considered by recalculating the protection under the new situation.

For empirical application, the relationships among the various protective devices are expressed precisely in algebraic form. The derivations and the formulas are contained in Appendix C. To apply the formulas we required an extensive body of data for each of the wide range of industrial activities covered: inputs and outputs, together with data on the magnitudes of the protective devices employed.

Our primary data source was the Central Bureau of Statistics' (CBS) annual survey of industrial establishments employing over 30 persons. With the cooperation of the CBS Industrial Statistics Section we were able to obtain detailed extracts from the returns of inputs, outputs, and indirect taxes, all at the establishment level. Confidentiality of individual returns was maintained by use of an identification code showing only industry, region, and establishment number.

The establishment data all refer to 1968, which was the latest year for which reasonably complete returns were available when we began this work. The results thus provide a picture of the situation in a period of relative economic stability. Liberalization, following the devaluation in mid-1967, was beginning, but the OGL list was largely confined to industrial materials,

23. For a discussion of the differences between a tariff and a quota when competitive conditions do not hold, see Jagdish Bhagwati, "On the Equivalence of Tariffs and Quotas," in R.E. Baldwin, *et al.*, eds., *Trade, Growth and the Balance of Payments — Essays in Honor of Gottfried Haberler,* Rand-McNally, Chicago, 1965. Bhagwati also analyses cases where there is monopoly holding of quotas, which is not of major interest in the Ghanaian case.

spare parts, and a few essential consumer items. The licencing system was running about as smoothly as in any year, and few tariff changes were instituted during the year.

Additional information not provided in the industrial statistics data had to be obtained from other sources. Our first step in this regard was to match each of the outputs and inputs listed by an establishment with the appropriate SITC 6-digit import item. For the quota premium rate on output we calculated the rate of excess of unit value of domestic output over the 1968 c.i.f. unit value of the competing 6-digit import item. We then calculated a weighted average quota premium (using domestic production at c.i.f. unit values as weights) for the establishment. For the tariff rate on output we calculated the ratio of 1968 duty collections for the matching SITC 6-digit item to the 1968 c.i.f. import values, and similarly for the sales tax rate on imports. The weighted average for the establishment also used weights at tax-free prices. We chose to use the collections rate rather than the scheduled rate because there are large discrepancies between the two due to numerous exemptions of duties granted various importers.[24] The difference between the scheduled and the collections rates is not trivial. Scheduled tariff collections on all imports would have yielded a tariff rate of 47.6 percent for 1968, whereas the actual collections rate for the same year was 20.1 percent.[25] On the grounds that it is virtually impossible to segment the duty-free and duty-paid markets in Ghana, we assumed that the tariff component of the domestic manufacturers' protection is only the average rate of duties and indirect taxes on competing imports, not the maximum.

Our approach to estimating the quota premium rate is subject to the usual shortcoming of unit value comparisons. In addition, it does not allow for real or imagined qualitative differences between the domestic and foreign goods, and hence does not tell us the extent to which the restrictive system allows the price of the domestic good to rise above what the price of that same good would be under free trade. Rather, it simply tells us how much the price of the domestic good exceeds the price of the foreign good. Ideally it is the former comparison that is of interest in considering the protection of domestic production: a with-versus-without comparison. At a minimum, the increase in the price of the domestic product due to the quota restriction is covered by the increase in the price of the foreign product due to tariffs and

---

24. As far as we could determine, the imports and duty collections (including sales tax on imports) are recorded at the same time. Hence a timing problem does not arise.
25. The scheduled rate was computed by determining the scheduled import duties (but not sales tax) for each SITC 6-digit item in the CBS, *External Trade Statistics,* December 1968, on the assumption that all imports of the item attracted full duty. The actual collections rate is from Table II-1 above.

indirect taxes. Hence whenever the nominal protection due to tariffs and indirect taxes exceeds the calculated quota premium (and the tariff is not redundant), or when we are unable to calculate a quota premium, we use the tariffs and indirect taxes on imports as our nominal rate of protection.

Turning to the input side, there are three types of inputs distinguished in our establishment data: materials, fuels and lubricants, and electricity. For materials, due to a general absence of quantity information, we were forced to settle for the inflation of costs due to tariffs and taxes, which is a minimum inflation that does not take into account the possibility of quota premia on these inputs. However, because most inputs were on OGL in 1968, this is not a serious shortcoming.[26] The inflation of material input costs that we did take into account are of two types:

(1) duties and indirect taxes paid on directly imported inputs; and

(2) in the limited number of instances where it occurred, higher cost importable inputs purchased locally.

For the first, we computed the rate by taking the ratio of duties paid to purchases of imported materials. For the second, we relied on the duty and sales tax collections on the matching SITC 6-digit imports as a proportion of the c.i.f. value of these imports, hence treating the importable inputs purchased locally as if they had been imported and duties paid on them. An average for each establishment was calculated, using weights at free-trade prices.

Petroleum fuels and lubricants constitute a relatively small proportion of most establishments' inputs, so we did not attempt a detailed disaggregation, but simply used the proportion of duties plus indirect taxes to total supply of fuels and lubricants to deflate use of petroleum fuels and lubricants.

Electricity comes largely from the Volta Dam, and is not directly subject to any trade distortion; consequently, we did not adjust use of electricity in our calculations.[27]

From what we have indicated so far, it is clear that our data and methods will subject our results to a number of qualifications. Specifically, we should note the following. First, our matching of domestic production and use of importable materials that are not directly imported with imports at the SITC 6-digit level was done to avoid the well known downward bias resulting from weighting tariff and quantitative premia rates by imports when items subject

---

26. To the extent that there were still quota premia on inputs, this procedure implicitly includes the input premia as part of the protection of value-added and output received by the producers. And in most cases producers do in fact receive the premia because licences for industrial materials go to actual users rather than intermediaries.

27. Additional data problems and methods are discussed in Appendix C.

to different rates are grouped. However, the result of this is the possibility of some arbitrarily narrow definitions of competing imports.

Second, our coverage is confined to an arbitrary selection of "large" establishments — these known to CBS and completing the 1968 annual detailed return less those whose returns we omitted because of inconsistent or incomplete data. Consequently, our results must be treated with some caution in drawing conclusions about the overall degree of protection of Ghanaian industrial activities. Rather, they are simply indicators of the wide range of protection enjoyed by Ghanaian industrial activities.

Third, we have no way of confirming the accuracy of our input—output data. There is the very basic problem of accurate accounting records. While we have eliminated some establishments because of incomplete or inconsistent returns, there probably remain others who had the foresight to enter any set of consistent numbers just to complete the form and avoid a call-back from a CBS official. This problem could have been minimized by undertaking the primary data collection ourselves, but only at the cost of a much more limited coverage. Beyond this, there is the problem of deliberately faked returns. Although the CBS assures the reporting firms that the return is confidential and will not be used for taxation or similar purposes, we are skeptical of the extent to which firms do report accurately. If a firm is keeping a double set of books, it is highly unlikely that it would use its private set to complete the questionnaire for the CBS, or anyone else. This possibility introduces a number of potential biases into our data. It means that we can generally expect the returns not to omit payment of duties on inputs and sales and excise taxes on output if they are liable for them. Hence, on the whole there is unlikely to be much understatement of these items. There is, however, the general incentive to overstate costs of inputs and understate the value of the output. This tends to reduce reported value-added, and where the effective rate exceeds the nominal rate this inflates the computed effective rate of protection.[28] At the same time, value-added at world prices is understated proportionately more than the effective rate of protection is overstated and as a consequence the computed net rate of protection is slightly understated.

The second major bias in our calculations arises from our inability to take into account possible quantitative premia on material inputs. This tends to reduce the computed value-added at world prices and hence inflate the computed effective rate of protection, where the effective rate exceeds the nominal rate. For the net rate of protection the overstatement of the effective rate

---

28. This is readily seen from equation (C.5), where V_j' is understated by the net amount of the understatement of X_j' and overstatement of $\Sigma_i X_{ij}'$.

of protection more than offsets the understatement of value-added at world prices. As a result, the net rate of protection is also overstated.

Finally, we have not taken into account the possibility that the structure of protection might have caused substitution in the input—output relationships.[29] For the industries considered we do not have enough observations or reasonably homogeneous inputs and outputs to estimate the substitution elasticities between inputs, and hence are not in a position to make the appropriate empirical adjustments of our estimates. If there is in fact a positive elasticity of substitution, the zero elasticity of substitution (i.e., fixed coefficient) assumption means that our estimates overstate the actual rates of protection.[30]

Putting these three biases together, we can unambiguously say that our computed effective rates of protection overstate the true picture where the effective rate exceeds the nominal rate. Our computed net rates of protection, however, are subject to offsetting influences which prevent an unambiguous statement concerning the bias, although our general presumption is that they are also overstated.

(c) Estimated rates of protection

We prepared estimates of protection for a broad range of industrial activities (Table III-5). For each activity there is an estimated rate of effective, net, and nominal protection. Each rate of protection is estimated initially on the basis of the quota restrictions (QR's). Then we estimated the element of protection due to the combined influence of tariffs, indirect taxes, and other non-quota elements (the tariff-tax system). The difference between the two indicates how much additional protection the licending system provided over and above the protection due to the tariff-tax system. These estimates all refer to 1968.

The estimates contained in Table III-5 are industry averages where data from more than one establishment were available. The average is a weighted average, using the share of value-added at world prices for the effective rates of protection and the share of output at world prices for the net and nominal rates of protection. This, of course, is not the same as calculating rates of protection from aggregated data, which implicitly weights by protected shares.

29. See J. Clark Leith, "Substitution and Supply Elasticities in Calculating the Effective Protective Rate," *Quarterly Journal of Economics,* Vol. LXXXII, No. 4, November 1968; and "The Effect of Tariffs on Production, Consumption and Trade: A Revised Analysis," *op. cit.*
30. See "Substitution...," *op. cit.*

Table III-5
Protection of Ghanaian industries, 1968 and 1970 (rates and standard deviations of rates in percentages, ranks in ascending order)

(1)	(2)	(3)		(4)		
	Industry			Effective rates of protection		
			No. of estb.	Quota restrictions (QR's)		
No.	Description	Notes		Rate	S.D.	(Rank)
1221	Gold mining	(9)	3	−12	6	(2)
1222	Bauxite mining	(9)	1	−3		(6)
1223	Manganese mining	(9)	1	−3		(7)
2010	Meat processing	(6)	3	35	92	(21)
2031	Fruit squash	(9)	1	−13		(1)
2039	Fruit and veg. processing	(5, 7)	1	498		(37)
2055	Coffee hulling	(7)	1	106		(27)
2061	Biscuits	(2, 7)	2	247	**	(33)
2082	Cocoa butter	(9)	1	−107*		(44)
2089	Confectionery	(7)	2	385	29668	(35)
2111	Distillery	(1, 7)	2	−312*	**	(46)
2131	Brewery	(3, 4, 7)	2	56	32	(25)
2140	Soft drinks	(2, 7)	4	20	17	(17)
2201	Processing raw tobacco	(7)	2	1803		(42)
2311	Kente	(9)	2	−3	6	(5)
2320	Knitting	(3, 6)	1	927		(40)
2411	Wearing apparel	(6)	13	749	521	(39)
2430	Shoes	(6)	20	1633	1507	(41)
2443	Mattresses	(1, 7)	1	2		(8)
2444	Towels, bedsheets, etc.	(1, 8)	2	23	70	(18)
2449	Blankets	(1, 3, 7)	1	53		(24)
2511	Sawn timber and lumber	(9)	34	10	6	(3)
2601	Furniture	(1, 7)	17	24	136	(19)
2609	Fixtures	(1, 7)	1	548		(38)
2720	Misc. paper	(1, 6)	4	11	35	(11)
2912	Handbags and luggage	(3, 7)	7	−192*	**	(45)
3003	Rubber processing	(7)	2	16	0	(13)
3119	Ind. chem.	(1, 8)	1	4		(9)
3121	Copra oil	(3, 7)	1	19		(16)
3122	Groundnut oil	(7)	1	108		(28)
3123	Palm oil	(3, 7)	1	14		(12)
3130	Paints	(6)	1	−653*		(47)
3193	Perfumes	(1, 6)	3	174	143	(32)
3194	Pharmaceut.	(1, 4, 7)	4	45	6	(23)
3195	Insecticides	(4, 6)	1	165		(31)
3196	Cosmetics	(1, 3, 6)	3	78374	78204	(43)
3197	Candles	(3, 7)	1	−7		(4)
3199	Misc. chemicals	(1, 6)	1	19		(14)
3412	Nails	(8)	1	19		(15)
3501	Al. ware	(2, 8)	3	30	67	(20)
3701	St. batteries	(6)	1	158		(30)
3703	Radio, etc.	(2, 8)	2	449		(36)
3709	Refrig.	(1, 6)	1	41		(22)
3920	Optical	(1, 7)	1	123		(29)
3949	Jewelry	(1, 7)	2	7	4	(10)
3959	Records	(7)	1	347		(34)
3990	Misc. plastics	(1, 8)	8	70	247	(26)

Table III-5 (continued)

(5)			(6)	(7)			(8)
Tariffs			QR− Tar.	Tar. + surchg.			Tar. + surchg. − QR
Rate	S.D.	(Rank)		Rate	S.D.	(Rank)	
−12	6	(4)	0	−13	7	(2)	−1
−3		(8)	0	−3		(8)	−0
−3		(9)	0	−3		(7)	−0
10	122	(13)	25	63	73	(25)	28
−13		(2)	0	−15		(1)	−3
498		(40)	0	478		(37)	−20
58		(28)	48	57		(23)	−49
247	**	(36)	0	246	**	(33)	−1
−107*		(46)	0	−105*		(44)	+2
385	29668	(38)	0	379	29197	(36)	−5
−312*	**	(47)	0	−277*	**	(46)	36
43	21	(25)	13	42	21	(20)	−14
20	17	(20)	0	19	17	(18)	−1
1803		(43)	0	1800		(39)	−3
−3*	6	(7)	0	−4	5	(6)	−1
927		(42)	0	1992		(40)	1065
389	252	(39)	361	926	589	(38)	176
36	96	(23)	1597	2045	1674	(41)	411
−4		(6)	5	−8		(4)	−10
23	70	(21)	0	188	592	(28)	165
53		(27)	0	52		(22)	−1
−12	7	(3)	2	−10	6	(3)	0
24	136	(22)	0	9	140	(12)	−15
548		(39)	0	−246		(45)	−794
11	36	(14)	1	14	37	(14)	3
−56*	**	(45)	−136	−30*	**	(43)	162
16	0	(16)	0	15	0	(15)	−1
4		(10)	0	−3		(9)	−7
19		(19)	0	9		(11)	−11
58		(29)	50	57		(24)	−51
14		(15)	0	12		(13)	−2
117		(1)	−770	−391*		(47)	262
174	143	(34)	0	340	272	(34)	226
45	6	(26)	0	42	8	(21)	−2
165		(33)	0	195		(30)	30
78374	78204	(44)	0	116993	116741	(42)	38619
−7		(5)	0	−8		(5)	−1
19		(17)	0	35		(17)	16
19		(18)	0	38		(18)	19
9	101	(12)	21	40	149	(19)	10
158		(32)	0	199		(32)	41
321		(37)	128	371		(35)	−79
41		(24)	0	189		(29)	+148
123		(31)	0	123		(27)	0
5	6	(11)	2	4	6	(10)	−3
198		(35)	149	196		(31)	−151
70	629	(30)	0	81	629	(26)	11

		(9)			(10)			(11)
		Net rate of protection						
		QR's			Tariffs			QR-Tar.
No.	Description	Rate	S.D.	(Rank)	Rate	S.D.	(Rank)	
1221	Gold mining	−6	3	(3)	−6	3	(4)	0
1222	Bauxite mining	−3		(4)	−3		(6)	0
1223	Manganese mining	2		(6)	−2		(8)	0
2010	Meat processing	5	16	(12)	2	20	(13)	3
2031	Fruit squash	−7		(1)	−7		(3)	0
2039	Fruit and veg. processing	82		(41)	62		(42)	0
2055	Coffee hulling	17		(26)	9		(23)	8
2061	Biscuits	92		(44)	92		(45)	0
2082	Cocoa butter	8		(18)	8		(20)	0
2089	Confectionery	81	13	(42)	81	13	(43)	0
2111	Distillery	28		(33)	28		(36)	0
2131	Brewery	46	31	(36)	35	21	(38)	11
2140	Soft drinks	6	13	(13)	6	13	(14)	0
2201	Processing raw tobacco	55		(40)	55		(41)	0
2311	Kente	0	5	(7)	0	5	(10)	0
2320	Knitting	112		(46)	112		(47)	0
2411	Wearing apparel	52	31	(39)	42	22	(39)	10
2430	Shoes	25	25	(31)	8	29	(18)	17
2443	Mattresses	1		(10)	−2		(9)	3
2444	Towels, bedsheets, etc.	1	10	(8)	1	10	(11)	0
2449	Blankets	25		(32)	25		(34)	0
2511	Sawn timber and lumber	−6	2	(2)	−8	3	(2)	2
2601	Furniture	6	10	(15)	6	10	(16)	0
2609	Fixtures	10		(21)	10		(24)	0
2720	Misc. paper	12	17	(23)	12	17	(26)	0
2912	Handbags and luggage	90	35	(43)	51	35	(40)	39
3003	Rubber processing	15	0.04	(25)	15	0.04	(28)	0
3119	Ind. chem.	1		(9)	1		(12)	0
3121	Copra oil	7		(16)	7		(17)	0
3122	Groundnut oil	46		(37)	25		(33)	21
3123	Palm oil	14		(24)	14		(27)	0
3130	Paints	47		(38)	−8		(1)	56
3193	Perfumes	29	29	(34)	29	29	(37)	0
3194	Pharmaceut.	19	6	(27)	19	6	(29)	0
3195	Insecticides	8		(17)	8		(19)	0
3196	Cosmetics	103	18	(45)	103	18	(46)	0
3197	Candles	−2		(5)	−2		(7)	0
3199	Misc. chemicals	6		(14)	6		(15)	0
3412	Nails	11		(22)	11		(25)	0
3501	Al. ware	4	14	(11)	−4	18	(5)	8
3701	St. batteries	21		(28)	21		(30)	0
3703	Radio, etc.	32		(35)	28		(35)	5
3709	Refrig.	9		(19)	9		(21)	0
3920	Optical	25		(30)	25		(32)	0
3949	Jewelry	9	5	(20)	9	7	(22)	0
3959	Records	155		(47)	88		(44)	67
3990	Misc. plastics	23	31	(29)	23	58	(31)	0

Table III-5 (continued)

Table III-5 (continued)

(12)			(13)	(14)			(15)			(16)
				Nominal rate of protection***						
Tar. + surchg.			T+S− QR	QR's			Tariffs			QR− Tar.
Rate	S.D.	(Rank)		Rate	S.D.	(Rank)	Rate	S.D.	(Rank)	
−6	4	(3)	−0	0	0	(1)	0	0	(1)	0
−3		(8)	−0	0		(1)	0		(1)	0
−3		(9)	−0	0		(1)	0		(1)	0
11	12	(21)	7	22	13	(20)	19	15	(21)	3
−8		(1)	−1	0		(1)	0		(1)	0
60		(39)	−2	88		(40)	88		(41)	0
9		(18)	−8	24		(22)	17		(20)	8
92		(44)	−0	103		(42)	103		(44)	0
8		(17)	−0	0		(1)	0		(1)	0
79	13	(41)	−1	105	20	(43)	105	20	(45)	0
26		(31)	−2	89		(41)	89		(42)	0
34	21	(36)	−12	54	23	(34)	43	13	(36)	11
5	12	(15)	−1	12	12	(12)	12	12	(12)	0
55		(38)	−0	64		(38)	64		(39)	0
−1	4	(11)	−1	7	5	(9)	7	5	(9)	0
241		(47)	129	124		(46)	124		(47)	0
106	38	(45)	54	63	31	(37)	53	23	(38)	10
87	43	(42)	63	58	21	(35)	41	11	(35)	17
−5		(4)	−6	5		(7)	2		(7)	3
2	82	(13)	2	9	20	(10)	9	20	(10)	0
25		(29)	−0	35		(30)	35		(32)	0
−6	2	(2)	0	0	0	(1)	0	0	(1)	0
−3	14	(6)	−9	15	9	(15)	15	9	(16)	0
−4		(5)	−14	16		(17)	16		(18)	0
13	18	(23)	2	21	13	(19)	21	13	(22)	0
29	50	(34)	−61	119	48	(45)	80	33	(40)	39
14	0.08	(24)	−1	17	0	(18)	17	0	(19)	0
−0		(12)	−1	29		(24)	29		(26)	0
3		(14)	−4	16		(16)	16		(17)	0
24		(27)	−22	58		(36)	37		(33)	21
11		(22)	−2	15		(14)	15		(15)	0
28		(33)	−19	69		(39)	3		(13)	56
76	46	(40)	47	49	31	(33)	49	31	(37)	0
18	6	(25)	−1	29	7	(25)	29	7	(27)	0
10		(19)	1	27		(23)	27		(25)	0
152	28	(46)	49	113	31	(44)	113	31	(46)	0
−3		(7)	−0	7		(8)	7		(8)	0
11		(20)	5	14		(13)	14		(14)	0
21		(26)	11	22		(21)	22		(24)	0
−1	19	(10)	−5	28	15	(26)	22	16	(23)	8
26		(30)	5	39		(31)	39		(34)	0
32		(35)	−0	40		(32)	35		(31)	5
42		(37)	33	31		(27)	31		(28)	0
25		(28)	0	32		(28)	32		(29)	0
8	7	(16)	−1	10	3	(11)	9	6	(11)	0
87		(43)	67	164		(47)	97		(43)	67
28	60	(32)	5	33	31	(29)	33	53	(30)	0

Table III-5 (continued)

		(17)			(18)
		Nominal rate of protection***			T+S
No.	Description	Rate	S.D.	(Rank)	−QR
1221	Gold mining	0	6	(1)	0
1222	Bauxite mining	0		(1)	0
1223	Manganese mining	0		(1)	0
2010	Meat processing	34	11	(28)	12
2031	Fruit squash	0		(1)	0
2039	Fruit and veg. processing	87		(38)	−1
2055	Coffee hulling	16		(18)	−9
2061	Biscuits	102		(42)	−1
2082	Cocoa butter	8		(1)	0
2089	Confectionery	104	20	(43)	−1
2111	Distillery	88		(39)	−1
2131	Brewery	42	13	(32)	−12
2140	Soft drinks	11	12	(12)	−1
2201	Processing raw tobacco	63		(34)	−1
2311	Kente	6	4	(9)	−1
2320	Knitting	252		(47)	128
2411	Wearing apparel	133	45	(44)	70
2430	Shoes	154	14	(45)	96
2443	Mattresses	1		(7)	−4
2444	Towels, bedsheets, etc.	11	95	(11)	1
2449	Blankets	34		(27)	−1
2511	Sawn timber and lumber	0	0	(1)	0
2601	Furniture	14	9	(13)	−1
2609	Fixtures	15		(16)	−1
2720	Misc. paper	25	14	(21)	4
2912	Handbags and luggage	82	29	(37)	−37
3003	Rubber processing	16	0	(17)	−1
3119	Ind. chem.	29		(23)	1
3121	Copra oil	15		(15)	−1
3122	Groundnut oil	36		(29)	−22
3123	Palm oil	14		(14)	−1
3130	Paints	40		(33)	−20
3193	Perfumes	96	50	(40)	47
3194	Pharmaceut.	28	7	(22)	−1
3195	Insecticides	33		(26)	5
3196	Cosmetics	168	29	(46)	55
3197	Candles	6		(8)	−1
3199	Misc. chemicals	18		(19)	4
3412	Nails	33		(25)	10
3501	Al. ware	24	10	(20)	−6
3701	St. batteries	80		(36)	41
3703	Radio, etc.	39		(30)	−1
3709	Refrig.	64		(35)	33
3920	Optical	32		(24)	−1
3949	Jewelry	3	6	(10)	−1
3959	Records	96		(41)	−67
3990	Misc. plastics	42	55	(31)	9

Notes and Sources to Table III-5

Notes: * Negative value-added at world prices.
              ** Negative value-added in one or more establishments of industry.
              *** Nominal rate of protection is the net effect of deflators on the left-hand side of (C-4), (C-11) and (C-14) assuming $1 = 1$ percent, $rb = 5$ percent, $r = 3$ percent.
              1. No data on quota premia for all establishments.
              2. No data on quota premia for one or more establishments.
              3. Domestic production exceeds 90 percent of total domestic use, valued at domestic prices.
              4. 90 percent or more domestic production under price control.
              5. Less than 10 percent domestic production under price control.
              6. More than 90 percent domestic output competing with items covered by surcharges.
              7. Less than 5 percent domestic output competing with items covered by surcharges.
              8. Between 5 percent and 90 percent domestic output competing with items covered by surcharges.
              9. Export industries, with zero nominal protection, or negative if subject to an export tax.
Source: See text and Appendix C.

Consider the initial situation of protection due to the QR's. There are several negative or near-zero rates of protection which reflect the effects of the protective structure in levying a taxing effect on inputs that exceed the subsidy effect on outputs. The most obvious cases are the export industries that cannot obtain any protection of output via the protective structure but are subject to the taxing effect of higher-cost inputs: gold, bauxite, manganese, mining, fruit squash, kente weaving, and sawmilling. In addition, there is one "import-substitution" industry, candles, that has negative protection, which means there is a negative import-substitution effect.

In the positive range of protection, there are a few cases of negligible protection to four cases of negative value-added at world prices. At the low end of the scale (less than 10 percent Effective Rate of Protection — ERP) are industries producing mattresses, industrial chemicals, and jewelry. Moderate levels are enjoyed by industries such as beer, blankets, and pharmaceuticals. High to very high effective protection is received by a long list ranging from groundnut oil and coffee hulling (just over 100 percent), through records (over 300 percent), radio and TV assembly (over 400 percent) to apparel (over 700 percent), and shoes and cosmetics (over 1000 percent).

There are four cases of negative value-added at world prices (indicated in the table by *). This simply means that the value of output deflated to world prices is less than the value of inputs, again at world prices. These are industries producing cocoa butter, distillery products, handbags and luggage, and paints. In the case of cocoa butter, which is an export industry, the cocoa beans are purchased at a subsidized price *vis-à-vis* the world market in order to receive protection.

Comparing the protection due to the QR's with that attributable to tariffs alone, there were 20 for which we do not have QR premia. Of the remainder, 13 had nominal protection due to QR's in excess of that due to tariffs and indirect taxes. In those cases where the QR premium we calculated was less than the nominal protection due to tariffs and indirect taxes, we assumed that at a minimum the establishment received the nominal protection due to the latter. This procedure implicitly assumes that the tariff is not redundant. In the seven cases where redundancy may be relevant (those where domestic production exceeds 90 percent of domestic use), there are two cases (brewery and travel goods) in which the nominal QR protection exceeds the nominal tariff protection. In the five other cases (knitting, blankets, copra oil, palm oil, and cosmetics) we do not have QR for two, while for the remaining three (knitting, copra oil, and palm oil) the nominal protection is probably overstated.

Our industry and protection data can also provide useful information on the protective effects of the surcharges introduced in August 1970. An important feature of the surcharges was that an item subject to surcharge was also placed under OGL. As a consequence the nominal protection granted an industry competing with surcharge-laden imports is equal to (or less than) the tariff and surcharge nominal protection: the QR was no longer binding. Hence the comparison between the QR protection and the tariffs-plus-surcharges protection indicates the changes in protection due to this liberalizing measure.[31]

Given the way the surcharges operated, it was possible for the surcharges either to increase or decrease the protection of output. And, of course, surcharges on importable inputs decreased protection. Assuming that the surcharges were fully applied,[32] we computed surcharge rates protecting outputs, and chargeable on importable inputs. We then recalculated surcharge inclusive of rates of protection. For completeness we also allowed for the elimination of the 1 percent import license fee, which was abandoned at the end of 1968.

The results of the surcharges ranged from substantial increases in protection to the imposition of negative protection on a previously positively pro-

---

31. We are assuming away major structural change within the industries between 1968 and 1970.
32. Because of the limited experience with the surcharge this was the only option open to us. In theory this is appropriate, as the surcharges are applicable to virtually all importers, including manufacturers exempt from regular duties. In practice, exceptions or evasions may be extensive.

tected industry. Of the twelve industries which had 90 percent or more of their output competing with imports subject to surcharge, only one had its protection reduced due to surcharges. Most of the industries which did not compete with surcharged imports were negatively affected via increased input costs, although some had small increases in their protection. Of the 35 industries not competing with surcharged imports, 27 had their protection reduced due to surcharges. This very mixed and discriminatory result is in sharp contrast with the equal treatment that would have been accorded all industries via an equal proportionate across-the-board tariff and export subsidy (or, of course, a devaluation).[33]

At the industry level it is clear that the 1968 protective structure in the Ghanaian industrial sector instituted vastly different stimuli between industries. And the changes instituted by the 1970 surcharges resulted in additional discriminatory changes in the protective structure, retaining the major differences between the protection enjoyed by the various industries.

The picture of substantial and apparently random variation is also found at the establishment level. The variation is evident when we consider the standard deviations of protective rates for individual establishments in the cases of multi-establishment industries. The industries with a large number of establishments such as apparel, shoes, sawmilling, furniture, and plastics all have standard deviations at least two-thirds the size of the average rate of effective protection. This is true for the basic protection due to tariffs as well as that due to QR's. Note also that the standard deviations of these industries did not decline with the introduction of the 1970 surcharges. The randomness is suggested by the lack of any significant relationship between the effective rate of protection and several potential explanatory variables. To test the possibility that differences in the rates of effective protection might be associated with certain establishment characteristics, we regressed the effective rate of protection under the quota restriction (QRERP) on: the number of years since production started (YSPS); a dummy for type of ownership (TOWND) set equal to unity for state and joint ownership and equal to zero for other types; a dummy for nationality of ownership (NOWND) set equal to unity for non-Ghanaian and mixed enterprises and equal to zero for Ghanaian; and finally a regional dummy (REGD) set equal to unity for the Accra-Tema capital district and equal to zero for all other regions. Our sample consists of 101 establishments with positive value-added at world prices, and for which the data were complete. The regression yielded the following result:

33. See J. Clark Leith, "Across-the-Board Nominal Tariff Changes and the Effective Rate of Protection," *Economic Journal,* Vol. LXXVIII, No. 312, December 1968.

$$\text{QRERP} = 2.4 \text{ YSPS} - 244.0 \text{ TOWND} + 414.8 \text{ NOWND} + 784.7 \text{ REGD}$$
$$\quad\quad (0.05) \quad\quad (-0.21) \quad\quad\quad (0.49) \quad\quad\quad\quad (0.94)$$

$$R^2 = 0.0178$$

None of the coefficients is significantly different from zero (*t* values in parentheses) and the explanatory power of the equation is very low.[34] These establishment characteristics thus do not offer an explanation of the variation in effective rates of protection.

The protection of Ghanaian industrial establishments appears to be largely random. When set against the declared policy of simply promoting industrialization *per se,* the rationale for this apparently random dissemination of protection is not at all obvious. Yet when we recognize that this protective structure developed over several years, with protective instruments frequently brought into play to achieve other objectives, and with a complexity that both researchers and policy-makers would find difficult to sort out, we conclude that the variability and randomness of the protection of Ghanaian industrial activities was largely unintended.

4. Domestic resource costs in manufacturing

The effective rates of protection we reported in section 3 demonstrate that the trade regime instituted resource pulls that differ substantially between activities of the industrial sector. The purpose of this section is to cite a similar piece of evidence, using a slightly different measure, which also shows wide variation in the stimuli afforded Ghanaian manufacturing activities.

William F. Steel's study of Ghana's import-substitution policies[35] contains a set of domestic resource cost (DRC) estimates for a sample of 41 Ghanaian manufacturing establishments. His data were collected directly from the firms, and cover the period mid-1967 through mid-1968. The scope of coverage is somewhat more limited than our ERP estimates, but by relying on direct collection he was able to check data more thoroughly and obtain more detailed information than we were able to.

The concept of domestic resource costs is closely related to both the effective exchange rate and the effective rate of protection. At the same time it is designed to take into account social opportunity costs which neither of

34. An identical regression, omitting the 2511 group (sawmilling) yielded similar coefficients and *t* values.
35. See W.F. Steel, "Import Substitution and Excess Capacity in Ghana," *Oxford Economic Papers,* New Series, Vol. 24, No. 2, July 1972, based on his unpublished Ph.D. thesis, M.I.T., 1970.

the other measures does directly. The DRC refers to the number of units of local currency required to earn (or save) a unit of foreign exchange. Hence it is denominated in new cedis per dollar just as the effective exchange rate. The similarity with the ERP is that it focuses on value-added in domestic production and takes into account the effect of the price distortions on both output and inputs. At the simplest level of similarity the ERP may be translated into the DRC in the same way as the nominal tariff is translated into the effective exchange rate (see Chapter II, section 3). Thus:

$$DRC = (1 + ERP)r \qquad\qquad (3.1)$$

where

DRC = domestic resource cost, N¢ per \$, ERP = effective rate of protection, and r = official exchange rate, N¢ per \$.

Typically, DRC estimates take into account not only the trade regime which the ERP focuses on, but also allow for the appropriate "shadow prices" or social opportunity costs of the primary factors, capital and labor.[36] When these are included, the relationship of equation (III.1) does not strictly hold. Differences of definition aside, the DRC estimate for a local activity is an indicator of the extent to which the distortions taken into account provide a stimulus to that activity relative to, say, the official exchange rate or some (usually higher) social opportunity cost of foreign exchange.

Steel's estimates of DRC's in the 41 firms he covered point to the same general conclusion about randomness of outcomes as our ERP estimates: there is wide variation in the economic returns to Ghanaian import-substitution industries: The DRC estimates (Table III-6) range from N¢ 0.29 per dollar to N¢ 30.55 per dollar and beyond into the range of negative value-added at world prices. Further, substantial differences between firms persist within industry groups. For example, in the textile industry the range is N¢ 0.44 per dollar to negative value-added at world prices. (The official exchange rate at the time was N¢ 1.02 per dollar.) In sum, using a different set of data and a different measure, Steel's DRC work and our ERP estimates suggest the same sort of conclusion: the resource pulls instituted by the restrictive system exhibited substantial and apparently random variation.

Steel also considered the extent to which DRC's were related to various characteristics of the firms. He found that the DRC was related: positively

---

36. Because capital costs are not consistently available from the CBS survey, we did not attempt to use the data collected for the ERP estimates to compute DRC rates.

Table III-6

Steel's domestic resource cost estimates, 1967–1968 (DRC in new cedis per dollar, ranks in ascending order)

	Industry group		DRC	Rank
11.	Rice milling		1.15	7 (tie)
20.	Food manufacturing		4.45	26
21.	Beverages		0.71	5
22.	Tobacco		1.15	7 (tie)
23.	Textiles	(a)	0.44	2 (tie)
		(b)	1.69	11 (tie)
		(c)	1.87	13
		(d)	−17.19*	33
		(e)	−12.27*	34
24.	Footwear and clothing	(a)	1.40	9
		(b)	1.96	14
		(c)	3.08	19
		(d)	−25.55*	32
		(e)	−7.15*	36
		(f)	−1.65*	39
25.	Wood and sawmills	(a)	0.67	4
		(b)	1.53	10
		(c)	2.69	18
27.	Paper		−7.82*	35
30.	Rubber products		4.05	23
31.	Chemicals	(a)	0.29	1
		(b)	0.44	2 (tie)
		(c)	1.69	11 (tie)
		(d)	6.97	27
		(e)	−1.93*	38
		(f)	3.39	20
33.	Non-metallic	(a)	1.00	6
		(b)	4.18	24
		(c)	30.55	31
		(d)	−2.93*	37
34.	Basic metals		8.59	28
35.	Metal products	(a)	2.24	15
		(b)	2.26	16
		(c)	2.57	17
		(d)	3.59	22
37.	Electrical machinery	(a)	3.50	21
		(b)	10.94	29
38.	Transport equipment		4.40	25
39.	Plastics, miscellaneous		23.96	30

Note: * = negative value-added at world prices.

Source: W.F. Steel, "Import Substitution and Excess Capacity in Ghana," *op. cit.*, Table A-1.

with size of firm, the capital/labor ratio, and assembly type operations; and negatively with capacity utilization.[37] He concluded that

> Inefficiency was found to be related to incentives established by foreign exchange policies. High effective protection resulting from restrictive tariffs on "non-essential" final goods encouraged final-stage assembly, which was significantly less efficient in utilizing resources than more integrated production. Large-size and relatively capital-intensive techniques similarly were associated with relatively inefficient production and were stimulated by licencing procedures, special concessions for capital, and minimum wages for labour. [38]

This did not augur well for the success of import-substituting industrialization as a dynamic source of growth.

.

37. See W.F. Steel, *op. cit.,* Table VIII. Nationality of ownership and state ownership were not significant.
38. *Ibid.,* p. 235.

CHAPTER IV

Growth factors

1. Introduction

Economic growth as a means of achieving high living standards has long been one of the primary objectives of Ghanaian policy. Attention has repeatedly been focused on measures to accelerate economic growth. A significant manifestation of this emphasis has been a series of development plans dating back to the 1920's.[1] With the attainment of independence in 1957 planning for growth and development was given a renewed emphasis and the preparation of a five year plan begun.[2]

In launching the plan on March 4, 1959, Prime Minister Nkrumah set out the objective: "to give us a standard of living which will abolish disease, poverty, and illiteracy, give all people ample food and good housing, and let us advance confidently as a nation."[3] The swing to socialism in the early 1960's changed the techniques, but not the objectives. The Seven Year Plan, designed within the guidelines of the socialist Program of Work and Happiness of the Convention People's Party, emphasized that the choice of a socialist form of society was designed to "assure Ghana a rapid rate of economic progress without destroying that social justice, that freedom and equality, which is a central feature of our traditional way of life."[4] And after the overthrow of President Nkrumah the National Liberation Council's Two Year Development Plan included both the short-term objective of providing the foundations of self-generating growth and the long-term objective of "an improved rate of growth of national income through a sustained high rate of development... ."[5]

---

1. The first plan was Governor Guggisberg's Ten Year Development Plan (1920–1930), designed to provide the country with an advanced physical and social infrastructure. In the post-World War II period the "ten year plan" was launched in 1951.
2. This is referred to as the Second Five Year Plan, while the 1951 plan is referred to as the First Plan.
3. Quoted by E.N. Omaboe in W. Birmingham *et al.*, eds., *A Study of Contemporary Ghana*, Vol. I, *The Economy of Ghana*, Northwestern University Press, Evanston, 1966, p. 446.
4. Quoted by Omaboe, *ibid.*, p. 453.
5. Republic of Ghana, *Two Year Development Plan: From Stabilization to Development for the Period Mid-1968 to Mid-1970*, Accra, 1968, p. 2.

The ambitious statements of intention have not been matched by performance. The key indicator of real per capita gross national product posted even a decline during the 1960's (see Table A-1). Further, if we consider the relationship between growth of factor supplies and growth of output, we discover not the usual positive residual, but a negative one. In real terms, the difference between the growth of output and the growth of factor inputs (weighted by 1960 factor shares) over the period 1960 to 1969 amounts to −16 percent.[6] The coincidence between the evolution of a restrictive trade and payments regime and the economic atrophy is obvious, and poses the question to be faced in this chapter: what effect, if any, did the restrictive system have on the factors directly influencing economic growth?

A generally necessary but by no means sufficient condition for growth in the productive capacity of an economy is accumulation and efficient use of capital. For this reason we begin with a review of Ghana's savings and investment performance (section 2). We then consider the nature of the relationships between the control system and the processes of saving and of investing (section 3). Finally, we examine in as much detail as possible the specific growth-related responses of economic units to the control system (section 4).

2. Savings and investment performance

During the 1960's Ghanaian savings and investment performance deteriorated rapidly. The available evidence indicates that the domestic savings potential was not tapped, with the result that savings as a proportion of income fell. Investment, often treated as an objective rather than a cost, was maintained via an import surplus, but with a very low productivity.

We shall first consider domestic savings. The savings series is derived as a residual, as no direct estimates are available. We deducted from total gross domestic fixed capital formation the contribution made by the import surplus to yield a rough approximation of internally generated savings (including depreciation) that were applied domestically (Table IV-1). Looking at the

6. The output measure is the real percentage growth of GDP, which grew by 24.5 percent (Table A-1). The growth of real capital stock was 103.1 percent, and the growth of labor force was 26.8 percent. Shares of output in 1960 were 0.18 for capital and 0.82 for labor. These data are from T.M. Brown, "Macroeconomic Data of Ghana," *Economic Bulletin of Ghana,* Second Series, Vol. 2, No. 1, 1972. Note that Brown's share of capital in output for 1960 is probably understated, resulting in an (absolutely) understated residual. For example, if the share of capital were 0.30 the residual growth would have been −25.2 percent. This calculation omits the contribution of land for which no data are available. In the context of Ghana in the 1960's this is not a major omission, for there was neither a major shortage of land nor a major increase in land under cultivation.

Table IV-1
Domestic capital formation and related macro variables at current market prices
(in millions of new cedis)

	Gross national product	Gross dom. fixed capital formation	GDFCF percent of GNP	Import surplus (IS)	Dom. sav. = GDFCF minus IS	Dom. sav. as percent of GNP
	(1)	(2)	(3)=(2)/(1) percent	(4)	(5)=(2)−(4)	(6)=(5)/(1) percent
1955	676	104	15.4	−9	113	16.7
1956	701	112	16.0	15	97	13.8
1957	734	112	15.3	21	91	12.4
1958	776	110	14.2	−30	140	18.0
1959	884	154	17.4	12	142	16.1
1960	945	194	20.5	50	144	15.2
1961	1,008	210	20.8	82	128	12.7
1962	1,084	184	17.0	30	154	14.2
1963	1,190	218	18.3	56	162	13.6
1964	1,345	232	17.2	36	196	14.6
1965	1,589	271	17.1	124	147	9.3
1966	1,779	246	13.8	66	180	10.1
1967	1,757	213	12.1	35	178	10.1
1968	2,028	224	11.0	−15	239	11.8
1969	2,285	242	10.6	−31	273	11.9

Sources: IMF, *International Financial Statistics,* 1971 Supplement; *Economic Survey,* 1969, for 1968 and 1969.

domestic savings relative to gross national product one sees that, despite the year-to-year fluctuations, there are three distinct periods: a moderately high rate in the pre-restriction period (1955−1961), a lower average level − by about 2 percentage points − in the restrictive period of the Nkrumah regime (1962-1965), and an even lower − by a further 3 percentage points − but more stable average level under the National Liberation Council government (1966-1969).[7]

A major shortcoming of the residual approach to calculating savings is that many of the errors and omissions in national accounts data are incorporated in our savings estimate. As a proportion of national product these errors may be small, but as a proportion of savings they are probably large. Nevertheless,

7. We have not included a similar calculation based on a constant price series, largely because the magnitude of the import surplus in constant prices fluctuates drastically from year to year due to the instability of cocoa prices, which in the Ghanaian case is not an exogenous price movement.

the changing pattern we observed in the series is so strong that it is difficult to imagine that data problems are entirely responsible.

On the investment side, gross domestic fixed capital formation relative to GNP, while highly variable as in any country, also shows some clearly discernible periods. From 1955 to 1960 with a relatively open economy, investment maintained a moderate level peaking in 1960 and 1961, then declining throughout the subsequent restrictionist period, and dropping further with the post-*coup* austerity.

Of more interest is the response of output to the substantial additions to capital stock, for this indicates the extent to which the capital was used productively. One measure is the incremental output—capital ratio. In order to smooth out erratic year-to-year fluctuations in the series we have computed three-year moving averages centered on the mid-year for each of incremental gross domestic product and gross domestic fixed capital formation, both in constant 1960 prices. While this is inevitably a crude measure, it does provide us with an indication of broad trends. The results (Table IV-2) strongly suggest that the overall productivity of capital declined sharply in the period

Table IV-2

Gross domestic product, gross domestic fixed capital formation; three-year moving averages of incremental GDP and GDFCF (centered on mid-year), and ratios of moving average GDP/GDFCF (constant 1960 prices, in millions of new cedis)

Year	GDP (1)	GDFCF (2)	Moving average increm. GDP (3)	Moving average GDFCF (4)	Ratio (5) = (3)/(4)
1955	710	120			
1956	752	120		118.7	
1957	776	116	18.0	117.3	0.153
1958	774	116	45.7	132.0	0.346
1959	889	164	60.0	158.0	0.380
1960	956	194	75.3	186.0	0.405
1961	990	200	49.7	192.0	0.259
1962	1.038	182	39.3	199.3	0.197
1963	1,074	216	35.7	206.3	0.173
1964	1,097	221	28.0	229.0	0.122
1965	1,122	250	13.0	226.0	0.058
1966	1,113	207	12.0	203.7	0.059
1967	1,133	154	9.0	167.7	0.054
1968	1,149	142	25.7	147.7	0.174
1969	1,190	147			

Sources: (1) and (2), *Economic Survey,* 1967 and 1969, for 1959 through 1969; Birmingham *et al., Economy of Ghana,* p. 50, for 1955 through 1958.

Table IV-3
GDP, capital stock, and output/capital ratios
(in millions of new cedis, constant 1960 prices)

Year	GDP (1)	Capital stock (2)	Output/capital ratio [(3) = (1)/2]
1955	710		
1956	752	417.6	1.8008
1957	776	504.53	1.5381
1958	764	583.8	1.3087
1959	889	701.61	1.2671
1960	956	842.15	1.1352
1961	990	979.61	1.0106
1962	1,038	1,091.3	0.9512
1963	1,074	1,229.84	0.8733
1964	1,097	1,363.33	0.8046
1965	1,122	1,516.88	0.7397
1966	1,113	1,616.19	0.6887
1967	1,133	1,656.03	0.6842
1968	1,149	1,681.36	0.6834
1969	1,190	1,710.18	0.6958

Sources: (1) same as in Table IV-2; (2) computed by T.M. Brown, *op. cit.*

following restrictions, plummeted to incredibly low levels in the late Nkrumah period and the austerity of the early NLC government, and only began to recover slightly in thc late NLC period.

A second, related, measure involves the use of a capital stock series as constructed by T.M. Brown.[8] The resulting output–capital ratios (Table IV-3) show a similar rapid decline in the average productivity of capital, in constant 1960 prices, which was checked only by 1969.

Several explanations of the deteriorating savings and investment performance of the Ghanaian economy are available. While a full explanation of the determinants is beyond our scope, an important issue requires our attention: what was the role of the restrictive trade and payments regime in the results we have just outlined? In answering this question we consider in the next section the mechanism whereby the restrictive regime was a permissive ele-

8.   T.M. Brown, "Macroeconomic Data of Ghana," *op. cit.* This series was built up by using Szereszewski's estimates of gross capital stocks for 1960 (as contained in W. Birmingham et al., *op. cit.*), and assuming that they were one-half depreciated at that time. Given this benchmark, annual stocks were estimated from this benchmark, using the perpetual inventory concept – with gross investment providing additions to, and depreciation in capital destruction providing deductions from, the stock for each period. The aggregate stock figures were built from three separate series: plant and construction, transport equipment, and machinery and equipment.

ment in the poor savings and investment performance. Then in section 4 we consider a number of specific ways in which the restrictive regime may have contributed to the situation.

3. Saving, investing, and the restrictive regime

In this section we examine the role of the restrictive regime, broadly defined, in making possible the poor savings and investment performance. Consider first the savings rate. Potential savers regard actual saving as costing them something-foregone current consumption. If the return to them in terms of increased future real consumption is not worth the cost they simply refrain from saving, preferring instead to consume today.

Ghana is a country with limited monetization. This combined with unresponsive nominal rates of interest in the monetized sector (see below) severely limits the opportunities to hedge against inflation via higher nominal rates of return on financial assets. As a result, the savings rate in Ghana is particularly vulnerable to inflation. When the control system closed the economy, permitting the emergence of domestic inflation (see Chapter II, section 6), potential savers appear to have discovered that the real gain from foregone consumption was less because of inflation. Evidently they responded as could be expected: savings rates declined. Our hypothesis is that this negative relationship between inflation and savings was more than mere coincidence.

Precise specification of the relationship between inflation and the savings rate is complicated by a number of factors. First, as we noted earlier, the savings series is far from ideal. The data are derived as a residual, with the resulting incorporation of errors and omissions in the savings series. A second difficulty arises from the fact that disaggregated data are not available, obviating study of the important individual sectors such as government, household, and business. Government saving is particularly difficult to deal with, because it may not respond to inflation the way the private sector does, and major policy shifts, such as the austerity of the NLC government, can mask the overall relationship. Third, the response of savings rates to inflation is slow and uncertain in Ghana, but annual data make it difficult if not impossible to discover meaningful lag relationships. For these reasons any estimate of an aggregate relationship between inflation and savings is open to wide margins of error.[9]

9. It is worth noting in passing that a simple naive model does seem to work. We regressed the savings rate on the inflation rate, using a dummy variable to capture the effect of the NLC austerity period in reducing government savings. To smooth out erratic year-to-year changes and to allow for the slow and uncertain response of savings rates to inflation we used the (weighted) average savings rate in percent over the previous three years (SAVE RATE) as our dependent variable for each year, and

The low productivity of investment also requires some explanation. In this, the key point is that investment is a cost to the economy because it uses up real resources. It is not an objective to be attained. Potential investors, however, only regard it as a cost to the extent that they bear the costs. If the system is such that the real benefits are overstated or real costs understated to the investor, the real productivity of investment will likely be low.

There were two ways in which such misstatements of real benefits and costs of investment arose. First, the restrictive trade regime changed the relative attractiveness of export- and import-competing production. Thus we saw in Chapter II, section 6 how the price-level-deflated effective exchange rates for non-cocoa exports declined relatively more than the rate for imports during the decade of the 1960's (Table II-8). And on the import side the licencing system induced quota premia which acted in addition to the effective exchange rate to further pull resources toward import-competing production. We then saw in Chapter III, section 1 the shifts in the structure of domestic production valued at current domestic prices. Export sectors such as mining, sawmilling and cocoa showed relative declines while the largely import-competing manufacturing sector moved ahead. To accomplish such shifts in the relative structure of domestic production required the transfer of real resources between the sectors. In nominal terms, output in the expanding sectors rose; but higher and higher cost resources were called upon to increase the output, so that the relative real expansion of output did not keep pace with the nominal. As a result, the real productivity of the resources drawn into the favored sectors deteriorated.

---

the average compound percentage rate of inflation from 3 years previous (INFL RATE) as the independent variable. From the savings rates and the inflation rates computed in this way (from Tables IV-1 and IV-5) we obtained the following result:

SAVE RATE = 15.64 − 0.323 INFL RATE − 2.57 D
            (29.94) (4.142)   (3.98)

R^2 = 0.85
D.W.= 1.41
D.F. = 8

(D = 0 from 1959 through 1966; D = 1 from 1967 through 1969)

The explanatory power of the equation is high; the coefficients are significant at the 1 percent level (two-tailed test); and the Durbin–Watson is inconclusive. The savings rate does appear responsive to the rate of inflation. An increase of 5 percentage points in the rate of inflation is met by a decrease of about 1.6 percentage points in the percentage of GNP saved. At the means, the elasticity of the savings rate with respect to the inflation rate is −0.145. In addition, the austerity of the NLC period apparently reduced the savings rate significantly.

Second, there emerged specific discrimination among otherwise equally productive sources and uses of investable resources. Different savers arbitrarily received different rates of return. And the available savings were distributed arbitrarily among investors. This arose from the increasingly noncompetitive segmentation of the Ghanaian capital market.

Since we have not dwelt on this theme in previous chapters, it merits some elaboration here. A highly developed capital market often contains numerous segments designed to provide a variety of instruments which differentiate among lenders and borrowers on various economic bases such as risk, size and term of investment. Such differentiation and a consequent appearance of segments is typically the result of a competitive market working to meet the special needs of a great variety of savers and investors. But because it is a consequence of a competitive market, each segment is linked closely with all others, and the system as a whole adjusts rapidly to the changing circumstances.

The segmentation of the Ghanaian capital market was in sharp contrast with such a competitive segmentation. The prime mover in the capital market was the government. It correctly recognized that an efficient well-developed capital market would be a major source of strength in promoting economic development. Its basic strategy — creating several new capital market institutions — was undoubtedly correct. The difficulties arose in the socially suboptimal policies followed by many of the capital market institutions, both old and new. As we noted above, low interest rates probably contributed to the deteriorating savings performance, while loan allocations unrelated to the real productivity of investment contributed to the falling productivity of capital. A further element, which we shall explore in the next section, was the distorted choice of techniques in production arising from non-price rationing of loans.

The government relied on the Bank of Ghana for a large proportion of the credit required to float the new institutions. The Bank's claims on the government grew rapidly from 1962 onwards, exceeding 30 percent of total domestic credit by 1965, and remaining above that figure since.[10] The extension of a large volume of credit to the government is not in itself an unusual development, as governments the world over frequently rely on the Central banks to finance their own deficits. It does however represent a change from the previous system in which government deficits were largely financed from abroad. No longer was the test of credit worthiness immediately faced as deficits expanded. Money creation could be used instead.[11]

10. See IMF, *International Financial Statistics*, Line 12c.
11. N. Ahmad has estimated that 36 percent of the government deficits in the period 1962 through 1965 were financed by money creation. Ahmad, *op. cit.*, Table 4, p. 43.

The government used its newly acquired credit not only to finance its day-to-day deficits, but also to direct large blocks of the funds at its disposal to a variety of new government financial corporations. First, in 1963, it established the National Investment Bank (NIB) as a loan window to "finance, promote and assist enterprises in all sectors of the national economy."[12] Using a paid-up capital beginning at N₵ 6.5 million (1963) and rising to N₵ 10.2 million (1970) — about 70 percent of which was paid by the government — and borrowing on the capital, the NIB has made loans, issued guarantees and purchased equity in a variety of projects.[13] It has undoubtedly met a demand for small and medium-sized loans (N₵ 10,000 to N₵ 1,000,000) on longer terms of three to twenty-five years that was not being met by other segments of the capital market. What is not so evident is whether or not the NIB has allocated capital as a scarce resource. Its loan rates, reportedly generous, have not been published. The NIB has not, however, generated a substantial return on shareholders' equity, yielding 2.64 percent (1968), 2.83 percent (1969), and 2.73 percent (1970).[14] In the absence of substantial default on risky investments this does not represent a high rate of return on the capital at its disposal.

A second government financial institution, the Agricultural Development Bank, has been operating under various names and forms since 1964. Its major function has been the provision of credit to agriculture, although it also accepts deposits. Its lending resources have been made up almost entirely of paid-up capital from the government and the Bank of Ghana, plus some borrowing, and very limited deposit accounts.[15] The infusion of capital into the agricultural sector was not insignificant relative to the commercial banks' activities in that sector. The ADB had outstanding loans exceeding N₵ 6 million at the end of 1970, compared with commercial banks' loans and advances outstanding of N₵ 10 million to the same sector at the end of 1969 (latest date figures available). However, relative to total commercial banks' loans and advances for all sectors (N₵ 149 million, end of 1969) the combined loans of the commercial banks and the ADB to the agricultural sector has been small, given the size of the agricultural sector in the economy. The rate charged on loans has ranged from 7 percent to 9 percent, based on factors such as the bank rate, the ADB's borrowing rate, the rate at other Gha-

---

12. National Investment Bank, *Directors' Report for the Year Ended 31 December,* 1969.
13. It of course has some additional functions including investment promotion, post-financing surveillance of projects, and consulting services.
14. Calculated from NIB profit statements and balance sheets for the years indicated.
15. While growing rapidly from a small base, at the end of 1970 deposits amounted to N₵ 368,000 compared with paid-up capital on N₵ 10,554,000, or 3.5 percent of the latter.

naian financial institutions, and the financial prospect of the project.[16] While clearly not a deliberate low-interest policy, given a similar level of rates by commercial banks, the interest rate range has been narrow and has not extended to levels that would permit loans to riskier ventures.

The most important government financial corporation by far, is the Ghana Commercial Bank. Established in the early 1950's, it has now become the largest commercial bank, with about 75 percent of the total commercial bank assets in the country by mid-1970, and is currently a highly profitable operation. In many ways it has met the original objective of setting the pace for the expatriate commercial banks, showing the way in expansion of branches and engaging in a less-risk-averting loan policy. It has, however, continued to pay the same low interest rates on deposits as its competitors.

Fourth, the Ghana Savings Bank was designed to provide a convenient deposit window for savers throughout the country. While it succeeded in doing that, its deposit rate has, along with the commercial banks, been low. [17] This, combined with the bureaucratic nature of the operation, kept the level of deposits at a relatively low and stagnant level throughout the 1960's. From N₵ 10 million at the end of 1960, deposits declined to N₵ 8.4 million at the end of 1963, and subsequently recovered to N₵ 9.7 million at the end of 1970.[18]

Fifth, a major segment of the organized mortgage market has been a small government-sponsored intermediary, the First Ghana Building Society. It has issued shares (mostly to the government) and accepted deposits with limited withdrawal privileges at interest rates in 1971 of 5 percent and 6 percent, but formerly 4½ percent and 5 percent. Its deposits were less than N₵ 270,000 at the end of 1969. Additional funds from shares amounting to N₵ 2.60 million enabled the Society to hold 651 mortgages at the end of 1969, valued at N₵ 2.63 million. Lending rates have been about two or three percentage points above the borrowing rates.[19]

The government did not confine its transfer of credit to its own financial institutions. Large amounts of capital were made directly available to government corporations. The original share capital was provided sometimes in total, sometimes in part, by the government. In addition, loans at zero interest rates were made in a variety of ways to several public enterprises. Occasionally these loans were in the form of advances to undertake specific activities, but more often than not they were made necessary by the public

16. Agricultural Development Bank, *Organization and Functions,* Accra, 1968.
17. To early 1971, the deposit interest rate was $2\frac{1}{2}$ percent, and subsequently 5 percent.
18. IMF, *International Financial Statistics,* 1971 Supplement, and December 1971.
19. See latest available First Ghana Building Society, *Annual Report,* 1969, Accra, March 1971. Since its inception in 1956 the total number of mortgages issued has been 838.

enterprise's deficit which the commercial banks would not cover. The data on such loans are limited, but what is known appears as a line in the government accounts (see Table IV-4).

Various other methods of borrowing from the government have been used by the state enterprises. For example, the Auditor General noted, in reporting on the last year of the Nkrumah era, instances in which state enterprises were unable to pay accrued indirect taxes such as Social Security Fund contributions and Sales Tax liabilities, and cases in which the authorized capitalization was exceeded by unauthorized investment in machinery.[20]

Two expatriate commercial banks, subsidiaries of Barclay's Bank D.C.O. and of the Standard Bank group, have a long history in Ghana, mostly financing the large traders and cocoa exports. While relatively less significant in the overall picture than they were during the colonial era — due to the growth of the Ghana Commercial Bank and the Bank of Ghana — their conservative practices seem to have set the tone in many aspects of commercial banking. For example, the interest rate on savings deposits since 1960 remained within one-half a percentage point of three percent. The prime rate on loans and overdrafts secured by government securities ran at $5\frac{1}{2}$ percent in the early 1960's, rising to 7 percent in the austerity period following the *coup*, then falling to $6\frac{1}{2}$ percent at the time of the 1967 devaluation — where it has since remained. Further, the unsecured loan rate range begins at only one-half to 1 percent above the prime rate, and rises to only 10 percent, a ceiling which remained constant throughout the 1960's.[21]

This quick review of segmentation in the Ghanaian capital market strongly suggests that segmentation developed not because the competitive market was at work, but often because the competitive market was suspended. For particular investors the admittedly imperfect capital market allegedly did not provide "adequate" or "cheap" enough capital, and special institutions were established to do just that, sheltering these investors from competing demands for capital. In a similar vein, developments on the savings side in no way suggest a competitive differentiation designed to provide for a variety of situations. Rather, the policy toward savers appeared to have been one of almost total neglect, with little long-term development of new instruments.

The noncompetitive segmentation of the organized and regulated sector of

---

20. See Republic of Ghana, *Report by the Auditor General on the Accounts of Ghana for the Period 1 January, 1965 to 30 June, 1966,* Accra, March 1968.
21. For details, see Bank of Ghana, *Report of the Board for the Financial Year Ending 30 June, 1970,* p. 59. Unfortunately no data are available on the actual rates at which loans were made, which might give a picture of more flexibility than the published rates do. However, the very strong impression one obtains in Ghanaian banking circles is that non-price rationing of credit is a major device extensively employed.

Table IV-4
Central government capital account
Payments: loans to public enterprises, 1961–1969 (in thousands of new cedis)

Year	Value
1961	2,968
1962	95
1963	–
1964	–
1965	26
1966	580
1967	333
1968	1,332
1969	–

Source: *Economic Survey,* 1969, p. 113.

the Ghanaian capital market has made it possible to maintain low nominal interest rates in the face of substantial changes in the domestic price levels. Two issues are important: the rate of inflation, and variations in that rate. Using the GDP deflator as a price index (Table IV-5), the average compound rate of inflation during the decade of the 1960's was nearly 8 percent per annum. There was, however, considerable year-to-year variation, such as the rapid inflation of 1965 and the deflation of 1966–1967. This experience, when set against the interest rates on deposits and loans in the organized institutional segments of the capital market, suggests that : (a) most deposit rates were on average negative in real terms; (b) few lending rates were much above zero in real terms; (c) changes in the rate of inflation were seldom reflected in deposit and lending rates. In sum, the institutional capital market's nominal rates were extremely low relative to, and unresponsive to changes in, the degree of domestic inflation.[22]

Given the negligible attention paid to pricing of capital in response to domestic developments, it is not surprising to find also a neglect of foreign developments. The use of capital account controls to isolate the domestic capital market from international capital markets could be considered an appropriate strategy. To the extent that the social marginal productivity of capital in the domestic economy exceeded the rate of return on capital abroad, the isolation of the domestic capital market from foreign influences could divert domestic savings to domestic uses which would be a social gain.

22. This does not suggest that individual institutions were behaving irrationally. On the contrary, the large volume of credit flowing through particular segments such as the commercial banks may have proved highly profitable.

Table IV-5
GDP deflator index, 1956–1969 (1960 = 100.0)

Year	Index	Percent change from previous year	From 3 years previous	
			Percent change	Annual compound rate (percent)
1956	91.97			
1957	92.32	0.38		
1958	101.11	9.52		
1959	100.11	−0.99	8.85	2.9
1960	100.00	−0.11	8.32	2.7
1961	103.20	3.20	2.07	0.7
1962	105.40	2.13	5.28	1.7
1963	112.48	6.72	12.48	4.0
1964	123.70	9.98	19.86	6.2
1965	144.60	16.90	37.19	11.1
1966	161.10	11.41	43.23	12.7
1967	156.93	−2.59	26.86	8.3
1968	179.90	14.64	24.41	7.5
1969	195.63	8.74	21.43	6.7

Source: Computed from GDP at current and at constant prices, *Economic Survey*, 1967 and 1969, for 1959 through 1969, and Birmingham *et al.*, *Economy of Ghana*, p. 50, for 1955 through 1958.

Yet despite the imposition of exchange control, the Ghanaian capital has remained linked to outside markets. Borrowers not satisfied in the domestic market, including the government, frequently turned to the international capital market, and often at substantially higher rates of interest. A large external debt was accumulated at rates of interest ranging from near zero up to 15 percent or more on suppliers' credit (Table IV-6). In addition to formally contracted loans, less explicit borrowing took place via devices such as the compulsory 180-day credit scheme on imports, arrears on foreign-exchange remittances for imports, and limitations placed on remittances by foreign-owned firms. [23] Ghana inevitably was charged interest on these loans either explicitly or implicitly, at rates which reflected the cost of capital in the supplying countries plus a risk premium to cover the lenders' uncertainty over Ghana's prospects. [24] In sum, Ghana borrowed substantial amounts from

23. The extent of the borrowing is impossible to estimate. Many of these devices can be circumvented in whole or in part.
24. This, of course, does not apply to funds which were blocked initially when exchange control was imposed.

Table IV-6
Externally held debt, 1968, 1969 (in millions of new cedis)

Item	End of June 1968	End of June 1969*
1. Government debt		
Stocks	2.9	3.2
IMF	104.2	106.7
Joint consolidated & misc. funds	15.7	6.3
Volta river project	82.2	82.2
Counterpart funds	15.8	27.7
Tefle bridge	5.1	5.1
USAID commod. prog.	4.1	5.6
W. Ger. commod. loan	8.3	8.9
UK loan	10.5	14.4
PL 480	25.9	28.2
Danish loan	0.1	0.2
2. Other debts**	90.2	38.2
3. Suppliers credits	372.6	374.5
Total	737.6	701.2

Notes: * Provisional.
          ** Arrears of trade bills, banking, and private sector debts.
Source: Bank of Ghana, *Report of the Board for the Financial Year Ended 30 June,*
          1970, p. 64.

foreign capital markets at rates far in excess of the rates paid on the domestic capital market.

Ghanaians also saved in foreign capital markets. Despite exchange control prohibition of capital transfers for such purposes, various devices have been available to the interested person, ranging from the purchase of foreign exchange on the black market through more sophisticated devices such as over-invoicing on imports. All typically involved a higher price of foreign exchange initially, but given the expectation that in the long run reconversion to local currency would involve at least an equal price of foreign exchange due to higher black market prices and/or official devaluation, the Ghanaian saver could in the long run expect to obtain both the higher rate of return offered on savings abroad and the possibility of a profit on the exchange transaction.[25] Hence, not only did Ghanaians borrow from abroad, they also lent abroad, both at higher rates of interest than obtained in most institutional segments of the local capital market, and at substantially higher transactions costs.

25. We are excluding consideration of capital flight for precautionary purposes.

Table IV-7
Selected interest rates in the UK and Ghana, 1960 to 1969 (percent)

	UK (averages for year)				Ghana, Commercial banks (end of year)			
Year	Treasury bills	Euro-dollar London	Gov't. bond yield (LT)	Gov't. bond yield (ST)	Savings deposits	6 month fixed deposit	Bills discounted	Loans secured
1960	4.88		5.43	5.60	3 to 3.5	2.5	7.0	5.5 to 7.0
1961	5.13		6.22	5.98	3 to 3.5	2.5	7.0	5.5 to 7.0
1962	4.18		6.00	5.31	3 to 3.5	2.5	7.0	5.5 to 7.0
1963	3.66	3.95	5.59	4.83	3 to 3.5	2.5	7.0	5.5 to 7.0
1964	4.61	4.32	6.03	5.54	3 to 3.5	2.5	7.0	5.5 to 7.0
1965	5.91	4.81	6.42	6.57	3 to 3.5	2.5	7.0	5.5 to 7.0
1966	6.10	6.12	6.81	6.77	3 to 3.5	2.5 to 2.75	7.5 to 9.5	7.0 to 9.0
1967	5.82	5.46	6.70	6.67	3 to 3.5	2.75 to 3.25	7.0 to 10.0	6.5 to 10.0
1968	7.04	6.36	7.40	7.59	2.5 to 3.5	2.75 to 3.0	6.0 to 10.0	6.5 to 10.0
1969	7.63	9.76	8.89	8.82	2.5 to 3.5	2.75 to 3.0	7.0 to 10.0	6.5 to 10.0

Sources: UK, from IMF, *International Financial Statistics*, 1971 Supplement. Ghana, from Bank of Ghana, *Report of the Board for the Financial Year Ended 30 June*, 1970, p. 59.

Despite these links with foreign capital markets, institutional segments of the Ghanaian capital market were largely unresponsive to outside developments. The restrictive trade and payments regime was an important permissive element, allowing domestic institutions the apparent freedom to proceed in their own way. An important example of this assumed independence was the lack of Ghanaian response to the rising nominal international interest rates in the period following 1963. As a proxy for foreign rates, consider the selected interest rates prevailing in the United Kingdom in contrast with the Ghanaian rates on deposits and loans (Table IV-7). Foreign rates began to rise from 1963 and almost doubled by 1969. Ghanaian rates did not respond, remaining constant until the deflationary period following the 1966 coup. Even with the 1966 adjustment, by 1969 Ghanaian rates were not nearly double those of 1963.

The strategy of developing new capital market institutions to meet the needs of the Ghanaian economy thus failed to develop a strong interconnected domestic capital market. Instead, there emerged several noncompetitive segments, largely isolated from one another and unresponsive to new economic situations. The strategy of isolating the domestic capital market from the rest of the world was not successfully implemented. Instead, reliance on international capital markets by both savers and investors continued, but the domestic capital market was largely unresponsive to international developments. These results suggest the possibility of major misallocations. The final task, to which we now turn, is to examine the consequences of the system.

4. Responses to the control system

The non-price rationing of the import licencing system and the segmented capital market were employed by the policymakers to ensure that particular activities were favored in the allocation of capital and of licences for imported materials. For the favored ones, the constraints of capital and imported materials were frequently eliminated over the relevant range of their potential demand. Yet output and employment did not respond as they "should" have to this generous treatment. Why? The answer lies in large part with the signals individuals received from the allocative system: cheap and relatively plentiful supplies of capital and imported materials for the favored ones. The response was to treat them as cheap and plentiful.

This section concerns the responses of various sectors of the economy to the control system. While the evidence is fragmentary and no single piece alone covers the entire picture, altogether the evidence which follows provides considerable insight into the response of economic units.

(a) Output and input intensities

Consider first the typical response of favored producers to the implicit subsidies arising from their special treatment by the licencing authorities and the capital market. A convenient method of specifying the way such favored producers respond to cheap and plentiful allocations of capital and foreign exchange is to start from an initial no-distortions situation and examine their response to a cheaper input. Assume that some inputs such as capital and foreign exchange are available to a producer at a fixed price but that at least one input, say labor, is available only at increasing costs. Assume further that the price of output is given for the producer. Given the price of output and the fixed-price inputs, the producer adjusts output to the point that his marginal unit cost of all the inputs equals the price of output. Now, keeping the unit price of output constant, introduce a subsidy in some form on one of the fixed-price inputs. For the same outlay the producer can purchase more inputs, enabling him to draw on higher cost variable-price inputs to the point again that his marginal costs are equal to the output price.

The input subsidy stimulates output. And if the production function is such that there is any substitution between the subsidized and other inputs, the subsidy also induces the producer to use that input relatively more intensively.

A subsidy on an input thus achieves two objectives: it stimulates output, and it induces the producer to use the subsidized input relatively more intensively. If these two objectives coincide, clearly the input subsidy approach is a simple two-pronged instrument that may be easier to employ than alternative combinations of instruments. However, when the objective is to expand output only but not induce a shift in relative input intensities, the input subsidy becomes a far less attractive instrument: it is less effective than an output subsidy of the same value, and has the unwanted effect of inducing substitution opposite to that desired. Yet Ghanaian policy during the restrictive period frequently resorted to implicit input subsidies in the form of cheaper capital and/or foreign exchange, together with plentiful supplies over wide ranges to favored recipients.

To examine this phenomenon in more detail it is useful to specify a functional form for the production function. At the industry level the most plausible, and at the same time convenient form of the production function is a Cobb–Douglas. Our empirical estimates reported below provide a reasonably good fit to this form. Also, the only other industry-level production function work on Ghana which we are aware of provides some support to the view that the elasticity of substitution in a variety of Ghanaian industries is not substantially different from unity. [26] There are, however, numerous

26. M. Roemer, "Elasticities of Substitution in Ghanaian Industry," mimeograph, Accra, September 1971. His estimates are based on pooled cross-section and time-series data for the period 1962 to 1968, and refer to value-added only, not (as our estimates do) to gross output.

theoretical and empirical problems associated with our use of a neoclassical production function[27] on the Ghanaian data, the most serious problem being the set of competitive assumptions underlying the analysis. While we do not wish to minimize these problems, the neoclassical production function does provide us with a convenient framework within which we can illustrate the direction of industry responses to the system. In other words, what follows should be taken as nothing more than illustrative of the general type of response exhibited by the Ghanaian industries.

Our Cobb—Douglas production function takes the form:

$$X = AK^{\alpha}L^{\beta}M_F^{\delta}M_D^{\gamma} \tag{IV.1}$$

where X = quantity of output, A = a constant, K = capital services used per period, L = labor services used per period, M_F = foreign materials consumed per period, M_D = domestic materials consumed per period, and the exponents are constant.

The response relationships of output and input intensities to a subsidy are readily specified.[28] The key is to identify one input as the constraint on expanding output. Given that, it is possible to derive expressions showing the expansion of output and the expansion of input uses in response to the introduction of subsidies. These are all functions of the input coefficients, the rates of subsidies on the inputs, and the elasticity of supply of the constraining input.

The remaining task is to apply the relationships to a few cases. First, we have estimated the Cobb—Douglas production functions for three industry groups using cross-section data from the 1968 Central Bureau of Statistics industrial survey.[29] We were limited to three groups because complete data were available on a sufficient number of establishments in only the shoe industry, the sawmilling industry, and the furniture industry. These nevertheless do provide a range of illustrative input intensities and differing characteristics.

Our data were the following:

(a) Output. We used value of gross output, as insufficient establishments reported quantities to permit us to construct quantity indexes.

(b) Labor. The total number of employees reported by the establishment was our indicator of labor inputs. Man-hour data were not reported.

(c) Capital. Depreciation data were reported, but not capital stock, so it was

27. For a useful discussion see: Murray Brown, *Theory and Measurement of Technical Change,* Cambridge University Press, Cambridge, 1966; and Marc Nerlove, *Estimation and Identification of Cobb—Douglas Production Functions*, North-Holland, Amsterdam, 1965.

28. The details are contained in Appendix D.

29. See Appendix C for further discussion of these data.

impossible to check the reasonableness of the depreciation figures. We experimented, using reported depreciation data in our estimates, and found none of the capital coefficients to be significant (and two were negative). Because capital services actually used is the variable we wish to employ, we also attempted to adjust the depreciation data for reported capacity utilization in the two industries for which this was possible, but again obtained inclusive results. We therefore fell back on non-wage value-added as our proxy for capital services.

(d) Imported materials. Here we simply used the value of imported materials consumed in production.

(e) Domestic materials. Again we used values of materials consumed, plus values of fuels and electricity consumed.

Equation (IV.1) is linear in logs, which we used as our estimating equation in the following form:

$$\log X = \log A + \alpha \log K + \beta \log L + \delta \log M_F + \gamma \log M_D$$

The resulting least squares regressions are set out in Table IV-8. The overall fits are high, and the important coefficients in each industry are significant. In the case of shoes the coefficient for domestic materials is not significantly different from 0 at the 10 percent level primarily because many establishments use no domestic materials, and others very limited amounts. For the same reason the foreign materials coefficients for sawmilling and furniture are not significant. The sums of the coefficients suggest the possibility of some limited scale economies in the furniture industry, but not the others.

The small number of establishments in most other Ghanaian industries made it impossible for us to do cross-section estimates of their production functions. As a consequence, our three industries do not include a representative of the numerous assembly-type import-substitution industries which frequently have only one or two establishments. Since these industries are an important part of the Ghanaian industrial picture, we have arbitrarily selected a "representative" case, that of a radio and television assembly operation, to supplement the illustrative calculations. Using the same variables as in our production function estimates, we calculated relative shares of output paid for capital, labor, imported materials, and domestic materials in place of our coefficients α, β, δ, and γ. These values were: $\alpha = 0.141, \beta = 0.090, \delta = 0.695,$ $\gamma = 0.074$. The sharp contrast with the other industries is evident in the dominance of imported materials.

Second, we require some indication of the degree of subsidies received by the industries. There is a variety of approaches available to specify these subsidies, depending on the norm chosen. The norms include various "shadow price" concepts such as the equilibrium price in the absence of distortions, or

Table IV-8

Regression results for Cobb–Douglas production functions cross section, 1968

Industry	Degrees of freedom	R^2	$\log X = \log A + \alpha \log K$	$+ \beta \log L$	$+ \delta \log M_F$	$+ \gamma \log M_D$	Sum of significant coefficients
Shoes	8	0.986	4.220 (6.425)** + 0.543 $\log K$ (6.020)**	+ 0.316 $\log L$ (3.318)**	+ 0.136 $\log M_F$ (1.566)**	+ 0.054 $\log M_D$ (1.095)	0.995
Sawmilling	19	0.985	1.113 (2.298)** + 0.181 $\log K$ (2.950)**	+ 0.050 $\log L$ (3.650)**	+ 0.004 $\log M_F$ (0.331)	+ 0.864 $\log M_D$ (13.250)**	1.095
Furniture	8	0.953	3.554 (3.593)** + 0.679 $\log K$ (3.393)**	+ 0.066 $\log L$ (1.791)*	+ 0.016 $\log M_F$ (0.527)	+ 0.423 $\log M_D$ (2.681)**	1.168

Notes: a. The values of R^2 not adjusted for degrees of freedom. b. t values in parentheses, * indicates significant at 10 percent level, and ** at the 5 percent level (one-tail test).

the marginal value of an actual restricted supply. Empirical estimation of such values, however, would require a major study in itself and would take us far beyond the scope of the present work. Instead, we have fallen back on the national average as the norm against which we judge whether or not a subsidy is involved.

For imported goods we must recognize that the average value of foreign exchange expended on them is made up of the various taxes on imports, both explicit and implicit, which we detailed in Chapter II, Table II-1. In addition there is the premium attributable to the restrictive licencing. On an economy-wide basis various "guesstimates" for 1968 have put this latter value at at least 15 percent of the official exchange rate. When added to the average taxes on imports of over 36 percent in 1968 (Table II-1) we have an average premium value of foreign exchange of 51.5 percent. For our illustrative purposes we have rounded this down to 50 percent, and on this basis calculated the implicit subsidy rates on imported materials contained in Table IV-9. We do not mean to suggest that these numbers are anything more than approximations of actual implicit subsidies, but they clearly illustrate (conservatively) the nature of the problem.

For capital, a convenient norm is the marginal productivity of capital derived from an aggregate nonagricultural production function study by Peter Newman. Using a cross section of the seven Ghanaian regions, he fitted a Cobb–Douglas production function for 1960. Given the capital coefficient and the capital stock, the marginal productivity of capital was 17.2 percent, before depreciation.[30] If we correct for depreciation by deducting from value-added, Brown's estimate of depreciation for the same year, the marginal productivity of capital is 14.9 percent.[31] Since this was for 1960, and since the actual productivity of capital has subsequently declined, a conservative illustrative magnitude might be on the order of 12 percent for 1968.

The actual rates at which these industries are able to obtain capital are equally elusive. However, to illustrate the significance of the issue at hand,

30. From Peter Newman, "Capacity Utilization and Growth," mimeograph, January 1970. The data by region for gross value-added and capital stock were from R. Szereszewski, Chapter 4, in W. Birmingham *et al., The Economy of Ghana, op. cit.* Employment data by region were from the 1960 census. His estimate was:

$$\log Y = 0.447 + 0.615 \log K + 0.371 \log L$$
$$(7.760) \qquad (3.235)$$

where Y = gross value-added at factor cost, K = capital stock (value), L = employment (numbers) in the nonagricultural sector: t-values are in parentheses, and R^2 = 0.990. The value-added was N¢ 418 million, and capital stock N¢ 1,500 million for 1960, which with the capital coefficient yields 17.2 percent as the marginal productivity of capital.

31. T.M. Brown, "Macroeconomic Data of Ghana," *op. cit.,* estimates depreciation for 1960 equal to N¢ 53 million.

Table IV-9
Implicit industry average subsidy rates on imported materials, 1968

Industry	Av. import tax rate (percent)	Adjust for other trade taxes (percent)	Total rate on imp. mat. (percent)	Implicit subsidy rate (percent)
	(1)	(2)	(3)	(4)
Shoes	28.08	10.40	38.48	7.68
Sawmilling	3.28	9.16	12.44	25.04
Furniture	4.12	9.21	13.33	24.45
Radio/TV	0	9.00	9.00	27.33

Sources: 1. Average import tax rate is total duties paid on imported materials with respect to imports of materials, weighted by use of imported materials. Data are from establishment returns to the CBS annual survey of industry.

2. The adjustment for other trade taxes takes into account the 180-day credit scheme on imports on the assumption that it increased the c.i.f. price by 5 percent (and thus is included in the base for the duty and other collections) plus the allowable 6 percent per annum (i.e., 3 percent of value) interest cost. This column also includes the 1 percent import licence fee in 1968.

3. This is the sum of columns (1) and (2).

4. The implicit subsidy rate is the difference between the norm of 50 percent premium and the rate in column (3) as a proportion of 100 percent plus the norm.

assume that they are able to obtain capital at the maximum unsecured loan rate of the commercial banks, a nominal 10 percent per annum. Taking into account the average compound rate of inflation in the period 1966 through 1969 of 6.7 percent, this suggests a real rate of access to capital at 3.3 percent per annum. And, *vis-à-vis* our norm of 12 percent, we are speaking of a subsidy rate on capital at 72.5 percent or to round down, 70 percent. At first glance this appears to be an excessively high subsidy rate, but when we note that most private industrial establishments are able to obtain capital at nominal rates much below 10 percent, and publicly owned industries often at zero nominal rates, this implicit subsidy rate appears to be very conservative. To be even more conservative, a 50 percent subsidy rate is also considered.

Finally, we need to specify the constraining input for each industry. On the basis of our subjective knowledge of the industries involved, we have selected labor as the constraining input for ·the shoe and radio—television assembly industries, primarily because these employ some high-skilled labor, which is likely to require higher wages in order to induce an expansion of supply. For the sawmilling and furniture industries we have assumed the constraining input to be domestic materials. Further, we have arbitrarily assumed that the elasticity of supply of each constraining input is unity.

Given our illustrative implicit subsidy rates, together with the industry

Table IV-10a

Responses of output to assumed subsidies on capital and imported inputs

Industry	Coefficients[a]				Constraining input[b]		dp_i/p_i		Output changes dX/X	
	Capital α	Labor β	For. mat. δ	Dom. mat. γ	Input name	Elast. assumed	$\mathrm{sub}_k=0.7$	$\mathrm{sub}_k=0.5$	$\mathrm{sub}_k=0.7$	$\mathrm{sub}_k=0.5$
Shoes	0.543	0.316	0.136	0	Labor	$e_l=1$	7.18	2.39	65.86	10.49
Sawmilling	0.181	0.050	0	0.864	Dom. mat.	$e_{md}=1$	0.29	0.16	0.66	0.32
Furniture	0.679	0.066	0	0.423	Dom. mat.	$e_{md}=1$	5.92	3.04	46.89	8.24
Radio/TV[d]	0.141	0.090	0.695	0.074	Labor	$e_l=1$	76.43	33.76	5,993.63	1,207.47

Table IV-10b

Responses of inputs to assumed subsidies on capital and imported inputs

Industry	Input changes[c]				Ratios output to input changes			
	Cap: dK/K		For. mat.: dM_F/M_F		Output/capital		Output/inp. mat.	
	$\mathrm{sub}_k=0.7$	$\mathrm{sub}_k=0.5$	$\mathrm{sub}_k=0.7$	$\mathrm{sub}_k=0.5$	$\mathrm{sub}_k=0.7$	$\mathrm{sub}_k=0.5$	$\mathrm{sub}_k=0.7$	$\mathrm{sub}_k=0.5$
Shoes	221.88	21.97	71.43	11.44	0.297	0.477	0.922	0.917
Sawmilling	4.52	1.67	–	–	0.146	0.192	–	–
Furniture	158.62	17.48	–	–	0.296	0.471	–	–
Radio/TV[d]	19,981.10	2,415.94	8,248.45	1,662.02	0.300	0.500	0.727	0.727

Notes: a. Only significant coefficients: those insignificant at 10 percent level set equal to zero. See Table IV-8 for estimated equations.
b. The proportionate price change dp_i/p_i is that of the constraining input.
c. Constraining input changes by the same proportion as its price changes (assuming its $e=1$).
d. Coefficients not derived from production function estimation. See text.
e. Subsidy rate on imported materials from Table IV-9.

coefficients, we have calculated response ratios of output and input uses for each industry. The results are contained in Table IV-10. The responses of output are large, ranging from 32 percent (sawmilling) on up to virtually infinity (radio and TV assembly). The magnitudes of the response arise mostly because of the subsidies on capital of 6 to 8.5 percentage points on the interest rate which amount to massive relative subsidies on the use of capital.

There is considerable variation between industries in the response of output. For similar input subsidy rates, the response of output depends directly on the size of capital and imported materials coefficients, and inversely on the size of the constraining input coefficient. Hence the large output response for the radio and television assembly industry arises mostly from the high foreign materials coefficient and the low labor coefficient. And the sawmilling industry's response is considerably smaller because of the relatively small capital coefficient and large domestic materials coefficient.

The elasticities of output with respect to subsidized input changes are low. Even for the very conservative assumption of a 50 percent rate of subsidy on capital, the elasticity of output with respect to capital addition is 0.5 or less. Imported material elasticities are not as low (largely because the subsidy rates are not as high as for capital), but even an 8 to 27 percent drop from a unitary elasticity is considerable cause for concern.

To sum up, using representative magnitudes of industrial structure and relative subsidy rates, we have illustrated in a Cobb—Douglas framework how: (1) output is generally highly responsive to relative subsidies on inputs; and (2) use of subsidized inputs increases at a relatively (sometimes considerably) greater rate than output. We emphasize that these results should be taken as nothing more than illustrative. If however these magnitudes are anywhere nearly representative of the Ghanaian situation, we now have a major clue in explaining the response of the industrial sector to the control regime. Cheap and virtually unlimited supplies of foreign exchange and capital for the favored ones stimulated output, but the use of imported materials accelerated and the output—capital ratio plummeted.[32]

The growth consequences of the set of policies which permitted large relative subsidies on capital and imported materials were serious. Favored sectors flourished.[33] Other sectors suffered seriously: access to capital and foreign exchange was, for most, blocked and little or no growth occurred.

---

32. Further, when we take into account the fact that a high proportion of recorded capital formation is made up of imports, the increased use of foreign exchange by favored recipients is further increased. In 1969 imports of durable producers' materials (mostly construction materials) plus producers' equipment amounted to N₵ 119.7 million while gross domestic fixed capital formation was N₵ 242 million (*Economic Survey,* 1969, pp. 117, 116).

33. See Chapter III.

The overall effect was one of stagnation accompanied by apparently worse capital and foreign-exchange "gaps" for the economy as a whole.

(b) Other responses

Other responses to the control regime suggest themselves. Overbuilding of plant, low capacity utilization, excessive inventories, limited technical progress, and diversion of entrepreneurial talent are commonly cited as problems arising from a control system. Undoubtedly in individual cases serious problems along these lines developed in Ghana during the control period. The available evidence, however, generally indicates that the case against controls on these grounds is not proven. The lack of proof may well rest on incomplete and unsatisfactory data. We suspect, however, that many of the problems associated with the import-substituting industrialization stemmed from problems other than the control system *per se.* Excessively long settling-in periods, combined with inexperienced management and labor were frequently responsible for poor performance in the industrial sector, rather than controls *per se.*

The evidence consists of a variety of isolated observations over the period, and some more detailed data for 1968. Consider first the issue of capacity utilization. During the late Nkrumah period (1964 and 1965) serious shortages of materials and spare parts were common, resulting in substantial underutilization of capacity (see Chapter II, section 5). In the immediate post-coup period low capacity utilization due to import shortages remained a serious problem. In setting out its plea for additional aid required for 1967, the NLC government put as its goal the attainment of "roughly some 50-55 percent of the theoretical 100 percent capacity on a one-shift basis."[34] Steel's interviews in 1968 of the 41 manufacturing firms in his sample found capacity utilization rates for 1967-68 ranging from 10 percent to 100 percent, with an average of less than 50 percent.[35] Finally, our data from the CBS 1968 Industrial Survey contained estimates of full capacity for some establishments which, given the reported actual output data, enabled us to compute capacity utilization rates. The range of capacity utilization rates was as broad as Steel's, with an unweighted mean of 57 percent and a standard deviation of 32 percent. The CBS Survey also contained responses from some establishments concerning the licences applied for and the licences utilized. This enabled us to compute licence utilization rates with respect to the licence

34. Republic of Ghana, *Ghana's Economy and Aid Requirements in 1967,* Accra, May 1967, p. 22.
35. W.F. Steel, "Import Substitution and Excess Capacity in Ghana," op. cit. He defined full capacity as "the realistic maximum level at which the firm would operate over a continued period of time if there were no restrictions in terms of demand or availability of inputs (at existing prices)," p. 225, footnote 4.

applications as a potential capacity utilization explanatory variable. While clearly subject to some serious shortcomings (e.g., unknown accuracy of responses, and inflation of licence applications), this ratio in theory represents the extent to which import licences actually made available and used corresponded to the desired flow of import licences.

These data permitted us to test the hypothesis that the rate of capacity utilization (CUT) is a function of licence utilization (LUT).[36] Regressing the former on the latter yielded the result:

$$CUT = 38.33 + 0.398 \text{ LUT} \qquad R^2 = 0.133$$
$$(1.25) \quad (1.96) \qquad\qquad DF = 25$$

The explanatory power of the estimated equation is low, the licence utilization coefficient is significant at the 5 percent level (one-tailed test), and the elasticity of capacity utilization in response to licence utilization at the mean is about 0.3 across the establishments. While the response of capacity utilization to licences is significant, licencing alone is not apparently a major determinant of capacity utilization.

Second, the existence of a licencing system could result in a diversion of investment flows into inventory holdings. We were unable to test this hypothesis fully. However, our 1968 cross-section data on the industrial sector enabled us to test the hypothesis that actual material inventories are a function of import dependency of inputs. Hence regressing material stocks at the beginning of the period as a percent of material used during the period (ST/USE) on the percent of imported material used in total material purchases (IMP/TOT) yielded:

$$ST/USE = 25.48 + 0.805 \text{ IMP/TOT} \qquad R^2 = 0.075$$
$$(1.480) \qquad\qquad DF = 27$$

The explanatory power of the estimated equation is very low and the coefficient is not significantly different from zero at a reasonable confidence level. We therefore reject the hypothesis that in the presence of the 1968 QR regime the more import-dependent an establishment the greater its inventory

36. The licencing argument follows from the point that availability of materials affect the level of attainable output. We also attempted to take into account the possibility that inventories of materials would perhaps have additional explanatory power. However, inclusion of the percentage of materials used during the period in stock at the beginning of the period did not yield a significant coefficient. Also, because the extent of the effect of LUT on CUT might depend on the import dependency of the establishment, we included the percent of imported materials in total material purchases as an explanatory variable. Again the coefficient was insignificant.

holdings. However, one will note that while the restrictive regime may shift the demand for inventories outward, it may also prevent the satisfaction of that demand. This can result in a situation where inventories can expand only when the QR system is relaxed, and if the relaxation of the system is not accompanied by an inward shift of the inventory demand, a substantial accumulation in inventories may well occur.[37]

Third, technical progress seems to have been absent during the period of the restrictive regime. Absent also is any major empirical work on the subject. However, as we noted in the introduction to this chapter, there was a negative residual between growth of output and growth of input at the aggregate national level. This clearly does not suggest the presence of substantial underlying technical progress.

Focusing more narrowly on inward transfers of technology, recent work by H. Baumann indicates that such transfers have been relatively limited. For example, a crude indicator such as patent applications by foreigners, 1963 to 1968, shows Ghana relatively low in relation to many other LDC's.[38] Baumann also constructed a composite index of technological transfer for a selected list of LDC's over the period 1958 through 1967, which again shows Ghana on the lower end of the scale relative to the other countries considered.[39]

Finally, the diversion of entrepreneurial talent from innovative endeavors is a potentially serious consequence of the restrictive system. The extent of the loss is impossible for us to quantify. The nature of the problem is, however, clear. As J.H. Mensah declared while he was Minister of Finance and Economic Planning, one of Ghana's major problems is weakness in her high level manpower:

> When one watches the cruel ineffectiveness with which so much expensively acquired equipment is operated in Ghana, when one realizes the inability of most parts of our administrative and managerial machinery to deliver the high quality performance which is required for a more rapid pace of national progress, then one realizes that Ghana may possess an articulate and polished elite in comparison with other African countries but she does not yet possess the managerial resources for running a fully modernized country.[40]

Yet because of the substantial gains to successful recipients of licences and other concessions and the large numbers of the available talent which were

---

37. For example, in 1965 and again in 1971, a surge of imports built up inventories largely in anticipation (subsequently shown to be correct) that a tight licencing system would return.
38. See H. Baumann, "Technological Change in Ghana's Economic Development," mimeograph, University of Western Ontario, January 1972, Table 1.
39. *Ibid.,* Table 5.
40. From a lecture delivered to the National Union of Students, Legon, 23 April, 1970.

required to administer the detailed regulations, a portion of the nation's entrepreneurial talents was diverted into coping with and running a control system. This was a serious loss.

5. Concluding remarks

We have presented a variety of evidence which links Ghana's control regime and its economic atrophy in the 1960's. We have shown that during this period both the savings rate and the productivity of investment declined significantly. The control regime was an important contributor to this poor performance. By choosing to employ controls to close the external deficit, pressure on domestic demand was vented on the domestic price level, resulting in reduced domestic savings rates. On the investment side the control regime shifted resources into favored activities with lower real productivity and isolated the domestic from the international capital market, making it possible to engage in discriminatory allocation of investment to less than optimal uses. Favored activities responded by using relatively more, not less, of the apparently "scarce" capital, foreign exchange and entrepreneurial talent.

In sum, there are reasonable grounds for attributing part of the poor growth performance to the control regime. It is important, however, not to overdraw the negative contribution of the control regime. The case against controls is largely that controls permitted errors in policy to have adverse effects on economic growth. Elimination of the set of trade and exchange controls employed for most of the 1960's could thus be expected to alleviate adverse growth effects only indirectly and with a long lag, providing ample opportunity for substitute policies to be instituted which might just as effectively stifle economic growth as the existing set of policies did.

Despite the slow and indirect ways in which the adverse effect emerged, during the second half of the 1960's the undesirable consequences of the control system received considerable attention. The result was an attempt to extricate the Ghanaian economy from the morass of trade and payments controls. Yet after four and one-half years the liberalization experiment failed, leaving the control regime fully intact. We turn now to focus on the liberalization experiment.

CHAPTER V

Liberalization

In July 1967 the National Liberation Council (NLC) government chose to devalue and launch the economy on an experiment with import liberalization. Four and one-half years later the liberalization had collapsed. The licencing system for 1972 was as restrictive as the system of a decade earlier. What led to this experiment? What were its essential features? And finally, what went wrong? It is to these and related questions that we now turn.

1. The devaluation decision

To see what led to the devaluation and liberalization, we resume our historical narrative, left off in Chapter II, with the situation at the end of 1966. At this point the economy was approximately back in the situation of 1962 through 1964. Numerous instruments had been brought to bear on the balance-of-payments problem. Yet the decline in reserves continued, and the prospect was dim that further measures to defend the official exchange rate would succeed in reversing the trend. At this point there began active consideration of what had long been regarded as the last resort: devaluation.

Conventional wisdom, based largely on a structuralist elasticity pessimism, continued to oppose devaluation as a means of achieving external balance. Yet the corruption of the late Nkrumah era, together with the severe austerity imposed on the post-coup economy for balance-of-payments reasons, combined to produce substantial dissatisfaction with the existing system as a long-term solution. A major body of domestic opinion, mostly the new commercial and industrial upper-middle class, viewed controls and austerity as undesirable, and an import liberalization as a means of discarding both.[1] There was a general recognition that no significant liberalization could be achieved without a devaluation. However, there was little recognition that control over aggregate demand would be more urgent in a liberalized system.

1. This view, for example, was reflected subsequently in the *Progress Party Manifesto,* Accra, 1969, p. 5, where trade controls were said to "have harmed the welfare of the consumer and prevented an orderly growth of the economy."

This failure would contribute eventually to the downfall of the liberalization experiment.

In official circles much the same line of reasoning prevailed and was reinforced by consideration of two external factors.[2] Private foreign investment was said to be discouraged by the increasingly evident exchange risk, and creditor and donor countries were unlikely to be generous unless Ghana put its balance of payments in order.

The need for external support was pressing. The gap between minimum foreign exchange requirements and expected earnings for 1967 amounted to N₵ 95 million according to a Bank of Ghana estimate.[3] On turning to the medium-term official creditors in late 1966, the NLC government obtained substantial rescheduling of the debts falling due through 1968, thus providing immediate breathing space, but no long-term relief.[4] And in early 1967 the IMF convened a meeting of Ghana's ten major western donor countries, with the result of increased aid offers. Yet neither of these forms of relief could be regarded as anything more than a short-term palliative. If external assistance were to continue for long, Ghana would have to put its balance of payments in order. Devaluation would provide such an opportunity.[5]

On July 8, 1967 the then Commissioner of Finance and NLC Member, Brigadier A.A. Afrifa, announced the devaluation. In doing so he skillfully attributed the continuing balance-of-payments difficulties to the inflationary policies pursued by Nkrumah, and put forward as the only alternative to devaluation a further expenditure reduction or a more restrictive licencing system, neither of which, he noted, were favorably regarded. At the same time he justified the "stabilization" (austerity) program of the previous 16 months on the grounds that it permitted devaluation from a position of strength. In summing up, he put forward devaluation as a necessary and logical decision taken in Ghana's own interest. No foreign pressure was either officially acknowledged or blamed, although in a post-devaluation press release E.N. Omaboe, Commissioner of Economic Affairs, is quoted as saying that "donor countries are no doubt going to be impressed by the boldness with which we have approached these chronic economic problems."[6]

2. See J.H. Frimpong-Ansah, "Stabilization and Development: Ghana's Experience," *Economic Bulletin of Ghana,* Second Series, Vol. 1, No. 1, 1970. Mr. Frimpong-Ansah was Governor of the Bank of Ghana from 1967 through 1972.
3. Bank of Ghana, *Quarterly Economic Bulletin,* January–June 1967, p. 3.
4. Payments due in 1966, 1967, and 1968 amounting to N₵ 180 million were reduced to N₵ 46 million in those years by shifting the debt into the future. This is discussed in more detail in section 3 below.
5. We are not aware, however, of any prior undertaking by Ghana to devalue or by donors to support the devaluation. And no such undertaking was officially acknowledged later by either side.
6. Quoted in *Legon Observer,* Vol. 2, No. 16 (4 August, 1967), p. 16.

The devaluation package itself emphasized the exchange rate adjustment, and did not involve an immediate large-scale liberalization of imports. The official price of foreign exchange was increased by about 43 percent, from N₵ 0.714 per dollar to N₵ 1.020 per dollar. In recognition that the purchasing monopsony for cocoa by the CMB fixed the producer price in terms of local rather than foreign currency, the producer price of cocoa was increased by 30 percent.[7] However, producer prices of minor agricultural exports controlled by the CMB were left unchanged for several months. As a small sweetener, the minimum wage was immediately increased by 7.7 percent (from N₵ 0.65 per day to N₵ 0.70 per day) and government wages and salaries were increased by 5 percent. Import levies on some essential commodities which typically did not contain a substantial quota premium were reduced. The liberalization component was mostly in the form of a long-term commitment to expand the OGL list and to permit more liberal remittances of profits. The immediate expansion of the OGL list covered only a few items, with a more substantial widening taking place when the regulations covering the 1968 calendar year were announced in the next month. The direction of the NLC liberalization policy was clear. What remained to be seen was how far the NLC would go towards complete liberalization of imports.

Public reaction to the devaluation is difficult to gauge, for without a parliament and a vigorous press, concerted adverse criticism was not a serious problem for the government. Perhaps the most representative adverse criticism of the devaluation appeared in the semi-intellectual *Legon Observer*, by a commentator under the pen name Kontopiaat. From a complaint about high living costs, he went on to rely mostly on an elasticity pessimism type argument. For exports he noted facetiously that his cocoa trees had suddenly stepped up their yield since the devaluation, and that he was seriously contemplating exporting mosquitoes to South Africa, snakes and scorpions to Rhodesia, snails and frogs to France. He argued further that since the world price of these primary commodities was fixed, one could not, for some unspecified reason, boost export revenues by devaluation. For imports he queried where could local substitutes be found? "We can surely use plantain fibre for wigs;...charcoal and palm oil for soap; and canes for hulahoops...; the list of local substitutes, you see, is quite impressive...".[8] Another major theme was that higher costs of imported machinery and materials adversely affected

7. Note that a devaluation provides an opportunity to increase the producer price without reducing government revenue *vis-à-vis* the pre-devaluation situation because the foreign price denominated in local currency also rises.
8. *Legon Observer*, Vol. 2, No. 19 (15 September 1967), p. 26.

business, particularly small Ghanaian businessmen relative to expatriate businessmen, the latter being somehow unaffected.

A sufficiently large grain of truth existed in each of Kontopiaat's major arguments to make them generally accepted among many of the opponents of devaluation. Most educated critics did not distinguish between low, but nevertheless significant, elasticities and the assumed zero elasticities. The complaint about higher living costs was typically based on a before–after rather than a with–without comparison: a valid judgment in the former case, but not in the latter. The burden on local manufacturers was somewhat more complex. Whether or not high input costs were offset by higher output prices in a before–after comparison depended largely on the degree of protection contained in the pre-devaluation quota premia.[9] In a with–without comparison local manufacturers could have expected higher input prices from suppliers even in the absence of devaluation.

The polemics of political debate aside, what were the economic effects of the devaluation? In particular, did it act to correct the external imbalance and permit import liberalization to proceed as promised? It is to this set of issues that we now turn.

2. Short-run effects of the devaluation package

Six years had passed since the open deficit in Ghana's balance of payments had been closed by the system of exchange controls and import licencing. The excess demand for real resources which generated the deficit had been vented on the domestic price level. As a result, the domestic prices of tradeables were out of line with international prices.

The objective of a devaluation in these circumstances is to bring the domestic prices of tradeables into line with the international price level and subsequently ensure that, at the new set of prices, a new excess demand for real resources does not emerge. Hence the primary focus of our analysis of the short-run effects of the devaluation is on domestic prices and aggregate expenditure. In addition, a devaluation almost inevitably alters the distribution of income, an issue that merits consideration.

(a) The impact of devaluation on domestic relative prices

The circumstances in which the 1967 devaluation was introduced are of fundamental importance in evaluating its impact. The restrictive trade and payments regime had been functioning for several years, bottling up the

9. This is discussed in more detail below.

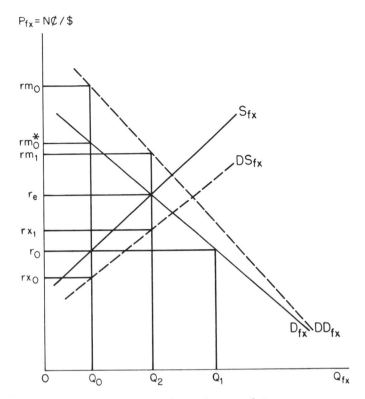

Fig. V-1. Foreign-exchange market.

excess demand and transferring its location from outside to inside the country. Of particular importance for our present discussion is the fact that the value of imports in terms of foreign exchange had already been restricted to less than the level that would obtain at an equilibrium exchange rate.[10]

This situation is illustrated by means of the usual heuristic presentation of the foreign-exchange market in Figure V.1. The vertical and horizontal axes measure the price and quantity of foreign exchange. For our purposes assume the dollar is the unit of foreign exchange and the new cedi the local currency. The demand and supply curves of dollars are represented by D_{fx} and S_{fx}. Assume that these arise only from imports and exports.

10. Further, the deflationary policy that had been followed for approximately twelve months meant that the latent excess demand was smaller than it would have been at a more acceptable (higher) level of domestic expenditure. This is considered further in section 2b below.

Underlying the generation and use of foreign exchange are the domestic markets in which exporters are paid and importers pay in local currency for the goods that enter the international markets. If there are trade taxes the rates at which domestic offers and demands of new cedis for dollars arise will differ from the rates at which the national offers and demands are made. On the export side, a tax means that exporters will receive fewer new cedis per dollar than the nation does. Thus we have drawn the domestic supply curve of dollars as DS_{fx}, which lies below the curve S_{fx} due to the export tax. If the export tax is some arbitrary sum (as in the case of Ghanaian cocoa) the precise relationship between the two curves is not clearly defined. On the import side, the domestic curve DD_{fx} lies above D_{fx} due to the import tariff.

The situation depicted in Figure V-1 is a closed deficit at the fixed exchange rate r_0. The excess demand of Q_0Q_1 is not satisfied because of either an unwillingness to draw down reserves by the amount necessary or simply the absence of adequate reserves. Assuming that exactly the quantity of dollars generated is made available for import (OQ_0), the ultimate purchasers of this value of imports pay Or_0 new cedis per dollar to purchase the foreign exchange, $rm_0^*rm_0$ in import tariffs, and $r_0rm_0^*$ to the recipients of the licence premium.

In these circumstances the fact that the dollar value of imports has already been restricted to less than the level that would obtain at the equilibrium exchange rate is readily apparent. Because of this previous restriction, a devaluation can aim at expanding both the quantity of foreign exchange earned and eventually the quantity of foreign exchange used. It need not aim at "the restoration of equilibrium in Ghana's balance of payment through stimulating exports and curtailing imports."[11] Rather, the appropriate objective is to permit an expansion of both the quantities of foreign exchange generated and used via an upward adjustment of the exchange rate to the point where the latent excess demand is eliminated due to expanding export earnings, and demand for imports is contained by price rather than licences.[12]

The achievement of the objective is by no means automatic. The presence of discretionary "distortions" on the import side, and in the case of Ghana on the export side, means that the devaluation will not be transmitted automatically to the markets for tradeables in the domestic economy. Consequently it is entirely possible to have a devaluation in which one or both of

11. CBS, *Economic Survey*. 1967, Accra, p. 31.
12. In the case of a downward sloping supply curve of foreign exchange (but assuming a stable market) a devaluation moves in the direction of equilibrium by contraction of both the quantities generated and used, but in a closed deficit, the contraction of the quantity used is clearly smaller than in the case of an open deficit.

the export and import sides is unaffected. The necessary discretionary changes may simply not be made.

On the export side, if the distortion is not an *ad-valorem* export tax, only by chance will the change in the new cedi price facing export producers reflect appropriately the rate of devaluation. For example, if the export tax is a residual between a fixed producer price and the world price, the local currency producer price must be increased for there to be any transmission of the devaluation. Movement along the curve S_{fx} arises because of movement along the domestic producers' supply curve, not the other way around. In terms of Figure V-1, if the price facing export producers does not reflect the devaluation, the quantity of foreign exchange supplied will not rise by the amount predicted from considering S_{fx} and the change in the official exchange rate.

On the import side it is important to distinguish between the immediate impact of the devaluation and the subsequent changes that may come about as the quantity of foreign exchange supplied increases. The immediate effect of the devaluation, assuming the dollar magnitude of the licences is kept constant, is to narrow the licence premium gap between r_0 and rm_0^* in Figure V.1.[13] If the devaluation does not entirely close this gap immediately (and it need not, for the expected expansion of the quantity supplied has yet to take place), the price facing ultimate domestic purchasers of imports is unaffected. Nothing happens to the level of foreign-exchange utilization unless the licencing authorities change the dollar value of licences issued. Later, as the quantity of foreign exchange available expands, the licencing authorities can increase the foreign exchange available for imports resulting in a movement down the curve DD_{fx} and an eventual elimination of the gap between the new exchange rate and the rate along D_{fx}. In sum, a devaluation on impact need not mean an increased price facing ultimate domestic purchasers of imports, and can eventually mean a decrease in that price.

In terms of this analytical framework, the changes in prices facing export producers are a useful measure of the extent to which the devaluation is transmitted to exporters. The prices facing purchasers of imports may initially not change at all. If they rise, the devaluation has on impact more than

13. Where imports are for resale, the premium gap is captured as the import items move along the resale chain from the licence recipient to the ultimate purchasers for final use. Where imports are for own use and (as in Ghana) there is no auction system for licences or resale is uncommon, the premium gap is implicit, arising from the quota restriction and the derived demand for the items imported for own use. The following discussion is phrased in terms of imports for resale. Hence for the case of imports for own use one should read "the implicit premium-inclusive price" in place of "the price facing ultimate domestic purchasers."

eliminated the licence premium, and if they eventually fall because the expansion of foreign-exchange earnings permits an increase in licences, the devaluation may be termed a success.

The issue arising from the 1967 devaluation is: to what extent was the external change in the new cedi price of a dollar transmitted to the domestic markets for tradeables? The relationships involved are readily expressed in algebraic form, which we have done in an appendix to this chapter.[14] Our measure relates the domestic price change to the foreign price change associated with the devaluation. The calculations generally involve comparisons between the weighted monthly average of the pre-devaluation period of January through June 1967 and the post-devaluation period of August through December 1967. (Devaluation occurred on July 8, 1967.) These periods were selected to be short enough to avoid extensive extraneous influences not associated with the devaluation, and at the same time long enough to iron out monthly fluctuations. The net result is an estimate of the percentage change in new cedis per dollar received by the export producers or paid by the ultimate import purchasers.

(1) Exports. Our calculations for the export side are contained in Table V-1. These should be taken as nothing more than a rough indicator of what in fact occurred. Several simplifications had to be made in order to arrive at these approximations. For export prices we used unit values from the export trade statistics. Producer prices of the CMB commodities were those paid at the buying stations scattered throughout the country. Producer prices of timber were derived by deducting the export taxes paid at the rates for 1966 for the pre-devaluation prices and the rates for 1968 for post-devaluation prices. Additional points are noted in Table V-1.

Turning to the results, there is some variation between commodities. In the case of cocoa, the CMB increased the producer price by 30 percent immediately after the devaluation. The export unit values rose by over 32 percent in the post-devaluation period, so that the market appears to have adjusted to a nearly complete transmission of the devaluation to domestic producers.[15] For timber, specific export tax levies were reduced immediately

---

14. See Appendix E.
15. Note that the change in export unit value is very nearly equal to the export price increase that would have been predicted had the producer price change exactly equalled the change required for full transmission (33 percent). See Appendix E for details of this calculation.

Table V-1
Transmission of 1967 devaluation to domestic prices of exports

Commodity	Percentage of exports 1966a	Post-devaluation index (pre-deval. = 100)		Percentage change, in new cedis per dollar
		Producer price	Export priceb	
Cocoa beansc	55.5	130.0	132.7	40.0
Cocoa butter	6.2	144.8	144.8	42.9
Timber (logs and sawn)d	11.3	128.0	126.4	44.6
Bauxite	0.8	138.9	138.9	42.9
Manganese	6.5	120.6	120.6	42.9
Diamonds	5.8	147.3	134.1	57.0
Gold	9.2	126.1	126.1	42.9
Kola nutsc	0.7	100.0	148.0	−3.5
Palm kernelsc	0.0001	114.5	135.1	21.0
Coffeec	1.2	111.0	68.2	132.6
Bananasc	0.0013	113.9	159.1	2.3
Shea nutsc	0.0027	104.2	88.1	68.8
Sub total and average	97.1			43.04
Otherse	2.9			42.86
Total and average	100.0			43.03

Notes: a. Export percentages derived from Central Bureau of Statistics, *Quarterly Digest of Statistics*, June 1968 — except for kola nuts, palm kernels, coffee, bananas and shea nuts, which were calculated from CBS, *External Trade Statistics* (monthly), December 1966.

b. Export unit values used to calculate export prices pre-devaluation (Jan.– June 1967) and post-devaluation (Aug.–Dec. 1967) were calculated from CBS, *Quarterly Digest of Statistics*, June 1968 and March 1969, except for kola nuts, palm kernels, coffee, bananas and shea nuts, which were calculated from CBS, *External Trade Statistics* (monthly), various issues, 1967.

c. These items are handled by the CMB, and the domestic prices are the producer prices paid by the CMB pre- and post-devolution. The cocoa bean price was changed shortly after devaluation: the producer price change for the others is the change from 1967 to 1968. See CMB, *Ghana Cocoa Marketing Board at Work*, Accra, 1968. Taking the producer price change as zero for these items yields the following change in new cedis per dollar in 1967 alone: palm kernels = 5.7237 percent; coffee = 109.5785 percent; bananas = −10.2015 percent; shea nuts = 62.0927 percent.

d. The domestic prices pre- and post-devaluation for timber were derived by deducting the export tax at the *ad valorem* equivalent for 1966 from the pre-devaluation export price and for 1968 from the post-devaluation export price. The export duties and export values are from CBS, *Quarterly Digest of Statistics,* March 1969.

e. Assumed full transmission.

after the devaluation. The change in domestic prices thus more than reflected the devaluation.[16]

The remaining items are minerals, and agricultural commodities handled by the CMB. The mineral exports, except for diamonds won by African diggers, were not subject to export tax either before or after the devaluation and hence there was no mechanism to prevent full transmission of the devaluation. A 9 percent export tax on diamonds won by African diggers was eliminated immediately after the devaluation, resulting in a larger price rise to domestic producers.[17]

The CMB is responsible for the purchase and sale of several minor commodities: coffee, palm kernels, copra, shea nuts, kola nuts, ground nuts, and bananas. Of these only coffee, shea nuts, kola nuts, and bananas were exported in 1966 and 1967. The CMB's response to the devaluation for these commodities was delayed until producer prices were set for the following crop year. And the response in general was considerably less than the devaluation. Taking into account trends in world prices however, and hence new cedi export prices, the net result was virtually no change in the producer prices relative to the international prices for bananas and kola nuts, and very large relative changes for shea nuts and coffee.

Putting all the export items together, the weighted average transmission of the devaluation was fractionally more than the 42.86 percent gross devaluation: for those commodities considered, the domestic price rise was 43.04 percent, and for all exports (assuming full transmission for the remainder) it was 43.03 percent.

16. Despite the relatively large change in prices facing domestic producers of timber, it is important to note that not only must the signal of the devaluation be transmitted to the domestic economy (which in this case it was), but it must be allowed to work. There is some evidence, however, that congestion at the port of Takoradi resulted in a smaller response of timber exports than might have been achieved. "Present facilities [at Takoradi], mechanical handling equipment, and methods are totally inadequate to handle expeditiously the present volume of traffic [of logs and sawn timber]," Nathan Consortium for Sector Studies, *Ports Study: Transport,* 1970, Annex V, p. 3.

17. This probably overstates the case substantially for diamonds as a whole. The diamonds that appear in the export statistics are almost entirely the product of large-scale operations, but in addition individual diamond diggers win what is reported to be a considerable amount of diamonds. However, the purchasing authorities reportedly pay low prices and purchase only from licenced diggers (and licences are difficult to obtain). Hence there is a substantial amount of outward smuggling that is not directly affected by the official exchange rate.

(2) Imports.[18] We turn now to the import side, focusing on items which are imported and resold. The issue here is: what was the direction and extent of the change in prices of imports facing the ultimate domestic purchasers of imports? The domestic market for imports in 1967 was almost totally under the influence of import licencing. And for most goods the binding constraint was the level of licences issued, not the duty-paid price. In these circumstances the result of a devaluation depends on both the local currency c.i.f. price change due to the exchange rate change and on the magnitude of the licences before and after the devaluation. Our focus is on the impact effect of the devaluation and hence the appropriate case is one in which the dollar value of licences is kept constant. It is only later when foreign-exchange receipts have risen that one can expect import licences to be increased.

To measure the percentage change in new cedis paid per dollar of imports we focused on the change in the domestic price. This assumes an infinitely elastic foreign supply of imports. We were unable to develop a complete measure of the changes in domestic prices of imports for resale, but as an approximate measure we resorted to changes in prices of importable items in the domestic wholesale price index. Our data consisted of the monthly reported wholesale prices of each importable item in the CBS Wholesale Price Index.

In virtually all cases the prices preceding devaluation were constant from three or more months. Following devaluation, some prices continued at their former level, and most of the remainder increased to some new higher level. In a very few cases there was a decline. Our measure of the change in price attributable to the devaluation was the difference between the pre-devaluation price and the new price, implicitly assuming that world prices of imports did not change. The new price was almost universally set and kept within the remaining months of the year, although the approach to the new price varied; in some cases the price rose bit by bit to the new level, and in others there was a sharp rise followed by a decline to the new price.

To arrive at a very rough estimate of the overall effect of the devaluation on domestic prices of importables for resale, we computed two import-weighted averages of the price changes, confining our attention to consumer goods.[19] For both averages we matched each importable item from the Wholesale Price Index with the SITC 3-digit group it most appropriately represented. In cases where more than one item fell in a 3-digit group we split

18. The cooperation of the Central Bureau of Statistics in arranging for detailed extractions from the Wholesale Price Index returns is gratefully acknowledged. J.E. Tandoh, the Government Statistician, and S.W.K. Sosuh, Chief of the Primary Statistics Division, were particularly helpful.
19. Consumer goods imports amounted to 31 percent of total imports in 1966, and 33 percent in 1967. See Table A-4a.

the group among the items. Our first average uses the import weights of only those 3-digit items covered. This is "Weight A" in Table V-2. Our second average, "Weight B," was computed by grouping the Wholesale Price Index items into the two major groups of consumer goods imports by end-use, durables and non-durables, and assigning each group the weight of the group in total consumer goods imports.

The results are suggestive, although clearly they are nothing more than crude indicators. The change in price for non-durables was more than 23 percent, while for durables the change was some 6 percentage points less. On average the price rise facing purchasers of imported consumer goods at the wholesale level was about 23 percent. In other words, about 55 percent of the devaluation was transmitted to domestic prices of imports for resale, resulting in some restrictive pressure (via price) on imports.[20]

The average, however, conceals three distinct types of situations. For those commodities that experienced no price change, there was some mopping up of the licence premium, but licences remained the binding constraint post-devaluation. For those that had a price change equal to the devaluation, there was no licence premium pre-devaluation, and the devaluation was fully transmitted to the ultimate domestic purchasers. For the intermediate situation, in which the price rise was less than the devaluation, there was some pre-devaluation licence premium, but this was entirely consumed, changing the binding constraint from licences to price, assuming no significant change in the magnitude of the dollar value of the licence issued. Hence for the second and third types, the authorities were in a position to abandon licences and adopt a liberalized approach for imports.[21]

Finally, two caveats are in order. We should note that our analysis concerns only consumer goods which normally are imported and resold. It does not apply to materials and equipment which frequently are directly imported for own use. For such cases we had no way of measuring the "invisible" licence premium arising from the quota restriction and the derived demand curve for directly imported items, despite the fact that it would be absorbed

---

20. The Wholesale Price Index also contains a number of items falling in the import categories of materials, equipment and fuels. Using the same procedure as for the consumer goods, we calculated that the price change for raw and semifinished materials was 19.86 percent, for capital equipment 36.33 percent, and for fuels and lubricants 5.57 percent.

21. Note that the test of whether or not licences could be abandoned without affecting the level of imports is not whether the scramble for licences by individual applicants continues. Each importer's share is still affected by the licencing system if licences are retained. This holds despite the fact that the constraint on total imports of a given good is now price rather than licences.

Table V-2

Changes in wholesale prices of importable commodities for resale following
1967 devaluation (percentages)

Imports by end-use group	Weight A (percent)	Weight B (percent)	Price change (percent)
1. Non-durable consumer goods	93.65	87.58	23.68
2. Durable consumer goods	6.35	12.42	17.11
Weighted average – weight A			23.26
– weight B			22.86

Notes: Weighting within groups by SITC 3-digit commodity imports for 1966.
Weighting between groups:
Weight A – 1966 SITC 3-digit commodity imports of those items covered.
Weight B – 1966 imports by end-use.

Sources: a. Weights within groups, and weight A between groups derived from 1966 import trade statistics, CBS, *External Trade Statistics of Ghana,* December 1966. Weight B from CBS, *Economic Survey,* 1969, imports by end-use.
b. Wholesale prices of individual commodities extracted from CBS Wholesale Price Index monthly returns from respondents.

in all or part by the devaluation. Second, we have not dealt with the inevitable speculative demand for imports that arises in a licence-restricted system. Whether or not this is affected by the devaluation depends crucially on the expected course of liberalization, but since it is licence constrained, it cannot be measured.

To sum up, the devaluation was approximately fully transmitted on the export side. On the resale import side the domestic price response to the devaluation was about 55 percent of the gross devaluation, within six months of the devaluation.

(3) Relative prices of tradeables and domestic goods. What remains to be considered is how the changes in the prices of tradeables compared with the changes in the prices of domestic goods. Did relative prices change? Our monthly data are limited to price indexes which have substantial elements of importable items. The only component which is clearly not dominated by importables is local foods. The monthly data for 1967 are set out in Table V-3. There was a clear decline in local food prices following the devaluation, with the overall result that the index was, on average, some fifteen points lower in the five months following the devaluation than during the six months preceding. While this was largely due to a good crop, the fact remains that relative to this set of home goods the prices of tradeables rose in the immediate post-devaluation period.

A similar picture emerges if we look at the National Accounts deflators,

Table V-3
National consumer price index, local foods component, and total 1967 (1963 = 100)

	Month	Local foods component index	Total index
	January	179.6	158.8
	February	172.5	156.1
	March	169.6	155.3
	April	173.0	157.5
	May	176.2	159.4
	June	182.5	163.7
	July	178.0	161.5
	August	168.6	157.1
	September	155.4	151.1
	October	156.6	152.7
	November	157.6	153.1
	December	164.5	157.1
Average	Jan.–June	175.6	158.5
Average	Aug.–Dec.	160.5	154.2

Source: *Economic Survey,* 1967, p. 149.

which are available only on an annual basis. We again get a picture of home-goods prices declining relative to tradeables. Recall from Table II-10 that when we isolate the domestic component of GDP, the deflator increased, but by only 1.1 percent from 1966 to 1968, compared with substantially greater rates of increase in the deflators for both exports and imports.

The available evidence, then, indicates that in the immediate post-devaluation period relative domestic prices shifted in the following ways: (a) local currency prices paid to export producers rose relative to the prices facing domestic purchasers of imports and home goods; and (b) local currency prices facing purchasers of imports declined relative to prices paid to export producers, but rose relative to prices facing purchasers of home goods.

(b) Domestic expenditure

The domestic expenditure-output balance is also likely to be altered when a devaluation occurs. It is important to note in this context that the Ghanaian economy had been on a deflationary path for approximately twelve months prior to the devaluation. As a result, the economy was in a position in which much of the required cut in real income had taken place already. Devaluation and accompanying policies would not be called upon to play a major role in further deflating the economy.

The magnitude of the prior deflationary policies is difficult to estimate precisely. What is clear is that in 1967 GDP in current prices was about 1 percent below the 1966 rate. This was primarily the result of a substantial cut in the government deficit. The financial deficit had fallen from an annual rate of approximately N₵ 101 million in the period January through June 1966 to a rate of N₵ 61 million in the twelve months prior to the devaluation (see Table V-5 below).

It is important to note also that the devaluation took place from a position in which the potential foreign exchange deficit had been kept closed, in part, by the system of exchange control and import licencing. The prior deflation and limitation of imports together thus meant that the task of the devaluation did not involve a substantial reduction of total real expenditure in general, and actual imports in particular.[22]

There are two important aspects of the change in the domestic expenditure-output balance when a devaluation occurs: (1) the direct effect of the devaluation package on the levels of expenditure and output; and (2) the fiscal and monetary policies accompanying devaluation. We begin with the former, and examine the effects of the devaluation package on each of the external and internal components of domestic expenditure.[23]

First, the devaluation increased the local currency value of domestic expenditure on imports more than it increased the local currency payments on exports, resulting in a net reduction of expenditure on domestic output. This effect follows when we start from an initial situation of imbalance in which imports exceed exports and when, in the short run, imports continue in excess of exports. Thus when the Central Bank is selling foreign exchange net to the public because imports exceed exports and the price of foreign exchange is increased, there is a net increase in the local-currency-denominated sale of assets to the public, and purchasing power is mopped up. On the import side, one must recall that we are unlikely to have any immediate change in the level of imports. Commodities subject to strict licencing had substantial quota premia and would continue at approximately the same level in the short run, with the result merely that the premia were absorbed by the devaluation. The licence recipients now had to pay a higher local currency

---

22. This is in contrast with the 1971 devaluation where a reduction of both domestic expenditure and imports was called for. We take this up in sections 4 and 5 below.
23. See R.N. Cooper, "Currency Devaluation in Developing Countries," *Princeton Essays in International Finance*, No. 86, June 1971, for a useful discussion of the problem in a more general context. Also, J.N. Bhagwati and A.O. Krueger take an overview of this issue in the analytical framework for this series: *Foreign Trade Regimes and Economic Development: Experience and Analysis* (publication forthcoming).

price to the Bank of Ghana. The other commodities not subject to severe licencing were largely "essential" imports which are price inelastic in demand. The devaluation did not eat up a quota premium. Rather, because of the inelasticity of demand the local-currency-denominated expenditure on these commodities was increased in the same way as by the imposition of a substantial excise tax, again transferring local currency funds to the Bank of Ghana. In the meantime, exports could not immediately respond. The Bank of Ghana purchases of foreign exchange from the exports would tend to offset the sales to importers, but because imports exceeded exports, the net effect was one in which the Bank of Ghana was selling assets to the public.

Second, the net domestic output-expenditure balance was virtually untouched by the devaluation and accompanying measures: if anything, the effect here was also deflationary. For one, by increasing the availability of imported spare parts and raw materials via the expanded OGL list, domestic producers were able to increase real domestic output. The evidence here is confined to the industrial sector, where the annual data suggest a reasonable recovery of value-added and gross output in 1968 over the stagnation of 1967 (Table V-4).

Domestic expenditure was also potentially subject to two other influences. There could have been a money demand effect in which the public decreased its spending in response to the higher prices of goods in order to restore the real value of its money holdings. However, because the devaluation was one in which quota premia were absorbed, and because exports are not consumed locally, prices of tradeables facing consumers did not rise by the full proportion of the devaluation. And due to the good harvest, prices of local foods declined in the period following the devaluation. The overall effect on the consumer price level was a slightly lower price level in the five months following the devaluation than in the six months prior (see Table V-3 above). Therefore, no immediate effect on the demand for money could be expected.

Table V-4
Gross output and value-added in industry at 1962 prices (in millions of new cedis)

Year	Gross output	Value-added
1962	122.4	81.2
1963	140.8	91.2
1964	147.9	95.0
1965	151.2	98.9
1966	173.0	120.1
1967	179.9	119.7
1968	204.0	124.4

Source: CBS, *Industrial Statistics*, 1966–1968, Accra, 1970.

The "sweeteners" thrown into the devaluation package to make it more acceptable were unusually small in the circumstances. In the face of a 43 percent devaluation, the 7.7 percent increase in the minimum wage and the 5.0 percent increase in government wages and salaries clearly were not large.[24]

The devaluation package itself thus had, on balance, a deflationary effect on the domestic economy. Yet an additional effort was made to dampen the level of domestic expenditure. Apparently the authorities expected the impact of the devaluation to be inflationary. This expectation arose in part from a failure to recognize the potentially deflationary effect of the devaluation in the circumstances of the 1967 devaluation, together perhaps with the popular confusion of a once-and-for-all price rise due to a tax or an exchange rate adjustment and a price inflation due to excess money demand.

The compensating policies that were introduced centered on the government deficit. The measure that most usefully sums up the overall situation is the net increase in the financial claims on the government – i.e., net government borrowing – contained in Table V-5. From the austerity budget of 1966–1967, the deficit was cut further in the twelve months following the July 1967 devaluation by about N₵ 16.5 million (from N₵ 61.1 million to N₵ 44.6 million. Without a more complete macro model, it is difficult to say whether this move was absolutely deflationary or simply less inflationary. In any case, the direction of the effect is clear. It was not, however, a severe cut back. The overall level of government current and capital expenditure was approximately N₵ 380 million in fiscal year 1967–1968.[25] The reduction in the deficit was thus only 4.3 percent of total government expenditures.

To sum up, the combined effect of the devaluation package and the government's fiscal policy does not appear to have been inflationary. On the contrary, the initial conditions surrounding the devaluation suggest that the

---

24. Cooper, *op. cit.*, p. 16 ff., lists a number of other effects which are frequently important in developing countries' devaluations. These include:
    (1) If the public had accumulated substantial inventories of goods in anticipation of the expected price rise from a devaluation, total expenditure by the public could drop until these excess inventories were depleted.
    (2) If there were a substantial private debt denominated in foreign currency, the devaluation could lead to serious bankruptcies.
    (3) New investment in export industries now favored by the devaluation could lead to an increased aggregate expenditure, but only if the real effect of the devaluation is expected to last (which was somewhat uncertain).
    None of these elements appear to have been significant in the case of the 1967 Ghanaian devaluation.
25. See: Republic of Ghana, *Financial Statement*, 1968–69.

Table V-5
Central government financial receipts, payments and deficits, fiscal years 1965–1969
(in millions of new cedis)

Year*	Months	Financial receipts	Financial payments	Deficit (Net borrowing)
1965	(Jan.-Dec.)	110.4	32.0	78.4
1966	(Jan.-June)	67.3	16.9	50.4 (= 100.8 annual rate)
1967	(July/66-June/67)	122.8	61.7	61.1
1968	(July/67-June/68)	80.4	35.8	44.6
1969	(July/68-June/69)	116.4	69.3	47.1
1970**	(July/69-June/70)	88.3	29.9	54.4

Notes: * The fiscal year was changed by the NLC government with transitional
half-year of Jan.-June 1966.
** Provisional estimate.

Source: Republic of Ghana, *Financial Statement,* 1968–69, and 1970–71.

growth of excess demand for real resources by domestic residents was dampened, and possibly even the absolute level of excess demand was reduced.

(c) Income distribution

A substantial shift in one major price, that of foreign exchange, inevitably
altered the distribution of income in the economy. The data available permit
us to consider only some broad aggregates:[26] the distribution between the
export- and import-competing producers; and the distribution between
capital and labor.

(1) First, the relative price shifts noted in the preceding discussion suggest
that there was a significant shift in the relative distribution of income in favor
of export producers. Looking at the immediate price effect alone, and ig-
noring any subsequent quantity responses, we know that an across-the-board
change in the prices of output and inputs results in an equi-proportionate
change in the producers' per-unit value-added.[27] Considering individual ex-

26. No data on distribution of income by either income class or functional class are
available. Some pioneering work by Kodwo Ewusi on the distribution of income
among wage and salary employees covered by the CBS, *Labour Statistics* is reported
in his "Notes on the Relative Distribution of Income in Developing Countries,"
Review of Income and Wealth, Series 17, No. 4, December 1971, pp. 371–73. However, since this work refers to only one functional class, it is of limited value in
assessing the effect of devaluation on the distribution of income between functional
classes.
27. See J.C. Leith, "Across-the-Board Nominal Tariff Changes and the Effective Rate of
Protection," *Economic Journal,* Vol. LXXVIII, No. 123, December 1968.

port sectors, cocoa farmers had their output price increased by 30 percent, and because their costs were little affected by the devaluation, were likely to have experienced an even greater increase in their per-unit value-added. Minor agricultural exports handled by the Cocoa Marketing Board were not affected immediately. The mining and timber industries received slightly more than the full benefit of the devaluation on the price of their output, and because not all their inputs are imported, had their total input costs increased by less than the rate of the devaluation, with the result that they benefited by more than the rate of the devaluation.

The import-competing sector, largely consisting of producers of items not classified as "essentials," had already received much of the price increase on outputs due to the import licencing, although as we noted above, there appears to have been some increase in the price of importables accompanying the devaluation. The rate of increase, however, was less than the proportionate increase in costs for the highly import-intensive industries, with the result that per-unit value-added for these activities did not increase by as much as the devaluation.

On balance, therefore, we may conclude that on impact the devaluation shifted the distribution of income in favor of existing export producers relative to import-competing producers.[28]

(2) A second question concerns the distribution of income between capital and labor. If the production functions are Cobb–Douglas, changes in relative factor prices are in the long run compensated by changes in factor techniques resulting in constant income shares for capital and labor.[29] In the short run, however, a shift in relative factor prices does change the income distribution for as long as the existing techniques of production remain in use. Hence, to the extent that the devaluation altered relative factor prices, the distribution of income was altered for the short run.

A careful study for the manufacturing sector by Michael Roemer[30] contains indexes for the wage–rental ratio over the period 1960–1970. The wage

28. This increase in "quasi rents" for exporters is of course the desired result of a devaluation in order to induce a relative shift of resources into export production and out of import-competing production. As resources shift, however, the quasi rents in export activities will fall.
29. There are numerous problems associated with the concept of an aggregate Cobb–Douglas production function: e.g., that it is impossible to derive an aggregrate production function which is independent of the prices of inputs and outputs. For a helpful discussion see A.A. Walters, *An Introduction to Econometrics*, Macmillan, 1968, pp. 305-314. Our approach, however, is a useful first approximation of the initial situation following a devaluation.
30. Michael Roemer, "Relative Factor Prices in Ghana Manufacturing," *Economic Bulletin of Ghana*, Second Series, Vol. 1, No. 4, 1971.

index Roemer employed was based on earnings in private manufacturing establishments. It shows a substantial rise in the cost of employing a unit of labor between 1960 and 1966, amounting to an average compound rate of 7.6 percent. His cost-of-employing-capital index takes into account the costs of domestic and foreign financing, costs of factory construction, as well as capital equipment costs. There was a gradual upward drift in the costs of financing, costs of construction, and costs of equipment. However, the two key policy variables, tariffs and the exchange rate, remained fixed through the period 1960 to 1966. As a result, the cost-of-capital index rose much more slowly than the wage index from 1960 to 1966, at about 3.8 percent per annum. Overall, the wage-rental ratio stood about 25 percent higher in 1966 than in 1960.[31]

The 1967 devaluation succeeded in returning the wage-rental ratio to approximately the situation which prevailed in 1960. The wage index continued to rise in 1967, but the cost of capital was increased substantially by the devaluation. Devaluation increased the local cost of foreign equipment and, via the import component of construction costs, the cost of factory construction. With the other components of the capital index maintaining their previous trends, the cost-of-capital index jumped in 1967 to the point that it roughly equalled the wage index for the same year. This evidence suggests, therefore, that on impact the devaluation significantly increased the relative cost of employing capital. In turn, this means that in the short run (before production techniques change) the distribution of income in the manufacturing sector was shifted relatively in favor of capital and against labor.[32]

A devaluation of the magnitude undertaken by Ghana in 1967 is a substantial shock to many sectors of the economy. After several years of gradually building up the disequilibrium excess demand, of containing it by other measures, and of the consequent redistribution of income, the sudden alteration of relative prices in itself sets up new disequilibrium forces. If these are in the right direction, the initial conditions created by the devaluation point to a correction of the original excess demand. And what we have demon-

31. We are simply summarizing the broad trends of Roemer's findings, with the result that we do not do justice to the careful detail of his analysis. He employs a variety of alternative assumptions concerning the life of assets, the ratio of domestic to foreign financing, and profits taxes. The details change with these alternatives, but the principal conclusions concerning the rise in the wage-rental ratio through 1966 and the substantial drop due to the devaluation remain unaltered.

32. Beyond the initial impact, it is worth noting that in 1968 and 1969 the wage index moved up faster than the cost-of-capital index, eroding about one-half of the effect of the devaluation on the wage-rental ratio.

strated in this section is that on impact the 1967 devaluation introduced a set of incentives which did in fact point the economy towards a reversal of its balance payments difficulties, and eventually, perhaps, to move to a liberalization of its international trade and payments regime. We turn now to a discussion of just what in fact did occur in the first few years following devaluation.

3. The medium-term effects of devaluation

Every Finance Minister who takes the momentous step of a major devaluation must impatiently wait to see whether or not it works — particularly if he remains in office long enough. Our reading of the experience prior to the 1967 devaluation was that failure to control aggregate demand, and hence in a licencing situation the domestic price level, was largely responsible for the balance-of-payments difficulties (Chapter II, section 6). In the previous section of this chapter we established that on impact the devaluation wrenched relative prices in the appropriate direction and was on balance deflationary. What remains to be seen is the subsequent response of the economy to the sudden readjustment produced by the devaluation. A basic question which must be answered is: did the devaluation make any significant difference to the balance-of-payments picture? A related question is: was the pre-devaluation experience a useful guide in predicting post-devaluation developments on the export and import sides?

A simple procedure aimed at answering these questions is to compare the actual export and import experience with the predicted, using the regression results from Chapter II, section 6. Before doing so, it is important to note the behavior of the variables in the years following devaluation. Aggregate demand resumed its expansion in 1968. Following a minor decline in 1967, in 1968 GDP in current prices was up 15.3 percent over 1966. And in 1969 it grew by a further 12.6 percent. Licencing was retained almost entirely intact in 1967, with about 3 percent of imports allowed under Open General Licence. Some liberalization occurred in 1968, and about 18.5 percent of imports came under OGL (see Table V-11 below). Prices declined in 1967, but the GDP deflator jumped in 1968 to a level 11.7 percent greater than 1966, and by an additional 8.8 percent in 1969. With no new changes in the nominal effective exchange rate facing non-cocoa exports, by 1968 the price-deflated rate fell to a level equal to that of 1964, and continued its decline during 1969.

These developments are of considerable significance, for it was not the devaluation alone that was at work over the medium term. Other key determinants of exports and imports — particularly aggregate demand and domes-

Table V-6
Actual and predicted values of non-cocoa exports and imports after 1967 devaluation
(in millions of new cedis)

	First year after devaluation*				Second year after devaluation*			
	Actual	Predicted	Difference (A–P) Absolute	Percent of predicted	Actual	Predicted	Difference (A–P) Absolute	Percent of predicted
Non-cocoa exports	85.3	93.5	–8.2	–8.8	87.4	90.2	–2.8	–3.2
Imports	314.0	322.0	–8.0	–2.5	354.4	363.8	–9.4	–2.6

Notes: * For non-cocoa exports the first year after devaluation is taken as 1968–1969, and the second 1969–1970. For imports the first year after devaluation is 1968 and the second is 1969.

Source: Actual values of non-cocoa exports from Table II-12; of imports, from *Economic Survey*, 1969. "Predicted" computed using regression results of Chapter II, section 6: non-cocoa exports from fit of equation (II.6), and imports from fit of equation (II.7).

tic prices — were also acting, but in the opposite direction to the devaluation. Consider now the responses of exports and imports to the devaluation and these subsequent developments (Table V-6).

(a) Non-cocoa exports

For non-cocoa exports, the change in the real effective exchange rate was substantial when compared with previous year-to-year changes. To respond fully to such a large change would undoubtedly require new investment, but new investment would be forthcoming only if it were clear that the devaluation in real terms was going to stick. As a result, the response was slower to emerge than the smaller year-to-year changes would suggest; in the first full year of 1968–1969 the response to the 1968 real effective exchange rate yielded an actual value of non-cocoa exports in constant prices of N₵ 85.3 million compared with a predicted value of N₵ 93.5 million. In the second year, 1969–1970, the actual response to the 1969 real effective exchange rate was much closer to the predicted, with the shortfall amounting to only 3.2 percent of the predicted.

As a check on the predictive power of our estimated equation we reran the regression for the entire period 1961–1962 through 1969–1970 with a separate dummy variable set equal to unity for each year after 1966–1967. This procedure reveals the extent to which the original regression tracked in the postdevaluation period. The result was:

$$\ln NCX_t = 2.778 + 0.4359 \quad \ln(EERX/P)_{t-\frac{1}{2}}$$
$$(9.89) \quad (6.28)$$

$$-0.1390\,D \cdot 1 \;-\; 0.0896\,D \cdot 2 \;-\; 0.0292\,D \cdot 3$$
$$(-4.50) \qquad (-3.01) \qquad (-9.59)$$

$$\text{Obs.} = 9$$
$$R^2 = 0.9359$$
$$\text{D.W.} = 1.727$$

where $D \cdot 1 = 1$ for 1967–1968 and zero for all other years, $D.2 = 1$ for 1968–1969 and zero for all other years, $D \cdot 3 = 1$ for 1969–1970 and zero for all other years. The dummy for 1969–1970 is insignificant, indicating that by then the relationship between the price-level-deflated effective exchange rate and non-cocoa exports was not significantly different from the previous relationship. However, the dummy variables for the two earlier years are significantly negative.

The failure of non-cocoa exports to rapidly reach their predicted levels merits an additional comment. First, the British devaluation of 16 percent in November 1967 reduced the effect of the Ghanaian devaluation in that market. Second, there were a number of difficulties encountered internally by potential exporters, particularly the timber export trade. Bottlenecks in rail transportation and at the port of Takoradi were frequent.[33] And until 1969, there were continuing complaints from timber producers about their difficulties in obtaining licences for equipment and spare parts from the import licence authorities. Third, the depletion of natural resource deposits (gold, diamonds, and manganese particularly) may have limited or prevented response to the increased effective exchange rate.[34]

Whether or not the devaluation could be termed a success in stimulating non-cocoa exports depends largely on the basis chosen for comparison. If the basis selected is a before—after comparison, the performance showed only a minor improvement: non-cocoa exports had by 1969—1970 only approximately reestablished the level of 1965—1966.

However, when both the exchange rate and the price level changes are taken into account, the response was approximately what could have been expected on the basis of previous experience. By 1969—1970 the rise in the domestic price level had absorbed much of the effect of the devaluation, and the real effective exchange rate was approaching that of 1965. A more appropriate basis for comparison, however, is the situation in the absence of the devaluation. Our fit of equation (II.6) yields a predicted constant price value of non-cocoa exports of N₵ 76.8 million for 1969—1970 at the old official exchange rate compared with the actual N₵ 87.3 million.[35] In other words, given the inflation, the devaluation yielded an increase of non-cocoa exports amounting to about N₵ 10 million or 14 percent over what would have been otherwise achieved for 1969—1970. In this connection it is important to recall the conclusion from section 2b above: on impact the combined effects of the devaluation package and the government's fiscal policy was not inflationary. Hence the inflation emerged after the devaluation had its initial impact, and was not an immediate consequence of the devaluation but was, as we argue later, attributable to subsequent, post-1967, expansionary policies.

(b) Cocoa exports

The effect of the devaluation on cocoa earnings is difficult to evaluate fully without a detailed econometric model of cocoa supply and demand. The

33. See Nathan Consortium for Sector Studies, *Ports Study: Transport,* 1970, Annex V.
34. This effect is more complex. Absolute depletion would, of course, prevent any response to increased price. Increased marginal costs due to lower-grade veins would, if occurring simultaneously, give the appearance of lower response to the higher price. However, the elasticity for a given price and marginal cost curve increases as the marginal cost curve shifts upward.
35. At the old exchange rate of N₵ 0.714 per dollar, the price-deflated effective exchange rate for non-cocoa exports would have been N₵ 0.363 per dollar.

important issues, however, are reasonably clear. Given the prices and market share at the time of the devaluation, the short- to medium-term response ratio of output to a change in the real producer price would have been about 0.17 (see section 2a). And given a medium- to long-run demand elasticity (absolutely) in excess of -1, we can evaluate the effect of the 30 percent increase in the nominal producer price accompanying devaluation on both output and earnings over the medium term of about three years.

The increase in the nominal producer price from N¢ 5.00 to N¢ 6.50 per headload which accompanied the devaluation could be expected to have the following effects. The short- to medium-term response would, in the absence of domestic price inflation, result in additional output on the order of about 6 percent. However, within three years the domestic price level wiped out the nominal producer price increase, with the result that the net effect on output and hence earnings was nil. Thus the circumstances surrounding the devaluation did not have a significant sustained effect on medium-term output or earnings from cocoa. It is however important to note that without the devaluation, which permitted the increased producer price without loss of government revenue, the continued rise in the domestic price level would have resulted in some medium-term declines in output.

While the policies accompanying devaluation resulted in little if any impact in the medium term, the long-term consequences for cocoa were far more serious. The long-run capacity, which requires time for new plantings to mature, is to a much greater extent affected by the real producer price than short-term output. Further, to induce new plantings, the real producer price must be above some minimum planting effort level. In terms of the 1967–1968 deflator, the minimum nominal producer price for new plantings was about N¢ 9.00 per 60-pound headload.[36] However, the price rise from N¢ 5.00 to N¢ 6.50 per headload accompanying the devaluation was not enough to reach the N¢ 9.00 minimum required at that time, with the result that there was no effect on long-run capacity. This perpetuated a zero plantings state that had persisted since 1964, with the predictable consequence of stagnating output in the 1970's.

The negligible impact of the devaluation does not mean that cocoa output and earnings remained unchanged. On the contrary, substantial changes in output and earnings did occur over the next few calendar years (Table V-7). The peak output of the 1964–1965 season is reflected in the high 1965

36. Bateman's recent work, "Cocoa Study," in *Economic Report*, Vol. IV, mimeograph, Washington, D.C., March 1972, indicates a minimum real producer price of N¢ 198 per ton to induce plantings in 1967–1968. This can be thought of as the intercept on the real price axis. Or course, as with any fitted function, actual observations will be scattered around the fit.

Table V-7
Exports of cocoa and cocoa products, 1965–1970 (quantities, thousands of long tons; values, millions of new cedis)

Year	Cocoa beans		Cocoa paste & cake		Cocoa butter		Total value	
	Quantity	Value	Quantity	Value	Quantity	Value	Millions of N₵*	Millions of $ **
1965	494	136.5	21	0.9	21	11.4	148.8	208.3
1966	392	103.1	24	1.2	39	11.5	115.8	162.1
1967 A	267	100.8	12	0.8	10	8.0	109.6	153.4
1967 B	63	29.9	12	1.7	13	14.5	46.0	45.1
1967	330	130.7	24	2.5	23	22.5	155.6	198.5
1968	330	185.6	23	4.5	20	24.1	214.1	209.8
1969	303	218.6	19	3.3	18	24.0	246.0	241.1
1970	362	300.4	17	3.9	17	27.3	331.6	325.0

Notes: * Items may not add to total due to rounding.
          **Conversion from N₵ to $ at $1.40/N₵ 1965 through 1967A, and at $0.98/N₵ 1967B (July–December) through 1970.
Sources: 1965-1969, *Economic Survey,* 1969; 1970, *External Trade Statistics,* December 1970; breakdown of 1967, *Quarterly Digest of Statistics*, December 1967. 1967A refers to January through June; 1967B refers to July through December.

calendar year sales volume. Subsequently the sales volume continuously declined until 1970, reflecting in large part the continuing decline in the real producer price in the mid-1950's, and the poor rainfall effect on the 1968–1969 season. Earnings in dollar terms, however, reached the 1965 level by 1968, and increased again in 1969. Output in 1969–1970 rose substantially, responding to the capacity additions of the late 1950's and early 1960's, together with current good weather and further increases in the producer price (to N₵ 7.00 for the 1968–1969 crop and N₵ 8.00 for the 1969–1970 crop) affecting output from existing capacity.

The revenue received from the post-devaluation sales was considerably in excess of what could normally have been expected. During the entire period from the bumper crop of 1964–1965 through 1970 the world cocoa market was in an unsettled situation. Not since the Korean war boom had the market taken so long to adjust to a new equilibrium. For Ghana the very serious price weakness of 1966 was followed by recovery in 1967 and 1968 to approximately the prices which the current actual volume would suggest. The price rise continued to 1969 and 1970, despite the fact that the decline in Ghanaian sales in 1969 was not substantial; in 1970 Ghanaian sales actually increased by about 20 percent. Ghana thus reaped a substantial windfall of cocoa receipts.[37]

(c) Imports

Turning to imports, our estimated equation describing the behavior of the import system takes into account only GDP and licencing, but not the price-level-deflated effective exchange rate facing importers, because the latter was not a restraining influence on imports during the period of licencing. It is conceivable that with the devaluation the price-level-deflated effective exchange rate could again become an active restraint on imports. However, it is clear from Table II-8 that the 1968 rate was considerably lower than the last few years before licencing was imposed. Consequently, even after devaluation it probably did not significantly affect the level of aggregate imports.

The growth of nominal GDP in 1968 and 1969 created pressure on the import system to increase the level of imports. The system responded to the pressure in much the same way as the pre-devaluation experience would suggest. Projecting our estimated equation (II.7) into the post-devaluation period yields predicted imports less than 3 percent higher than the actual imports for the years 1968 and 1969 (Table V-6). Performing a check similar to our check on the export equation, we re-ran the import equation (which was based on data covering 1955 through 1966) for the full period 1955 through 1969 with an additional dummy for each year after 1966. The result was:

$$M_t = 114.9 + 0.1205 \text{ GDP}_t - 32.10 \text{ DLIC} - 35.53 \text{ D} \cdot 1$$
$$(3.560) \qquad\qquad (-1.287) \qquad\quad (-0.9091)$$

$$- 17.85 \text{ D} \cdot 2 - 8.891 \text{ D} \cdot 3$$
$$(-0.4097) \qquad (-0.1816)$$

$$\begin{aligned} \text{Obs.} &= 15 \\ R^2 &= 0.776 \\ \text{D.W.} &= 1.278 \end{aligned}$$

None of the dummy variables is significant, with the t value for the 1969 where DLIC = 1 for all years when licicensing was enforced (1962, 1963, 1964, 1966, 1967, 1968, 1969) and zero for all other years; D·1 = 1 for 1967 and zero for all other years; D·2 = 1 for 1968 and zero for all other years; D·3 = 1 for 1969 and zero for all other years.
dummy being particularly small. We may therefore conclude that GDP in

---

37. The windfall of 1970 is discussed in more detail in section 4 below.

current prices and the licencing dummy of the pre-devaluation experience continued to explain the level of imports in the post-devaluation period. The system governing imports does not appear to have changed significantly with the devaluation.

(d) Capital flows

The remaining major item that might be expected to respond to the devaluation is autonomous capital flows, both private and official. As noted in Chapter II, prior to the devaluation private direct investment was felt not to be responding to the more favorable climate created by the National Liberation Council, and donor countries were not anxious to support an untenable balance-of-payments situation. The devaluation was expected to have a favorable effect on both. To sort out the facts, we have enumerated in Table V-8 the various sources of capital inflows (gross, not net) over the period 1965 through 1968.

Private capital inflows fluctuated substantially over the period. The major source of variation is investment by the Volta Aluminum Company (Valco). The timing here relates to the bringing into production of a smelter associated with the completion of the Volta Dam. Official capital inflow for the Volta River Authority (VRA), which built the dam, shows a similar time pattern for the same reason. Further, the Valco agreement provides for an enclave type of activity; investment, repatriation of funds, imports, and exports are all carried out in dollars at the company's own discretion. The entire operation may be considered largely as an electricity export contract denominated in dollars. Consequently, the Valco inflow in Table V-8 has little to do with the exchange rate, or for that matter with any other Ghanaian policy short of contract abrogation. Of major interest then is the total excluding Valco. This exhibits no substantial difference in dollar terms between the year before (1966) and the year after (1968) devaluation.[38]

It would be unwise to draw any strong conclusions from this limited set of data. It is simply suggestive of the sort of argument that appears in the literature on foreign investment; the exchange rate is only one of many kinds of influences on private capital flow. Most of the other influences, such as

---

38. One might also want to exclude from consideration reinvested profits on the grounds that such reinvestment is largely due to exchange control regulations blocking full remittance of profits; and the private suppliers' credits could be excluded because they are usually denominated in a foreign currency. This leaves only the "others" category, including direct investment – which also shows little change between 1966 and 1968.

Table V-8
Private and official capital inflows, 1965—1968 (in millions of US dollars)

	1965	1966	1967	1968
Private				
Reinvested profits	13.4	12.6	12.6	8.4
Valco	23.2	40.9	16.9	2.6
Private suppliers' credits	–	–	2.9	3.9
Others	0.3	6.2	5.6	5.8
Total	38.4	59.6	38.0	20.8
Total excluding Valco	15.1	18.8	21.2	18.1
Official				
OECD donors	–	7.8	15.0	39.3
Suppliers' credits	82.9	30.8	9.1	0.2
Volta River Authority	19.3	14.8	2.7	
Others	2.8	0.8	0.3	0.6
Total	105.0	54.3	27.1	40.1
Total excluding suppliers' credits & VRA	2.8	8.7	15.3	39.9

Sources: 1965 and 1966: Republic of Ghana, *Ghana's Economy and Aid Requirements in 1967*. Accra, May 1967. Converted from pre-devaluation N₵ at rate $1.40/N₵.

1967 and 1968: Republic of Ghana, *Ghana's Economy and Aid Requirements January 1969—June 1970*. Accra, March 1969. Converted from post-devaluation N₵ rate $ 0.98/N₵.

ability to repatriate profits, are not directly affected by the exchange rate. Hence a devaluation alone is unlikely to produce a noticeable increase in the private capital inflow. And it evidently did not for Ghana.

Official capital flows, paradoxically, are more sensitive to the exchange rate. Determined in part by the development "needs" of the recipient but also in part by the donor's sense of the appropriateness of the recipient's policies, they are affected to a substantial degree by the visible measurable policy changes in the "correct" direction. A devaluation in the face of balance-of-payments difficulties is taken as a clear signal that the "appropriate" economic policies are being followed and hence that the country is deserving of support. This was in part the view taken by major OECD donor countries in response to the Ghanaian 1967 devaluation. A moderate inflow for 1966 to support the new NLC government was doubled in 1967 and more than redoubled in 1968.[39] The official expectations were thus substantially realized.[40]

The gain from increased official capital inflows was in serious danger of being swamped by large repayments falling due on substantial medium-term suppliers' credits contracted by the Nkrumah government. Some relief had been obtained in a December 1966 debt-rescheduling agreement covering payments due through December 1968.[41] However, by not changing the debt schedule for 1969 and later years, a substantial hump for 1969 remained, with over N¢ 80 million or about 20 percent of exports falling due in that year.

Facing the prospect of a major debt repayment burden in 1969, Ghana turned to her creditors a second time in October 1968. Again only limited relief was obtained. This time medium-term debts due from January 1, 1969 through June 30, 1972 were shifted forward to the period 1974-1981.

The original medium-term debt schedule is compared with the revised 1966 schedule and the 1968 schedule in Table V-9 on the assumption that no new debt is incurred. The net result of the two reschedulings was to provide immediate relief for 1966 and 1967 and, in the years 1968 through 1971, a 47 percent cut in payments falling due. In the new schedule, however, the situation reverses by 1972, with higher payments falling due from then on. And because of moratorium interest on the rescheduled amount of about 6 percent per annum, the total payments were increased by about 25 percent.

The medium-term suppliers'-credit debts were clearly the most pressing, but by no means the only debts facing Ghana. Short-term debts in the form of arrears, trade credits, bank loans, and net IMF position were also falling due, together with a long-term debt arising from major capital projects undertaken in the past, such as the Volta Dam. Even after the 1968 rescheduling of medium-term debts, the overall schedule on existing debts for 1969 through 1981 promised little relief for the 1970's (see Table V-10). The somewhat more sympathetic attitude of donors in the 18 months following the 1967

39. At the same time reliance on official suppliers' credits was almost completely abandoned.
40. The actual inflow data probably overstate the increased commitments because the lag between commitment and utilization was being reduced as the Ghanaian authorities became more familiar with the intricacies of aid administration.
41. Payments on approximately N¢ 180 million of outstanding medium-term debt falling due between July 1, 1966 and December 31, 1968 – plus arrears accumulated prior to July 1, 1966 – were consolidated. Eighty percent of the consolidated amount was shifted to the period 1972-to-1979, with 20 percent to be paid between July 1, 1966 and December 31, 1968. These and other details are taken from Norman L. Hicks, "Debt Rescheduling and Economic Growth in Ghana," USAID Mission to Ghana, *Research Memorandum No. 8,* Accra, May 1969.

Table V-9
Medium-term debt schedules (in millions of new cedis post-devaluation)

Year	Original schedule	After 1966 rescheduling	After 1968 rescheduling	Net relief Original minus 1966	Original minus 1968
1966	52.7	8.1	8.1	44.6	44.6
1967	64.5	8.6	8.6	55.9	55.9
1968	63.1	29.2	29.2	33.9	33.9
1969	59.0	82.6	33.9	−23.6	25.1
1970	50.5	58.8	22.6	−8.3	27.9
1971	37.8	49.5	26.6	−11.7	11.2
1972	21.1	37.3	38.3	−16.2	−17.2
1973	14.4	33.5	41.2	−19.1	−26.8
1974	10.9	32.6	44.8	−11.7	−33.9
1975	5.6	31.0	49.1	−25.4	−43.5
1976	3.8	31.5	53.6	−27.7	−49.8
1977	2.5	31.3	52.4	−28.8	−49.9
1978	1.6	31.8	52.0	−30.2	−50.6
1079	0.7	15.5	34.7	−14.8	−34.0
1980	0.7	0.7	27.4	0.0	−26.7
1981	–	–	24.6	0.0	−24.6
Total	436.8	482.0	547.1	−45.2	−110.3

Source: Norman L. Hicks, "Debt Rescheduling and Economic Growth in Ghana," US AID Mission to Ghana, *Research Memorandum No. 8,* Accra, 1969.

devaluation had provided Ghana with some temporary relief from the immediate pressure arising for 1969, together with a relatively smooth debt schedule for the 1970's. However, Ghana did not obtain any substantial cancellation of debts.

To sum up, in the medium-term the devaluation did affect the merchandise trade account by about the magnitudes expected from previous experience. The devaluation, however, could not and did not do more than that. Resumption of gradual domestic price inflation was eroding the effect of the devaluation for both non-cocoa and cocoa exports, and the pull of aggregate demand was continuing to raise the level of imports. In a before-after comparison, the net merchandise balance for 1968 and 1969 was little different from the situation of 1962 or 1964. It is important to note, however, that the merchandise balance would have shown a substantially greater deficit in the absence of the devaluation.

On capital account the only noticeable change following devaluation was a somewhat more sympathetic view by the donor countries, which materialized in the form of increased aid flows and a smoothing of the debt schedule.

Table V-10
Short-, medium-, and long-term debt schedule (in millions of new cedis)

Year	Short-term	Medium-term	Long-term	Total
1969	30.9	33.9	15.0	79.8
1970	52.8	22.6	15.2	90.6
1971	44.7	26.6	16.4	87.7
1972	26.3	38.3	17.3	81.9
1973	16.1	41.2	19.1	76.4
1974	11.6	44.8	20.4	76.8
1975	9.6	49.1	21.8	80.5
1976	8.6	53.6	22.2	84.4
1977	4.5	52.4	22.4	79.3
1978	4.5	52.0	23.3	78.8
1979	4.5	34.7	23.6	62.8
1980	4.5	27.4	23.3	55.2
1981	4.5	24.6	22.7	51.8

Notes: Short-term includes arrears, trade credits, IMF (net), and bank loans. Official suppliers' credits only considered under medium-term. Long-term includes private suppliers' credits. This schedule refers to the situation after the 1968 rescheduling.

Source: Norman L. Hicks, *op. cit.*

Overall, the medium-term result of the devaluation was largely one of preventing further deterioration. The substantial readjustment necessary for a sustained liberalization did not emerge. Yet the NLC government had committed itself to a limited liberalization. As General Afrifa had declared in his devaluation announcement: "It is as you know the firm objective of the NLC to free our foreign trade payments from all artificial restrictions and controls."[42] The Progress Party government elected in 1969 was committed to a more sweeping dismantling of the control system.[43] Were these commitments to be honored, and if so in what way?

4. The import liberalization experience, 1967–1970 (Phase IV and return to Phase I)

Import liberalization began almost immediately after the devaluation and continued an uneven but uninterrupted expansion through the next four and one-half years. The attempt was cautious. Expansion of the OGL list was

42. Reproduced in, Bank of Ghana, *Report of the Board for the Financial Year Ended 30 June,* 1968, p. 43. This was somewhat qualified by the far more restricted commitment to place a very limited list of items on OGL.
43. See quotation from the *Progress Party Manifesto,* note 1 above.

spread over several years. Begun by the National Liberation Council (military) government, it was continued by the elected Progress Party government of Prime Minister K.A. Busia which took office in October 1969. A commitment to liberalization was an important component of the Progress Party's platform, and during its 27 months in office the Busia government continued to move towards total liberalization of imports.

The drive towards import liberalization appeared, on the surface at least, to be successful. For the first three and one-half years the trade balance did not move into a serious deficit position. And there was an increased reliance on price instruments rather than quantitative restrictions to control imports. As licences were removed from substantial portions of the import bill, surcharges on de-licensed imports were introduced. Initially then the import liberalization appeared to be designed to substitute price for quantitative restriction of imports. A further resort to price instruments came in the form of an announced subsidy for nontraditional exports.

In the latter stages of the liberalization, however, it became apparent that the objective was to increase the level of imports — an objective far more difficult to sustain in the absence of continued export growth. The initial success of the liberalization in increasing imports was due not so much to the underlying strength of the situation as to an unusual set of external circumstances. Foreign-exchange receipts were buoyed by exceptional cocoa earnings and substantial aid flows, plus debt-service relief.

When these external factors, particularly the cocoa market, adjusted to normal levels in 1971 it became obvious that a severe cut in imports was necessary. In a desperate move to correct the enormous imbalances that had arisen, a massive devaluation of nearly 80 percent was undertaken at the end of December 1971. This proved to be the final straw for large segments of the population already restive with the Busia government. Colonel I.K. Acheampong and his associates led a successful military coup in mid-January 1972. The new government revalued the exchange rate, wiping out two-thirds of the devaluation, repudiated some of the suppliers'-credit debt, unilaterally rescheduled much of the remainder, and reinstated strict import licencing. The import liberalization was finished.

In this section we trace the major developments during the liberalization episode in order to sort out their precise nature, timing and magnitude. This will enable us to consider in the next section the successes, failures, and neglect present in the Ghanaian liberalization experiment.

The OGL system for imports was the major vehicle of the liberalization. A small but crucial step in expanding the OGL list had been made in late 1966. Following a policy declaration which noted, among other points, that the aim of the government was not to continue these controls permanently but rather to have most essential commodities imported on OGL,[44] specific additions were made to the OGL list for 1967 which broke with the past. Up to this point the OGL list was largely confined to personal items and minor border trade. The list for 1967, however, added specified pharmaceuticals, fertilizers, hand tools for cultivation, fishing gear and a few industrial materials. The list was not long, and the total volume of imports under OGL in 1967 amounted to only 3.15 percent of total imports (see Table V-11 below). This was the first time since 1961 that the OGL was deliberately expanded and not quickly reduced again.

The devaluation announcement reaffirmed the intention to liberalize, and specifically to "include on OGL virtually all industrial and agricultural spare parts and chemicals, nearly all pharmaceuticals, and insecticides...."[45] In the next month, regulations for 1968 were published which contained these and other major additions to the OGL list,[46] with the result that 1968 OGL imports amounted to 18.5 percent of a substantially increased total import bill.

The following year, when regulations were announced for 1969, a further substantial addition was made to the OGL list. Again the result was an increased volume of imports under OGL: some 27.8 percent of an enlarged import bill. With this substantial portion of imports contemplated under OGL, the policy makers recognized that some dampening of the demand for delicenced imports would be necessary. The result was a surcharge on most OGL imports introduced in February 1969.[47] The surcharge rate, however, was low: only 5 percent of the c.i.f. value.

The last budget of the National Liberation Council government was presented to the country in July 1969 by J.H. Mensah, Commissioner of Finance.[48] The budget placed considerable emphasis on export promotion.

44. *Commercial and Industrial Bulletin,* 7 October 1966.
45. General Africa, reproduced in the Bank of Ghana, *Report of the Board for the Financial Year Ended 30 June,* 1968, p. 42.
46. For the first time, apparently, the OGL list, as well as the restricted list, was defined in terms of the SITC trade classification.
47. National Liberation Council, *Decree 325,* Gazetted 13 February, 1969. Exceptions to the surcharge were household effects, single copies of printed matter, pets, pharmaceuticals, textbooks, and fish caught by Ghanaian-owned vessels.
48. Mensah, trained at the London School of Economics and Stanford University, was regarded as one of the most promising and capable economists available to the government. His previous experience included four years on the faculty of the University College of the Gold Coast (now the University of Ghana), three years as an economist at UN Headquarters, followed by four years (1961–65) in the National Planning Commission, Accra, where he was the leading architect of the Seven Year Development Plan. He then went to the UN Economic Commission for Africa, returning to Ghana as Commissioner of Finance in April 1969.

Schemes were announced which would provide exporters of manufactures (except products of the woodworking and metal processing industries) with: rebates of up to 50 percent of their company tax liability; a cash bonus of 10 percent on incremental exports; replacement of licences on imported materials used; and drawback of duties and indirect taxes on materials used for export. Also announced was a subsidy of one-third of the internal transportation costs of moving secondary species of timber to harbor for export or elsewhere for processing or sale in the local market.

While of limited scope, these schemes could have resulted in a significant incentive to the eligible firms. However, administrative complications or delays in implementation made all of them inoperative from the firms' viewpoint. The procedures for drawbacks on indirect taxes and duties, and the procedures for obtaining export licences were so complex that only large firms could hope to cope, let alone find it profitable to participate.[49] The export bonus scheme was not enacted until April 1971, some 21 months after announcement, the delay apparently being due to "the long drawn-out discussions" with the IMF.[50] And the timber transport subsidy scheme had still not been implemented by the time of the 1970 budget a year later.[51]

The process of import liberalization was continued with the announcement in September 1969 of the OGL list for 1970. The elected Progress Party government, which took office shortly thereafter, retained the list until the budget for fiscal year 1970/71 was presented in August 1970, except for the addition of some "essential" food items in March 1970. The result for the first 8 months of 1970 was 39.4 percent of all imports coming under OGL.

The first budget of the Progress Party government was presented to Parliament in August 1970 by J.H. Mensah, now Busia's Minister of Finance. This marked a renewed drive towards liberalization in fulfillment of the Progress Party commitment to eventually abandon licencing.[52] Almost 60 percent of all imports for the remainder of the year came under the new OGL listing. Mensah also renewed the policy of surcharges on OGL imports, but abandoned the single rate. Instead, he introduced surcharges on most OGL imports, with rates which varied from 5 percent to 150 percent of c.i.f. value. Items subject to surcharge were automatically placed on OGL, although not

---

49. This was partially admitted even by J.H. Mensah, now Minister of Finance, in his 1970 *Budget Statement,* Accra, 25 August, 1970. On the drawbacks, he noted, "...so far very few applications have been received..." (p. 34). With respect to the company tax rebate, he said, "It has been decided this year to add to these tax incentives a simplification of doing export business" (p. 34).
50. *Ibid.,* p. 35.
51. *Ibid.,* p. 35.
52. See *Progress Party Manifesto, op. cit.,* p. 5.

all OGL items were subject to surcharge. The rationale of the differentiated surcharges was apparently a combination of a desire to capture for government revenues the quota premia on newly freed imports, together with a recognition that the demand for such imports had to be dampened.[53] The full protective consequences were apparently not taken into account prior to the budget.[54]

An instrument employed to achieve more than one objective, as the surcharge was, is bound to encounter serious difficulties in achieving all the objectives assigned to it. Such was the case with the differentiated surcharges. They do not appear to have had a major dampening effect on imports, did not generate a substantial additional revenue, and considerably altered the protective structure.

The additional collections of surcharges amounted to only approximately N₵ 7.3 million during the rest of 1970, or 5.4 percent of total imports and 8.9 percent of OGL imports for September through December 1970. This is a rough estimate arrived at by assuming that the January-through-August 1970 rate averaged the same as 1969. (Surcharge collections in all of 1970 amounted to N₵ 10.7 million.)

We have seen the jumbled protective consequences of this in Chapter III above. The surcharges substantially increased the protection of some industries, but many others had their protection reduced — some to the extent that previously positive protection was turned into negative protection. Consumers and industrial users of commodities subject to substantial surcharges were quick to complain. Some minor adjustments were made, but the widely differentiated structure remained intact.

An administrative change introduced in August 1970 also involved a loosening of OGL. Commitment forms for OGL were abandoned. These had been used since 1967 and were ostensibly designed to ensure that where possible commodity aid would be utilized rather than OGL. Commitment forms were issued by the licencing authorities on application to cover most commercial imports available under OGL. This enabled the licencing authorities to keep tabs on OGL imports and to increase utilization of commodity aid. To our knowledge, it was not used deliberately to restrict imports, but by its nature did involve an administrative hinderance.

A further change announced in the 1970 budget was an increase from $2\frac{1}{2}$ percent to 5 percent in the interest rate on Post Office Savings deposits. Although postal savings were not large, this move represented an important break with the past neglect of incentives to save. Implementation was some-

---

53. See *Budget Statement* for 1970–1971, Accra, 25 August, 1970.
54. The most serious omission was a failure to recognize fully the cost-increasing effect of surcharges on inputs for firms which received no additional protection of output.

Table V-11
Open general licence imports, 1967–1970

Group	Value (millions of new cedis)					
	1967	1968	1969	1970A**	1970B**	1970
0 Food and live animals	6.86	6.35	8.94	37.44	23.53	60.97
1 Beverages and tobacco	0	0	0	0	0	0
2 Crude materials, inedible	0.03	0.04	0.06	0.01	0.39	0.40
3 Mineral fuels and lubric.	0.04	0.35	0.35	0.72	--	0.72
4 Animal and veg. oils and fats	0	0	0	0	0	0
5 Chemicals* and pharm.	0.67	20.44	33.56	27.27	12.65	39.92
6 Manufactured goods	0.14	4.73	17.80	13.48	12.42	25.90
7 Machinery and transport equip.	0	22.79	31.48	26.25	24.84	51.09
8 Misc. manufactured articles	0.26	0.34	2.27	2.32	1.50	3.82
9 Misc. n.e.s.	0	0	0	0	0	0
Total	8.00	55.04	94.46	107.49	75.33	182.82

Group	Percentage composition of OGL					
	1967	1968	1969	1970A**	1970B**	1970
0 Food and live animals	85.75	11.54	9.46	34.83	31.24	33.35
1 Beverages and tobacco	0	0	0	0	0	0
2 Crude materials, inedible	0.375	0.07	0.06	0.01	0.52	0.22
3 Mineral fuels and lubric.	0.50	0.64	0.37	0.67	0	0.39
4 Animal and veg. oils and fats	0	0	0	0	0	0
5 Chemicals* and pharm.	8.375	37.14	35.53	25.37	16.79	21.84
6 Manufactured goods	1.75	8.59	18.84	12.54	16.49	14.17
7 Machinery and transport equip.	0	41.41	33.33	24.42	32.97	27.95
8 Misc. manufactured articles	3.25	0.62	2.40	2.16	1.99	2.09
9 Misc. n.e.s.	0	0	0	0	0	0
Total	100	100	100	100	100	100

Table V-11
(continued)

Group	Percentage of all imports*					
	1967	1968	1969	1970A**	1970B**	1970
0 Food and live animals	15.88	12.45	16.20	72.43	84.65	76.72
1 Beverages and tobacco	0	0	0	0	0	0
2 Crude materials, inedible	0.82	0.64	1.11	0.22	12.04	4.25
3 Mineral fuels and lubric.	0.26	1.63	1.53	4.34	0	2.96
4 Animal and veg. oils and fats	0	0	0	0	0	0
5 Chemicals* and pharm.	2.62	66.02	83.68	87.85	70.86	81.64
6 Manufactured goods	0.19	6.20	18.27	18.68	43.24	25.68
7 Machinery and transport equip.	0	26.51	33.31	34.99	74.95	47.25
8 Misc. manufactured articles	1.69	2.44	15.55	20.89	28.48	23.33
9 Misc. n.e.s.	0	0	0	0	0	0
Total	3.15	18.55	27.83	39.36	58.84	45.58

Notes: * OGL and total imports exclude Valco imports of aluminum. Excluded from OGL imports are several minor items such as headloads of foodstuffs, single copies of books and periodicals and some spare parts which are not separately identified in the *External Trade Statistics.*
           ** 1970A refers to January through August, and 1970B refers to September through December, to take into account a major expansion of OGL from August 25, 1970.
Source: Compiled from OGL lists published in *Commercial and Industrial Bulletin,* and corresponding import values recorded in *External Trade Statistics.*

what slower than the "immediate effect" promised in the budget speech: ten months passed before the increase took effect.

The import liberalization approach was selective in its incidence. Given the gradualist strategy adopted, and the differentiated compensating taxes (surcharges) on OGL, no other option appeared viable. The result was substantial variation in the proportion of OGL imports by major groups (see Table V-11). By the end of 1970, 70 percent or more of food, pharmaceuticals, and machinery imports were on OGL.[55]

55. Further, most fuels and lubricants were licenced in name only, with the volume of licencing based on actual demand. Hence SITC section 3 was also in effect almost completely liberalized.

From the perspective of late 1970, substantial progress had been achieved in liberalizing imports in the three years since devaluation. This had been made possible, in large part, by exceptionally large foreign-exchange receipts from cocoa and from aid donors. While the latter could be expected to continue for a few more years, the cocoa market windfall of 1970 could not.

In the post-Korean boom period a significant and relatively stable negative relationship between Ghana's cocoa volume and price had existed. Such a relationship provides a useful device both for evaluating the extent to which current cocoa receipts are normal, and for forecasting expected receipts on the basis of crop reports. While such an exercise was not, to our knowledge, explicitly undertaken, it is useful to do so in order to illustrate the approximate magnitude of the windfall of foreign-exchange receipts for 1970 and the adjustment necessary in 1971.

One such relationship between cocoa volume and price is:

$$\ln\ CXP_t = \alpha + \beta \ln\ CXV_t + u_t \tag{V.1}$$

where:

CXV_t = index of cocoa-bean export volume

CXP_t = index of cocoa-bean export price

Using annual data for the period 1955 through 1969,[56] we obtained the following fit:

$$\ln\ CXP_t = 8.655 - 0.8893 \ln\ CXV_t$$
$$\quad\quad\ (16.75)\quad (-7.51)$$

$$
\begin{aligned}
\text{Obs.} &= 15 \\
R^2 &= 0.8128 \\
\text{D.W.} &= 1.468 \,.
\end{aligned}
$$

In turn, substituting the actual volume index of 89 for 1970, we obtain a predicted price index of 107, compared with the actual index of 173. Translated into values, this means that the actual 1971 receipts of $ 294.4 million for bean exports alone were $ 112.1 million (or N₡ 111.4 million at the 1970

---

56. Source: IMF, *International Financial Statistics,* 1971 Supplement, Ghana, pages, volume index from line 72a and price index from line 74a (1963 equals 100 for both indexes), and Price Index converted to dollar terms, using IFS dollar export unit values for period 1967 through 1969.

exchange rate) greater than could be expected from past relationships.[57] With a windfall of such a magnitude the goods and services deficit of only N¢ 15 million during 1970 appears much less of a success. Put another way, approximately 27 percent of the 1970 import bill was financed by the cocoa windfall.

Moving into 1971, with an expected volume of sales approximately equal to that of 1970, the predicted bean price based on the fit of equation (V.1) above would be US $ 22.51 per hundred pounds. And as 1971 proceeded the actual price received did fall towards that level. During the first quarter the price averaged $ 28.66, and in the second quarter, $ 24.41, continuing to fall for the remainder of the year.[58] On the basis of this information, a prediction made towards the middle of 1971 would put estimated cocoa receipts for the current year nearly $ 100 million less than during 1970. Yet with the further liberalization of mid-1970, imports were continuing to grow at a substantial rate: 20 percent greater in the first half of 1971 than in the corresponding period of 1970. It is within this context that the Finance Minister set about the task of drawing up the 1971 budget.

J.H. Mensah presented the second budget of the Progress Party government to Parliament in late July 1971. The major feature was a drive toward total liberalization of imports.[59] At the same time it reflected the increasingly complex nature of the policy mix adopted to deal with the growing balance-of-payments pressure while at the same time pursuing import liberalization. The OGL list was extended further: over 76 percent of imports were free of direct control.[60] Surcharges were extended to specifically licenced imports and, correcting a major anomaly, government imports (including exempt public corporations) were now subject to import taxes.[61] Further, a 25 percent tax was levied on most non-commodity current payments, reducing the discrimination in favor of invisibles over goods imports.[62] Retreat-

---

57. If we were to take a shorter period, thus placing more weight on the later part in which Ghana was experiencing a reduced share of the world market, the price response which would have been predicted to the increased volume of 1970 would have been even greater than fitted relationship based on 1955 through 1969 data. Such a measure would mean an even larger calculated windfall for 1970.

58. See IMF, *International Financial Statistics*, June 1972.

59. The details which follow are taken from the *Budget Statement for 1971-72*, Accra, 27 July, 1971, unless otherwise indicated.

60. This figure is calculated by applying the new list to 1970 imports.

61. A Central Bureau of Statistics tabulation of government imports alone (excluding exempt public entities) for 1970 indicates that government imports amounted to 8.5 percent of total imports.

62. Remittances of current profits which had previously queued were now guaranteed but subject to a 25 percent tax. Transfers of foreign exchange for travel, payments of commissions, interest and headquarters expenses were also subject to a 25 percent tax. Airline and shipping remittances for other than merchandise imports, remittances for insurance, and student remittances were subject to a 10 percent tax.

ing to a limited extent from liberalization, the restricted and banned lists were expanded. And both to contain the surge of food imports as well as to encourage local production, some food items — including rice, sugar, and fresh or frozen fish which had been subject to low rates of duty and surcharge — were withdrawn from the OGL list.

In a move accompanying the budget, the export bonus (subsidy) for non-traditional exports which had finally been enacted earlier in the year was increased from 10 percent on incremental values to 25 percent of the total value.[63] The 25 percent bonus was also applied to tourist purchases of local currency with convertible foreign exchange. In a related move, the procedures for tax and duty drawbacks on exports had been simplified, making it feasible now for exporters to take advantage of these provisions.[64]

The Finance Minister also took a major if incomplete step toward monetary reform. Recognizing that the nominal interest rates were far too low to attract a major volume of savings, he announced that commercial banks were to increase their rates of interest on savings and time deposits from the previous $2\frac{1}{2}$-3 percent to a minimum of $7\frac{1}{2}$ percent, and to pay interest at the rate of 1 percent on demand deposits. In addition, the bank rate was increased from $5\frac{1}{2}$ percent to 8 percent. An accompanying set of instructions to the commercial banks set the ceiling on loan rates at 11 percent, up from the previous 10 percent.[65]

The resumption of normal cocoa prices was also creating budgetary problems. The cocoa export tax, a progressive function of the local currency export price, was yielding considerably less revenue than in the previous year. Projected total revenues at existing tax rates indicated a decline in revenues amounting to N₵ 121 million from the 1970–1971 revenues of N₵ 490 million. As a small partial remedy, an additional tax on income was introduced under the label: National Development Levy. Nevertheless, proposed internal borrowing amounted to N₵ 129 million, in contrast with actual borrowing of N₵ 49 million and N₵ 40 million in the two preceding fiscal years, plus a N₵ 25 million withdrawal from reserves.

In pushing forward with import liberalization, the government was convinced that this would be the means whereby it could pull the economy out of the doldrums. This opinion, however, was by no means unanimous in the country or even within the government. Strong pressures for the abandon-

63. *Legislative Instrument 700*, 2 July, 1971, Gazette notification, 6 August, 1971.
64. *Commercial and Industrial Bulletin,* 25 June, 1971.
65. Bank of Ghana, *Notice to Banks,* No. 71/2. We understand that the Bank of Ghana subsequently removed the ceiling on loan rates for all but loans to agriculture.

ment of liberalization continued to be exerted.[66] Time was running out if the import liberalization was to be completed successfully.

Yet several problems remained. With cocoa export revenues declining to more normal levels, and with the continued liberalization of imports, the average level of import taxes would have to be substantially higher to hold the de-licenced imports within reasonable bounds. However, the nominal effective exchange rate facing imports was only 4.5 percent greater in 1971 than in 1968, and even lower than in the second (post-devaluation) half of 1967. At the same time the domestic price level had continued to rise in the period since 1968: the consumer price index for 1971 was 21.4 percent greater than for 1968 and 31.2 percent above the 1967 average.[67] In real terms then, the effective exchange rate facing imports was declining at the same time as a major liberalization of imports was proceeding. The entire approach to liberalization had changed. Initially the liberalization had been an attempt to substitute an approximately equivalent price restriction for the discarded quantitative restrictions. Now however the liberalization had become a switch from a closed to an open deficit financed by the cocoa boom and aid donors.

For the industrial sector the haphazard protective structure that had been further complicated by differentiated surcharges continued to reflect historical accidents rather than a carefully designed industrialization strategy.

Non-cocoa exports remained in a state of relative neglect and at the same time unnecessary regulation. Export promotional schemes had appeared and disappeared with monotonous regularity. After two years of promises a scheme was now being implemented, but exporters could legitimately query, would it last? Further, timber and most minor agricultural crops remained under marketing boards of dubious promotional value.

The interest rate changes and related requirements dealing with government securities and expansion of credit, while laudable in intent, were not well designed to achieve the thoroughgoing interest rate reform which would be necessary to unify the segmented capital markets we described in Chapter IV. Further, the new regulations created a serious problem in squeezing the commercial banks' profitability by narrowing the gap between deposit and loan rates. Instead of encouraging a competitive bidding for deposits and active pursuit of non-prime borrowers, the regulations made it unprofitable

---

66. In partial reply to his critics, J.H. Mensah concluded his budget speech with the Akan proverb, "When the gun is hot it is the stalwart who still carries it near his bosom." *Budget Statement for 1971-72,* Accra, July 1971.

67. Central Bureau of Statistics, *Newsletter,* 20 April, 1972. The national accounts data do not at the time of writing extend beyond 1969, so that we are unable to continue the GDP deflator series.

for banks to accept time and savings deposits, or to make risky loans with high administrative costs.

Finally, the overall deficit budgeted for fiscal year 1971–1972 promised to place continued upward pressure on domestic demand and prices, with the consequent erosion in real effects of the higher nominal deposit interest rates, export subsidies, and import taxes introduced in the same budget.

The evidence was rapidly accumulating. The open deficit without the cocoa windfall could not be sustained. Strong medicine would be required to keep imports under control and to save the liberalization. The trade account surplus which Ghana had run since 1967 no longer existed. Yet it had been used to cover the perennial services and transfers deficits as well as debt service payments plus (in 1970 particularly) repurchase of substantial IMF drawings that had been made in 1966 and 1967. During 1971 these payments continued, along with the trade deficit, with the result that foreign-exchange reserves were reaching a perilously low level: $ 40 million at the end of the third quarter in 1971, or less than half the trade deficit accumulated in the first three quarters of 1971.

Discussions of solutions began within the government; later the IMF was consulted about reopening the standby credit. The Fund apparently was very discreet, not even suggesting that a devaluation would be a necessary component of any package. The government, however, quickly focused on devaluation as a simple single solution, not only to the balance-of-payments problem, but to a variety of other problems: the complex set of policies that had accompanied introduction of liberalization could be abandoned while at the same time saving the liberalization; and the large fiscal deficit could be ameliorated, easing the excessive aggregate demand pressure that was building up.

The solution adopted was devaluation. The decision rested largely with Prime Minister Busia. In the preceding months he had taken increasingly more control over economic decisions, and had become convinced that a devaluation would provide a once-and-for-all solution. The Minister of Finance, J.H. Mensah, was known to oppose devaluation as a "crude and blunt instrument." However, he did not resign when the Prime Minister decided to devalue.

The Prime Minister announced the devaluation in a broadcast to the nation on December 27, 1971.[68] The speech placed major emphasis on the turmoil in the world economy, and suggested that measures which had previously been introduced, such as the surcharges, had been "to try to forestall the economic problems that were moving in on us from overseas."[69] The devalua-

---

68. The text of the Prime Minister's speech is reported in the *Ghanaian Times*, Tuesday, December 28, 1971.

69. *Ibid.*

tion announcement itself was buried in a list of specific measures being taken "to simplify the increasingly complex structure that the individual measures have tended to create."[70]

The size of the devaluation was almost incredible. The exchange rate against the dollar was hiked from N₡ 1.02 per dollar to N₡ 1.82 per dollar, a rise of 78.2 percent. To this must be added the fact of the dollar devaluation itself, announced a few days earlier, making the depreciation against other currencies even greater. The weighted (by trade shares) average depreciation against all currencies was reported as 92 percent.[71]

The net devaluation was somewhat, but not substantially, smaller on the import side. Surcharges were abolished, lopping off approximately ten percentage points of the gross devaluation. The taxes on other current payments, which had been introduced in August of the same year, were also abolished. No data are yet available on the actual magnitude of collections, but if they were fully enforced they would have amounted to no more than 20 percent on approximately one-fifth of total current account payments. Overall, the net devaluation on the current payments side was about twelve percentage points less than the gross.

On the earnings side, the 25 percent export and tourist bonuses were abolished. The affected items, however, accounted for less than 10 percent of total current account receipts. More important was the decision for cocoa. The producer price was increased by only 25 percent (from N₡ 8.00 to N₡ 10.00 per headload) effective from the next mid-crop season.[72] Similar price increases were promised to producers of other agricultural crops handled by the Cocoa Marketing Board. Other traditional exports, timber and minerals, received the full benefit of the devaluation. The extent of the net devaluation for current receipts thus varied considerably among cocoa, other traditional exports, and nontraditional exports. Overall, however, because of the dominance of cocoa, the net was significantly less than the gross.

A minor concession in the form of increased government wages was also offered to partially offset the price increases arising from the devaluation. The increase ranged from $33\frac{1}{3}$ percent for the lowest-paid to zero for those earning over N₡ 1,000 per year.[73]

Following his outline of the devaluation package, the Prime Minister went on to note that he hoped these measures "will enable the government to carry

70. *Ibid.*
71. Ghana Commercial Bank, *Monthly Economic Bulletin,* December 1971.
72. Most of the current crop had already been sold by the cocoa farmers.
73. This item was vaguely stated in the Prime Minister's speech, so that it could have been taken, and was taken by many, to mean a $33\frac{1}{3}$ percent increase in the minimum wage, although the actual meaning of the regulation was as stated above.

further the policy of liberalization which it has pursued since coming into office." He referred again to the "world-wide economic and financial turmoil," before concluding with a call for exporters "to show greater energy and initiative," and an admonition that "for the rest of us, I know these measures will make imported goods much dearer [but will] ...so create more employment for our own people and generally help our economy. This is the best way of promoting self reliance."[74]

Considering the huge size of the devaluation, there was curiously little discussion of it, or attempt to explain why so large a devaluation had been undertaken. Apparently the Prime Minister believed that a massive devaluation would solve the balance-of-payments problem for years to come, leaving him free to concentrate on other issues. More than that, however, appears to have been behind the decision on size. Clearly the first several percentage points would be taken up in substituting devaluation for the surcharges and other taxes and subsidies, so that to have any net impact the devaluation would have to be larger than the existing effects of the recently introduced taxes and subsidies. Beyond that, however, the devaluation was evidently being used as a fiscal device. A major consideration in determining the size of the devaluation was the revenue requirements of the government. With a large government budgetary deficit looming, a substantial devaluation promised to provide a major addition to government tax revenues, particularly via the cocoa export tax. The cocoa export tax schedule is steeply progressive on the cocoa price denominated in local currency. Hence with the near doubling of the local currency, unit-value cocoa exports would provide a substantial boost for government revenue.[75] A further consideration, but clearly not uppermost in the minds of the inner decision-makers, may well have been that aggregate expenditure in local-currency terms would also be dampened in a manner similar to that of the 1967 devaluation. A devaluation about twice as large as that of 1967 would have a substantial deflationary impact on domestic expenditure. In addition to the effects arising from the initial excess of imports over exports (see Chapter V, section 2b, above), one could in this case expect a money demand effect: the public would reduce expenditure to restore the real value of its money holdings.

Whatever the underlying reasons, the rate chosen meant a huge cut in real income for the economy as a whole, with its immediate incidence on heavy

---

74. The Prime Minister's speech, *op. cit.*
75. At the same time, since government appropriations had already been fixed in terms of cedis, the devaluation would not immediately increase government expenditures. Heavily import-dependent Ministries, such as Defence, thus found the real value of their appropriations slashed.

net users of importables.[76] The aggregate excess demand for real resources that had been allowed to develop over the previous few years had been vented this time on the import binge of 1970 and 1971. It could not now be continued. This situation was in sharp contrast with the position of the economy prior to the 1967 devaluation, where internal deflation and strict limitation of imports had prevailed for the twelve months leading up to the devaluation. Rather, it corresponded more closely to the situation of early 1966 when the contraction of available external resources had meant a substantial cut in real income, in that case via a tightening of import licencing.

The Prime Minister made no attempt in his speech to indicate the magnitude of the cut in real income that would now be necessary, perhaps recognizing the parallel between his situation and that of Nkrumah in January 1966. The import volume for 1972 would have to be reduced by at least one-third of the 1971 volume, and perhaps more, if forthcoming obligations, particularly the large debt-service payments, were to be met. Whatever the set of policies adopted, that was the magnitude of the task, and that was the magnitude of the shock to the economy.

The shock proved to be too much for major segments of the Ghanaian society. Existing dissatisfaction with the Busia government was crystallized, and on January 13, 1972, a previously little-known colonel of the army, I.K. Acheampong, seized the opportunity to lead a successful military coup while Prime Minister Busia was out of the country for medical treatment. High on the list of justifications for the coup was "the inefficient management by that [Busia] Regime of our economy.... It [the coup] was staged...to save the country from total economic collapse."[77]

The new government quickly announced that it would reexamine both the devaluation and Ghana's external debt problem. In the interim it introduced an import-subsidy program on some essential consumer goods (milk, sugar, baby food, sardines, machetes, bar soap, and cod fish), and ordered that these commodities were to be sold at pre-devaluation prices.

Twenty-two days after the coup, Colonel Acheampong, Chairman of the National Redemption Council, and Commissioner for Finance and for Economic Affairs, announced a major new set of economic policies. The key-

---

76. It is important to recognize that the increased prices of importables arising from the devaluation will normally affect both purchases and sales by the same proportion. Hence the devaluation has a net taxing effect only on net purchasers of importables. Net sellers of importables, such as domestic manufacturers of tradeables using imported materials, will on the other hand be net gainers from the devaluation. The view that a devaluation has a net taxing effect on them via increased costs of importable inputs is thus purely myopic.

77. Colonel I.K. Acheampong, quoted in the *Daily Graphic,* Accra, 18 January, 1972.

stone was a selective debt repudiation, accompanied by a revaluation of the cedi to N₵ 1.28 per dollar, and a reimposition of strict import licencing.[78]

Even selective debt repudiation was something neither the National Liberation Council government nor the Progress Party government of Prime Minister Busia had been willing to do. Yet the total annual debt service burden was amounting to some 20 percent of normal export earnings. Creditor governments guaranteeing suppliers' credit had indicated no willingness to extend the repayments over a longer period without charging moratorium interest at approximately 6 percent. In both of his budgets the previous Finance Minister, J.H. Mensah, had complained about the lack of sympathy on the part of the creditor governments, and had staked out Ghana's position as requiring "a long term settlement which allows the economy of Ghana to begin restoring its basic strength before payments have to be resumed," and does not increase the level of debt by means of moratorium interest.[79]

Colonel Acheampong now reiterated the Ghanaian position, "that our foreign exchange resources simply could not at once sustain the debt service obligations and meet our minimal development targets," and complained that "the creditor countries...have proved singularly unsympathetic and unresponsive to our well documented case."[80] Short-term and long-term debts were validated. However, he came down hard on suppliers'-credit debt. He: (a) repudiated "all contracts which are vitiated by corruption, fraud and other illegality," including those with a specific list of companies having an original face value of $ 94.4 million, while at the same time offering "to go to arbitration in respect of all disputes arising from our action," with the IBRD's International Centre for the Settlement of Domestic Disputes as arbiter;[81] (b) refused to accept the rescheduling entered into by the two previous governments, particularly the $72 million moratorium interest; (c) set out conditions which suppliers' credits contracted before the overthrow of Nkrumah must prove in order to establish the validity of their claims (valid contracts not vitiated by fraud, corruption or other illegality, and only for projects technically and economically viable and productive — the onus of proof being on the creditor); and (d) unilaterally rescheduled the remaining suppliers'-credit debts on terms similar to the IBRD's soft-loan window, the International Development Association.

78. *Vis-à-vis* the original parity of N₵ 1.02 per dollar, this meant a 25 percent devaluation against the dollar, and a depreciation (weighted by trade shares) of 36 percent against all currencies. In addition, Colonel Acheampong let stand several measures which Busia had announced at the time of the December 1971 devaluation, including the abolition of surcharges, taxes on invisibles, and the national development levy.
79. *Budget Statement* for 1971–1972, p. 21.
80. *Ghanaian Times*, 7 February, 1972.
81. *Ibid.*

It was a dramatic and, many would argue, a long overdue move against this all-too-common carpetbagger device of selling capital equipment. However, this alone would not provide the magnitude of relief required for Ghana's balance of payments. At best it postponed about 10 percent of Ghana's foreign-exchange bill over the next few years.[82] Far more severe cuts in foreign-exchange use were required, and for this Colonel Acheampong chose licencing, accompanied by a revaluation of the cedi.

The experiment with import liberalization was ended. The gains from import liberalization did not appear sufficiently large to make the shock of the massive December 1971 devaluation acceptable as a means of saving it. Yet that devaluation had been assigned a task far greater than saving the liberalization. Not only had it been used as a substitute for the complex set of liberalization taxes and subsidies, but it had been used simultaneously in an attempt to achieve two other objectives: an enormous cutback of imports, and reduction in the accumulated excess demand for real resources.

The most unpopular aspect was the reduction in real income it implied. Yet the liberalization and the devaluation bore the brunt of the criticism. They were the scapegoat, while the true culprit — the previous set of policies which had been designed to obtain a higher level of consumption for Ghanaians than the available resources would permit — escaped detection. For the new government the unpleasant task of facing up to the necessity of cutting back the standard of living remained. It would now have to administer an import program via licencing of approximately the same magnitude as had been implicit in the original devaluation. Hence the immediate real income difference between the two schemes was nil.[83] Curiously, though, a given volume of foreign-exchange use at a lower cedi price to the initial recipients seemed preferable to the same volume at a higher cedi price.

How successful the new set of policies would prove to be remained uncertain. One thing was certain: import liberalization was finished.

5. Import liberalization — a total failure?

In the ultimate test — survival — the import-liberalization experiment failed. Yet such a test provides us with no clue as to the source of the failure.

82. The immediate net gain was also reduced by the response of those creditor nations who were also aid donors, some of whom tended to reduce their long-term aid commitments.
83. While this is true for the very short run, the import program under licencing in the medium term will be smaller than under the devaluation because export earnings will be smaller.

Was import liberalization inherently inappropriate in the Ghanaian context? Or was it a suitable policy poorly implemented? Or were there mistakes outside the realm of liberalization that brought about its failure?

A positive answer to each question could readily be constructed, depending largely on the breadth with which liberalization is defined and which instruments of economic policy are taken as given. By selecting the appropriate set of assumptions, either explicitly or implicitly, about what is given and what is not, it is possible to prove a great variety of conflicting propositions about the import liberalization. Such is the nature of the political debate that ensues from the Ghanaian liberalization experience.

Our purpose here is not to enter the political debate. Rather, the purpose of this section is to elucidate the economic issues involved. In particular, it is useful to know which elements of the experiment could be considered successful, and which failures. And more importantly, our purpose is to draw whatever lessons we can from the experience. We begin with a narrow frame of reference in which we consider only the transfer of items from the Specific Licence (SL) list to the Open General Licence (OGL) list.

We have seen how the absolute value of OGL imports grew over the period 1967 through 1970 (Table V-11). Hidden within this overall growth were the initial reaction to placing an item on OGL and subsequent growth of items remaining on OGL, mixed in different proportions each year. At the same time it is important to note what was happening to imports that were still under licence. To sort out the details we have separated the items placed on OGL for a given year and traced the performance of those items only through the year before they were placed on OGL, and through as many subsequent years as possible. The results are contained in Table V-12.

Beginning with the items placed on OGL in 1967, we see that the value of imports of those same items was slightly less during their first year on OGL than during the previous year, while they had been under licence, and that imports of those items did not grow substantially over the subsequent years. Since the items involved were mostly food, pharmaceuticals, and spare parts, it is not surprising to find that licences had previously been issued virtually on demand.

The items placed on OGL for the first time for 1968 encompassed a number of chemicals (including manufactured fertilizers), manufactures, and machinery. During the first year on OGL, these items increased by 11.2 percent over the previous (licence) year, which is high in terms of the historical growth of imports, but substantially lower than the 16.6 percent overall increase in imports that year. They continued to grow during their second and third years on OGL, but still at a slower rate than total imports.

Items added to OGL for 1969 began to include substantially more manufactured items that had formerly been subject to stricter licencing. The result

Table V-12

OGL imports* year prior to placing on OGL and subsequent years (in millions of new cedis)

First placed on OGL for year	Value of imports during cal. year indicated					Change from previous year							
	1966	1967	1968	1969	1970	1967 Value	1967 Percent	1968 Value	1968 Percent	1969 Value	1969 Percent	1970 Value	1970 Percent
1967	8.2	8.0	7.3	9.5	9.4	−0.2	−2.4	− 0.7	− 8.8	+ 2.2	+30.1	− 0.1	− 1.1
1968		43.0	47.8	53.8	60.5			+ 4.8	+11.2	+ 6.0	+12.6	+ 6.7	+12.5
1969			24.1	31.2	40.8					+ 7.1	+29.5	+ 9.6	+30.8
1970**				27.9	50.6							+22.7	+81.4
1970 Aug. additon					21.5								
Imports new to OGL	0	8.0	47.8	31.2	72.1	+8.0		+39.8		−16.6		+40.9	
Imports previously on OGL	0	0	7.3	63.3	110.7			+ 7.3		+56.0		+47.4	
Total on OGL	0	8.0	55.1	94.5	182.8	+8.0		+47.1		+39.4		+87.3	
Licenced imports	250.1	246.3	241.5	244.9	218.2	−3.8		− 4.8		+ 3.4		−26.7	
Total imports	250.1	254.3	296.6	339.4	401.0	+4.2	−1.7	+42.3	+ 16.6	+42.8	+14.4	+61.6	+18.1

Notes: * OGL and total imports exclude Valco imports of aluminum. Excluded from OGL imports are several minor items, such as headloads of food-stuffs, single copies of books and periodicals, and some spare parts which are not separately identified in the *External Trade Statistics*.

Sources: See Table V-11.

   ** Imports first placed on OGL for the year 1970 refer to those added effective January 1, 1970 and early in the year: the August 1970 additions are excluded.

was a more substantial jump in imports of those items over the licenced value of the previous year — and a further increase of about the same proportion in the next year.

The final year for which we have the detailed trade data necessary to make these calculations is 1970. The items added for 1970 were entirely food. (We are excluding the items added in August 1970.) The result was a very substantial surge of delicenced imports.

At the same time as newly delicenced imports were experiencing considerable growth (1969 and 1970), the volume of SL imports was not adjusted to compensate for the switch of items to OGL. Thus in 1969 the licence budget no longer had to provide for the NȻ 24.1 million (1968 value) transferred to OGL. Instead of delicencing by this amount, or otherwise making some allowances for reasonable growth among the remaining items on SL, the total value of licenced imports grew by NȻ 4.4 million. The growth of imports of the items remaining under licence was thus NȻ 27.5 million, or a 12.7 percent increase over those same items in 1968.

For 1970 the transfer of items to OGL and the change in SL imports is not as clear because of the addition to OGL of several items in August 1970. Excluding those items added in August, the previous year's value of newly delicenced imports amounted to NȻ 27.9 million, which is only slightly larger than the decline in SL imports for all of 1970. However, this substantially overstates the reduction of licencing in response to the transfer of items to OGL because some portion, probably about one-half, of the value of items transferred to OGL in August would already have been issued with licences, and at the same time those added in August 1970 had been imported under SL in 1969. Hence we again find a gap between the value of items transferred to OGL and the expected reduction in SL imports.

A simple standard against which we may judge this growth of SL imports is the cumulative value of delicenced imports, using the value of the year prior to delicencing. This is a minimum value because it does not allow for the growth which would have taken place in delicenced imports had they remained under licencing. Items switched to OGL in 1969 and in 1970 had a total value of NȻ 52.0 million in the year prior to delicencing, yet over this same period the value of SL imports fell by only NȻ 23.3 million. In other words, over one-half of the effect of transfer from SL to OGL was absorbed by increased licences for those items which remained on the SL list.

What lessons can be drawn from this experience? Two major influences were at work to increase the flow of imports: the release of pent-up demand as items were transferred from SL to OGL, and overall aggregate demand growth, which could now be vented on imports rather than domestic prices. Potential restraining influences on OGL imports were surcharges plus aggregate expenditure control — and on the remaining imports, licences. The evidence strongly suggests that none of the restraining influences was adequate.

The surges of OGL imports in 1969 and 1970 to satisfy the pent-up demand indicate that surcharges were far from adequate to capture the previous quota premia and hence contain that demand. Further, the subsequent high growth rates of OGL imports suggest that aggregate demand pressure remained too strong to keep freed imports from growing too rapidly. This placed a serious strain on the import liberalization. Such a strain by itself would have been temporarily tolerated. However, at the same time as freed imports were increasing substantially, the stringency of licencing was greatly relaxed, allowing imports still under SL to take up much of the value of items transferred to OGL. This Ghana could not afford simultaneously with the chosen approach to OGL. In sum, the rapid growth of imports was due both to an expanding OGL system with inadequate restraints in the form of surcharges and control over aggregate demand, and to a licencing system with inadequate restriction of those items still within its purview.

Difficult and complex as was the basic task of freeing imports from licencing, economic policy is made in a far broader framework. Numerous objectives must be considered and numerous instruments employed. Liberalization of imports cannot be treated in isolation from this broader framework of government economic policy. Because liberalization was only one of several objectives, and because of the limited number of effective instruments available, it could therefore be argued that liberalization had to be compromised in a less than optimal solution. Such an argument, however, ignores an important trait of the broader framework of economic policy. All instruments are now variable, and it is therefore potentially possible to assign instruments to targets on the basis of the two important principles: (a) there should be a number of effective instruments at least equal to the number of desired independent targets; (b) instruments should be assigned to targets on the basis of their relative effectiveness in affecting the targets.[84] Without such an assignment of instruments to targets it becomes far more difficult, if not impossible, to achieve the desired overall solution. While this is not the place to launch an extended discussion of the theory and application of general economic policy in Ghana, two major problems associated with the import-liberalization experience suggest that the failure of liberalization was in part due to the broader failure of general economic policy in Ghana.

First, throughout both the period of restriction and the period of liberalization there was a serious proliferation of policy instruments. By the late 1960's the accumulated assortment of instruments, acting in uncertain ways

84. These are, of course, the well-known Tinbergen and Mundell points. For the former, see J. Tinbergen, *The Theory of Economic Policy,* North-Holland, Amsterdam, 1952, Chapter 5; and for the latter, R.A. Mundell, *International Economics,* Macmillan., New York, 1968, Chapter 14.

on a variety of targets, made the effective formulation of economic policy an incredibly difficult and complex task. The direction and magnitude of the effects of the introduction of new policies and changes in old ones was frequently uncertain, and occasionally perverse. The task of planning and coping with such a complex and detailed system was far beyond what could reasonably be expected from even the best possible cadre of economic planners. Caught up with the hopeless task of coping in the small, policy formulation and implementation in the large was inevitably neglected. As a result, it is relatively easy to look back, as we do now, to find serious errors in the formulation and implementation of major policies. Two examples stand out: the differentiated surcharges, and the size of the 1971 devaluation.

The primary objective of surcharges introduced in 1970 was to dampen the pent-up demand for the newly freed imports, yet secondary objectives which could have been achieved by use of other instruments also played a role in the specification of the surcharge rates, with the consequence that the surcharges accomplished neither the primary nor the secondary objectives.[85] To achieve the primary objective while minimizing the disturbance of other policies, it would have been far more appropriate to employ uniform surcharges on freed items. A secondary objective, to discriminate between luxury and other imports (which the differentiated quota premia reflected) could have been achieved by the more appropriate instrument of indirect taxes applied to both domestic and imported goods.

In a similar manner, the major objective of the 1971 devaluation was to restore external balance while substituting devaluation for other equivalent (and therefore not independent) instruments. But because the 1971 devaluation was from an open deficit situation, it was also used in an attempt to achieve a secondary objective, internal balance. To achieve both objectives with the single instrument the devaluation had to be much larger than necessary to achieve the primary objective alone, which ended in shocking the economic and political system beyond acceptable limits. This contrasts with the 1967 devaluation, which had been assigned a considerably more limited task — restoration of external balance from a closed deficit position. And it accomplished this task to the extent possible. It had not been used also to achieve a massive cut in real income, for that had been done prior to the devaluation and was thus not associated with devaluation *per se.*

This leads us to the second important issue, the periodic jolts administered to the economy since the beginning of the 1960's. As disequilibria built up, typically little was effectively done to alleviate the situation until the last possible moment. Then, because the massive size of the disequilibrium re-

---

85. See section 4 above.

quired an equally massive adjustment, a drastic change had to be introduced. Such fillips produced severe shocks to the Ghanaian economy and society at large, so severe in fact that twice they were quickly followed by military coups. It is worth emphasizing that the shock of readjustment was the problem, not devaluation, which was merely the instrument employed by Busia in 1971 to implement the readjustment. Licencing and austerity had been used by Nkrumah in early 1966 to bring about readjustment following the import binge of 1965. Although the instruments were different, the shock to the society and the consequences for the national leaders were the same.[86]

Regardless of the device employed to bring about adjustment, it is clear that when adjustment became necessary large discrete changes were far less acceptable than small continuous changes of the same total magnitude. Successful formulation and implementation of economic policy requires more than determining the correct instrument and the correct magnitude: it also requires a careful attention to the time path of its incidence. Without such attention, the shocks administered by the inevitable adjustments were unacceptable.

The major lessons of the import-liberalization experience are clear. In the face of rapidly growing aggregate demand financed by an unusual cocoa windfall, and without adequate surcharges, by mid-1970 the liberalization had been carried too far. In broader terms, liberalization did not succeed because economic policy formulation and implementation failed. Bogged down in the complexities of a detailed control system, the government committed periodic policy blunders, placing the liberalization in jeopardy, unable to withstand the inevitable shock of massive readjustment.

86. The source of financing for the disequilibrium does not appear to have had a significant influence on the outcome. A careful examination of the balance-of-payments accounts (Table A—3a) suggests that the rapid growth in the absolute size of current account debits was financed differently in the Busia period than in the Nkrumah period. In 1970 the increase in current account debits over 1969 was more than financed by increased merchandise earnings, mostly due to the cocoa windfall. In 1971, when merchandise earnings returned to their 1969 level, the current account debits remained at about their 1970 level without the available financing of extra merchandise credits. Financing came largely from increased credits on the monetary authorities' account (two-thirds) plus increased capital account credits (one-third). Contrast this experience with the two cases of rapidly expanding current account debits under Nkrumah. In both 1960—1961 and 1965 the increased current account expenditures were financed only minimally by additional current account earnings, and only about one-third by increased monetary account credits. The major source for Nkrumah was increased capital account credits — i.e., increased external borrowing.

CHAPTER VI

Concluding remarks: major lessons of the Ghanaian experience

Ghana's experience with exchange and import controls has not been happy. In the 1960's the control system produced such dissatisfaction that a serious and prolonged attempt was made to liberalize the system. Yet in the end liberalization collapsed. What are the major lessons of both failures, and how might they be avoided in the future? These concluding remarks are to set out our own broad assessment of the lessons to be drawn from what Ghana has endured.

Failure to recognize the old adage that quantitative controls work best when they are needed least lies at the heart of the matter. During both the period of tight controls and the gradual liberalization, apparently redundant supportive policies received little attention. Aggregate demand for foreign-exchange use was allowed to increase rapidly without continuous compensating adjustments to the nominal effective exchange rates to keep them in line with sustainable real rates. The quantitative controls consequently had to bear an increasingly greater burden as the effects of the supportive policies were eroded. This burden proved to be far greater than they could support.

The case against quantitative controls then was that too much was asked of them: they failed to restrict the level and allocate the composition of foreign-exchange use in a satisfactory way. At the same time, a proliferation of restrictive instruments designed to shore up the control regime compounded the policy-makers' difficulties in maintaining control over the economy. The direction and magnitude of the effects of both old and new policies became so complex that it was frequently impossible for policy-makers to evaluate the effects of changes which were introduced.

Within this ambience several serious consequences of the system emerged. First, the restrictive regime contributed to the economic atrophy of the 1960's. The combination of inflation and massive discrimination between activities was too much for the economy to withstand without suffering. It is difficult to distinguish clearly the individual influences at work, but there is a strong presumption that a significant share of the blame for reduced domestic savings rates, low productivity of investment, and poor export performance must fall on the control regime.

Second, the broad objective of industrialization was almost completely obscured in the indiscriminate distribution of protection. Both the tariff-indirect tax system and the quantitative restrictions created a protective structure with substantial variation among industrial activities. Variation *per se* is not necessarily undesirable if it is based on evidence of divergences between private and social values or the existence of major externalities. Yet no such evidence existed. Variation of protection between activities was at best random and unpredictable.

Third, the administrative system proved incapable of consistently careful management of foreign exchange. Both the heavy borrowing by Nkrumah and the cocoa windfall of Busia were predictably short-lived. When the plethora of foreign exchange had been spent, crises ensued. To solve the crises, the policy-makers typically resorted to a drastic change in one major policy — either reimposition of strict import licencing (1961, 1966, 1972) or a substantial devaluation (1971). The shock of the readjustments required by these drastic changes had a serious unsettling effect on the economic and social fabric of Ghana. In a state of shock, the socioeconomic system required considerably more time to recover than would have been required from a consistent series of gradual policy shifts. Further, the state of shock seemed to preclude attention to follow-up policies necessary to ensure the success of the initial policy adjustment.

Finally, economic planning became bogged down in a frantic attempt to cope with an incredibly complex and detailed system. Policy-makers found themselves caught up in running the control system. Planning in the large was abandoned to the press of planning in the small. Serious errors in policy formulation and implementation inevitably followed. The brave new sense of direction and purpose of the early days of Ghanaian independence was lost. It was lost, but not forever. "Each thing that goes away returns and nothing in the end is lost." [1]

1. Ayi Kwei Armah, modern Ghanaian novelist, the opening sentence of his *Fragments,* Houghton Mifflin, Boston, 1969, p. 1.

APPENDIX A

GENERAL STATISTICAL TABLES

Table A-1
Ghana: GNP and population,* 1956–1969

	1956	1957	1958	1959	1960
GNP at current prices (in millions of new cedis)	702	734	776	884	946
GNP at constant (1960) prices (in millions of new cedis)	748	770	760	879	946
GNP per capita at current prices	150	154	160	180	141
GNP per capita at constant prices	159	162	157	179	141
Population (in thousands)	4,691	4,763	4,836	4,911	6,777

Annual rates of growth for	1957/56	1958/57	1959/58	1960/59
GNP at current prices	0.0456	0.0572	0.1392	0.0701
GNP at constant prices	0.0294	−0.0130	0.1566	0.0762
GNP per capita in current prices	0.0267	0.0390	0.1250	−0.2167
GNP per capita in constant prices	0.0189	−0.0309	0.1401	−0.2123
Population	0.0153	0.0153	0.0155	0.3800

1961	1962	1963	1964	1965	1966	1967	1968	1969
1,008	1,084	1,190	1,345	1,589	1,779	1,757	2,028	2,285
976	1,028	1,056	1,085	1,093	1,099	1,116	1,120	1,158
146	153	164	180	207	224	216	242	266
142	145	145	145	142	138	137	134	135
6,960	7,148	7,340	7,537	7,740	7,945	8,139	8,376	8,600

1961/60	1962/61	1963/62	1964/63	1965/64	1966/65	1967/66	1968/67	1969/68
0.0655	0.0754	0.0978	0.1303	0.1814	0.1196	−0.0124	0.1542	0.1267
0.0317	0.0533	0.0272	0.0275	0.0074	0.0055	0.0155	0.0036	0.0339
0.0355	0.0479	0.0719	0.0976	0.1500	0.0821	−0.0357	0.1204	0.0992
0.0071	0.0211	0	0	−0.0207	−0.0282	−0.0072	−0.0219	0.0075
0.0270	0.0270	0.0269	0.0268	0.0269	0.0265	0.0244	0.0291	0.0267

Sources: GNP at current prices, GNP at constant (1960) prices, GNP annual rates of growth, GNP per capita: 1960 through 1969, from *Economic Survey, 1969*, p. 15.
GNP at current prices, 1956 through 1959, from *Economic Survey, 1967*, p. 13.
GNP at constant (1960) prices, 1959, *Economic Survey, 1967*, p. 107; 1956 through 1958, D. Walters, *Report on the National Accounts of Ghana, 1955–1961*, Tables I, III, pp. 2-4.

Population: United Nations *Demographic Yearbook, 1969*, p. 136, for years 1960 through 1969.
United Nations *Demographic Yearbook, 1964*, p. 120, for years 1956 through 1959.

* Population estimates prior to 1960 census regarded as an underestimate.

Table A-2
Ghana: price indices, 1956–1971

	1956	1957	1958	1959	1960	1961	1962	1963
GNP deflator index (1960=100.00)	93.85	95.32	102.11	100.57	100.00	103.28	105.45	112.69
Wholesale price index (1963=100.00)	–	–	–	–	–	94.8	103.0	100.0
Consumer price index (1963=100.00)	78.7	79.4	79.4	81.6	82.4	87.5	95.6	100.0

	1964	1965	1966	1967	1968	1969	1970	1971
GNP deflator index (1960=100.00)	123.96	145.38	161.87	157.44	181.07	197.32	N.A.	N.A.
Wholesale price index (1963=100.00)	107.1	124.3	124.2	130.0	153.5	166.3	174.9	N.A.
Consumer price index (1963=100.00)	112.2	140.8	148.2	139.3	153.2	160.7	166.5	174.7

Sources: GNP deflator index:
  Computed from GNP at current and constant prices, *Economic Survey,* 1967 and 1969, for 1959 through 1969; and Birmingham *et al., Economy of Ghana,* p. 50, for 1956 through 1958.
Consumer price index:
  International Monetary Fund, *International Financial Statistics,* 1971 Supplement, pp. 90, 91, for 1956 through 1969; and *ibid.,* December 1972, pp. 152, 153, for 1970 through 1971.
Wholesale price index:
  International Monetary Fund, *International Financial Statistics,* 1971 Supplement, pp. 90, 91, for 1961 through 1969; and *ibid.,* December 1972, pp. 152, 153, for 1970 through 1971.

Table A-3a

Ghana: balance of payments, 1956–1971 (in millions of U.S. dollars)

	1956 Credit	1956 Debit	1957 Credit	1957 Debit	1958 Credit	1958 Debit	1959 Credit	1959 Debit	1960 Credit	1960 Debit
A. Goods and services	264.60	295.4	287.84	320.60	328.72	287.56	349.72	369.04	364.0	458.92
Merchandise, f.o.b.	239.12	230.44	261.24	249.48	299.88	218.68	316.40	299.04	333.76	348.04
Transportation and mdse. ins.	3.92	31.36	4.48	34.72	5.04	32.76	8.4	33.04	7.56	45.08
Investment income	14.0	15.68	14.56	16.80	14.56	18.20	14.0	18.48	12.32	27.72
Other	7.56	17.92	7.56	19.60	9.24	17.92	10.92	18.48	10.36	38.08
Net goods and services	—	30.80	—	32.76	41.16	—	—	19.32	—	94.92
B. Transfers	2.80	5.60	1.96	5.88	2.52	9.52	1.68	7.84	1.96	15.40
Transfers: private	0.28	2.52	0.28	2.52	0.28	6.44	0.28	5.32	0.56	12.32
Transfers: central gov't.	2.52	3.08	1.68	3.36	2.24	3.08	1.40	2.52	1.40	3.08
Net transfers	—	2.80	—	3.92	—	7.00	—	6.16	—	13.44
Net current account	—	33.60	—	36.68	34.16	—	—	25.48	—	108.36
C. Capital flows (net)	49.0	—	19.04	—	—	39.20	54.04	—	159.60	—
Capital NIE: private	—	2.8	—	11.48	—	11.48	22.40	9.8	10.36	—
Capital NIE: central gov't.	45.92	—	31.08	3.36	—	17.08	42.56	11.2	138.6	1.68
Commercial banks: assets	5.60	—	—	0.56	—	9.80	4.48	—	—	13.16
Deposit money banks: liab.	0.28	—	3.36	—	—	0.84	5.60	—	25.48	—
D. Net monetary authorities	—	7.84	9.52	—	—	2.52	—	24.92	—	27.72
Monetary gold	—	—	—	—	—	—	—	—	—	5.6
IMF accounts	—	—	—	—	14.56	14.56	15.12	19.88	—	—
Other assets	—	7.84	7.28	—	—	2.52	—	20.16	15.68	39.20
Other liabilities	—	—	2.80	—	—	—	—	—	1.40	—
Net errors and omissions	—	7.56	8.12	—	7.56	—	—	3.64	—	23.52

Table A-3a (continued)

	1961 Credit	1961 Debit	1962 Credit	1962 Debit	1963 Credit	1963 Debit	1964 Credit	1964 Debit	1965 Credit	1965 Debit
A. Goods and services	362.4	494.4	347.9	410.6	340.1	448.0	354.2	429.1	358.7	570.8
Merchandise f.o.b.	332.5	384.7	319.9	310.1	307.0	336.6	321.4	321.5	321.2	439.4
Transportation and mdse. ins.	8.6	52.2	10.6	49.4	12.8	48.0	21.2	53.2	23.7	64.1
Investment income	10.0	25.4	8.4	22.6	8.1	33.3	6.0	23.8	4.4	31.4
Other	11.3	32.1	9.0	28.5	12.2	30.1	5.6	30.6	9.4	35.9
Net goods and services	–	132.0	–	62.7	–	107.9	–	74.9	–	212.1
B. Transfers	2.8	17.9	3.6	17.0	4.4	20.6	2.1	24.0	8.3	19.2
Transfers private	0.6	13.1	0.2	14.0	0.6	17.0	1.6	21.7	4.7	19.2
Transfers: central gov't.	2.2	4.8	3.4	3.0	3.8	3.6	0.5	2.3	3.6	–
Net transfers	–	15.1	–	13.4	–	16.2	–	21.9	–	10.9
Net current account	–	147.1	–	76.1	–	124.1	–	96.8	–	223.0
C. Capital flows (net)	128.2	–	81.9	–	96.0	–	75.1	–	149.5	–
Capital NIE: private	2.6	15.4	22.1		30.9		35.9	4.8	87.9	2.0
Capital NIE: central gov't.	198.0	67.7	52.3	6.1	97.5	42.8	81.6	31.5	102.1	52.8
Commercial banks: assets	40.5	–	10.0		3.6		0.2		1.2	
Deposit money banks: liab.	–	29.8	3.6		6.8			6.3	13.1	
D. Net monetary authorities	23.3	–	2.3		40.1		18.8		63.7	
Monetary gold	–	–	–		–		–		–	
IMF accounts	–	–	14.3		–		–		–	
Other assets	39.1	17.3	–	18.4	40.8		26.0	21.8	49.4	10.6
Other liabilities	1.5	–	6.4		0.4	1.1	14.6		78.9	54.0
Net errors and omissions	–	4.4	–	8.1	–	12.0	2.9		9.8	–

Table A-3a (continued)

	1966 Credit	1966 Debit	1967 Credit	1967 Debit	1968 Credit	1968 Debit	1969 Credit	1969 Debit	1970 Credit	1970 Debit	1971 Provisional Credit	1971 Provisional Debit
A. Goods and services	315.2	432.7	314.6	383.9	356.0	396.0	389.4	426.1	466.7	481.8	364.8	485.1
Merchandise f.o.b.	280.3	320.7	284.1	265.3	318.4	270.8	348.3	290.1	424.3	336.6	324.4	338.3
Transportation and mdse. ins.	18.2	56.4	18.0	51.9	21.6	51.4	20.0	65.1	25.6	71.0	23.5	70.2
Investment income	4.2	24.3	3.2	27.4	2.9	35.0	5.3	42.0	2.8	43.1	3.0	44.7
Other	12.5	31.3	9.3	39.3	13.1	38.8	15.8	28.9	14.0	31.1	13.9	31.9
Net goods and services	—	117.5	—	69.3	—	40.0	—	36.7	—	15.1	—	120.3
B. Transfers	10.1	17.7	4.7	19.9	5.1	21.0	4.8	17.1	5.6	16.9	6.9	14.6
Transfers: private	4.1	16.5	1.7	17.2	1.5	17.4	0.8	14.0	2.0	13.8	3.5	11.7
Transfers: central gov't.	6.0	1.2	3.0	2.7	3.6	3.6	4.0	3.1	3.6	3.1	3.4	2.9
Net transfers	—	7.6	—	15.2	—	15.9	—	12.3	—	11.3	—	7.7
Net current account	—	125.1	—	84.5	—	55.9	—	49.0	—	26.4	—	128.0
C. Capital flows (net)	105.0	—	34.3	—	38.0	—	60.8	—	53.2	—	84.9	—
Capital NIE: private	56.1	6.9	34.7	3.4	22.9	3.1	10.2	1.2	20.5	1.7	77.0	—
Capital NIE: central gov't.	57.1	7.9	26.5	7.1	45.5	24.7	57.6	21.7	62.5	17.1	39.6	10.3
Commercial banks: assets	—	1.7	1.7	—	0.7	—	—	0.1	—	3.8	—	21.4
Deposit money banks: liab.	8.3	—	—	18.1	—	3.3	16.0	—	—	7.2	—	—
D. Net monetary authorities	18.2	—	42.0	—	8.0	—	2.7	—	—	34.3	30.0	—
Monetary gold	—	—	—	—	—	—	—	—	—	—	—	—
IMF accounts	46.9	—	18.8	—	10.9	—	—	5.4	11.6	23.2	9.3	31.7
Other assets	27.0	25.8	18.4	3.4	6.7	16.3	37.0	—	22.0	33.2	52.4	—
Other liabilities	—	29.9	27.1	18.9	6.7	—	—	28.9	—	11.5	—	—
Net errors and omissions	1.9	—	8.2	—	9.9	—	—	14.5	7.5	—	13.1	—

Sources: IMF, *Balance of Payments Yearbook*, various issues.

Table A-3b

Ghana: foreign-exchange reserves: absolute; percent of exports; percent of imports, 1956-1970

	1956	1957	1958	1959	1960	1961	1962	1963
Foreign-exchange reserves (end of year in thousands of new cedis)	379,622	342,918	362,454	339,242	297,270	147,392	144,836	85,580
Value of exports (in thousands of new cedis)	173,198	183,204	209,116	226,718	231,979	228,981	230,097	217,619
Value of imports (in thousands of new cedis)	177,840	193,370	169,186	226,049	259,235	286,826	235,084	260,775
Foreign-exchange reserves as percent of exports	219.18	187.18	173.33	149.63	128.15	64.37	62.95	39.33
Foreign-exchange reserves as percent of imports	213.46	177.34	214.23	150.07	114.67	51.39	61.61	32.82

	1964	1965	1966	1967	1968	1969	1970
Foreign-exchange reserves (end of year in thousands of new cedis)	66,581	26,249	41,165	17,400	22,200	19,100	27,800
Value of exports (in thousands of new cedis)	229,279	226,883	191,394	246,800	342,040	397,658	467,379
Value of imports (in thousands of new cedis)	243,184	320,051	250,647	261,523	314,032	354,391	419,046
Foreign-exchange reserves as percent of exports	29.04	11.57	21.51	7.05	6.49	4.80	5.95
Foreign-exchange reserves as percent of imports	27.38	8.20	16.42	6.65	7.07	5.39	6.63

Sources and note: See next page.

Sources and note for Table A-3a

Sources: Value of exports

CBS, *Economic Survey*, 1969, Table 14, p. 35, for years 1959 through 1969.
CBS, *Statistical Yearbook*, 1965-66, Table 109, p. 145, for years 1956 through 1958.
Ghana Commercial Bank, *Annual Report for the Year Ended 30th June*, 1971, Table 1, p. 44, for year 1970.

Value of imports

CBS, *Economic Survey*, 1969, Table 14, p. 35, for years 1959 through 1969.
CBS, *Statistical Yearbook*, 1965-66, Table 109, p. 145, for years 1956 through 1958.
Ghana Commercial Bank, *Annual Report for the Year Ended 30th June*, 1971, Table 1, p. 44, for year 1970.

Foreign exchange reserves

1956: Bank of Ghana, *Report of the Board for the Financial Year Ended 30th June*, 1960, Appendix 5.
1957 through 1962: Bank of Ghana, *Report of the Board for the Financial Year Ended 30th June*, 1965, Table 9.
1963 through 1966: Bank of Ghana, *Quarterly Economic Bulletin*, July-December, 1966, Table XIII.
1967 through 1970: Bank of Ghana, *Report of the Board for the Financial Year Ended 30th June*, 1971, Statement 20, p. 60.

Note: Reserves include Central Bank, Commercial banks and Treasury and other official institutions for 1963—1969. Reserves include Treasury, Bank of Ghana, Cocoa Marketing Board, banking institutions, local authorities, higher educational institutions and other official and private institutions for 1956 through 1964. Reserves are as of end of period, valued at the exchange rate existing at the time.

Table A-4a

Ghana: commodity composition of trade, 1956–1970 (in thousands of new cedis and in percentages)

Imports by SITC Sections

	0		1		2		3		4		5		6	
	Value	Percent of total	Value	Percent of total	Value	Percent of total	Value	Percent of total	Value	Percent of total	Value	Percent of total	Value	Percent of total
1956	28,238	15.88	8,498	4.78	638	0.36	10,180	5.72	238	0.13	12,406	6.98	65,348	36.75
1957	34,876	18.04	7,848	4.06	734	0.38	13,690	7.08	332	0.17	14,388	7.44	68,942	35.65
1958	29,348	17.35	7,462	4.41	922	0.54	12,560	7.42	384	0.23	13,216	7.81	58,038	34.30
1959	38,230	16.91	8,540	3.78	744	0.33	12,620	5.58	280	0.12	17,974	7.95	72,966	32.28
1960	42,008	16.21	7,576	2.92	684	0.26	13,578	5.24	444	0.17	19,032	7.34	79,590	30.70
1961	52,472	18.64	7,022	2.49	1,750	0.62	13,066	4.64	908	0.32	20,242	7.19	88,924	31.58
1962	46,278	19.43	2,652	1.11	1,576	0.66	14,641	6.15	646	0.27	19,353	8.13	81,081	34.05
1963	36,903	14.16	2,388	0.92	1,860	0.71	15,268	5.86	1,678	0.64	19,153	7.35	84,271	32.34
1964	40,083	16.50	1,414	0.58	1,994	0.82	14,149	5.82	2,898	1.19	14,974	6.16	79,325	32.65
1965	35,329	11.11	2,299	0.72	3,077	0.97	13,169	4.14	2,999	0.94	20,147	6.33	108,444	34.09
1966	39,287	15.64	2,402	0.96	2,327	0.93	10,579	4.21	2,615	1.04	16,621	6.62	77,109	30.70
1967	43,210	16.52	3,403	1.30	3,672	1.40	15,474	5.92	3,427	1.31	32,756	12.53	72,258	27.63
1968	51,013	16.25	5,035	1.60	6,277	2.00	21,488	6.84	3,952	1.26	48,349	15.40	76,265	24.29
1969	55,178	15.57	1,611	0.45	5,393	1.52	22,871	6.45	5,862	1.65	55,093	15.55	97,438	27.49
1970	79,474	18.97	3,924	0.94	9,420	2.25	24,358	5.81	3,835	0.92	66,874	15.96	100,847	24.07

Table A-4a (continued)

Exports by SITC sections

	0		1		2		3		4		5		6	
	Value	Percent of total	Value	Percent of total	Value	Percent of total	Value	Percent of total	Value	Percent of total	Value	Percent of total	Value	Percent of total
1956	104,392	66.54			36,412	23.21							15,964	10.18
1957	102,206	62.97			59,384	36.59							598	0.37
1958	125,532	67.34			59,898	32.13							712	0.38
1959	140,876	69.36			61,354	30.21							708	0.35
1960	136,312	65.97			69,396	33.58							728	0.35
1961	142,986	68.49	182	0.09	61,120	29.28	28	0.01	48	0.02	126	0.06	1,908	0.91
1962	143,148	68.97	50	0.02	55,654	26.81	20	0.01	330	0.16	190	0.09	3,098	1.49
1963	144,693	74.15	2	0.001	44,084	22.59	152	0.08	172	0.09	312	0.16	2,538	1.30
1964	147,792	70.83	4	0.001	53,570	25.67	2,088	1.00	10	0.004	496	0.24	2,314	1.11
1965	150,110	72.23	0	0	50,259	24.18	2,118	1.02	7	0.003	306	0.15	1,644	0.79
1966	119,584	68.60	17	0.009	46,890	26.90	953	0.55	39	0.02	379	0.22	837	0.48
1967	159,005	70.93	0	0	47,538	21.21	1,575	0.70	325	0.14	826	0.37	9,347	4.17
1968	219,261	70.05	0	0	59,265	18.94	1,741	0.56	12	0.003	737	0.24	27,443	8.77
1969	189,292	61.54	2	0	63,507	20.65	2,080	0.68	79	0.03	745	0.24	44,878	14.59
1970	337,478	73.33	0	0	61,745	13.42	668	0.15	267	0.06	402	0.09	33,206	7.22

Table A-4a (continued)

Imports by SITC sections

	7		8		9		
	Value	Percent of total	Value	Percent of total	Value	Percent of total	Total
1956	34,220	19.24	14,492	8.15	3,574	2.01	177,834
1957	33,004	17.07	16,060	8.31	3,496	1.81	193,370
1958	30,360	17.94	13,894	8.21	3,002	1.77	169,186
1959	51,212	22.66	20,248	8.96	3,234	1.43	226,044
1960	67,432	26.01	25,278	9.75	3,598	1.39	259,222
1961	66,166	23.50	26,876	9.55	4,136	1.47	281,562
1962	51,784	21.74	17,651	7.41	2,492	1.05	238,156
1963	74,141	28.45	21,347	8.19	3,604	1.38	260,611
1964	71,259	29.33	15,045	6.19	1,834	0.75	242,974
1965	104,096	32.72	23,249	7.31	5,309	1.67	318,116
1966	82,190	32.72	15,160	6.04	2,907	1.16	251,199
1967	70,424	26.93	15,350	5.87	1,529	0.58	261,503
1968	85,968	27.38	13,950	4.44	1,637	0.52	313,935
1969	94,518	26.67	14,601	4.12	1,827	0.52	354,391
1970	108,132	25.80	16,376	3.91	5,805	1.39	419,047

Table A-4a (continued)

Exports by SITC sections

	7		8		9		Others		Total
	Value	Percent of total	Value	Percent of total	Value	Percent of total	Value	Percent of total	Value
1956							126	0.08	156,894
1957							116	0.07	162,304
1958							264	0.14	186,406
1959							166	0.08	203,104
1960							204	0.10	206,640
1961	912	0.44	710	0.34	754	0.36			208,772
1962	1,946	0.94	682	0.33	2,440	1.18			207,556
1963	1,494	0.77	216	0.11	1,472	0.75			195,134
1964	972	0.47	224	0.11	1,186	0.57			208,656
1965	1,522	0.73	86	0.04	1,772	0.85			207,823
1966	2,909	1.67	407	0.23	2,317	1.33			174,332
1967	536	0.24	114	0.05	4,889	2.18			224,156
1968	388	0.12	69	0.02	4,074	1.30			312,990
1969	257	0.08	107	0.03	6,650	2.16			307,596
1970	240	0.05	95	0.02	26,131	5.68			460,232

Table A-4a (concluded)

Imports by end-use

	1. Consumer goods		2. Materials		3. Capital equipment		4. Fuels and lubricants		Total
	Value	Percent of total	Value	Percent of total	Value	Percent of total	Value	Percent of total	Value
1956	96,278	54.14	45,730	25.71	26,920	15.14	8,910	5.01	177,838
1957	109,932	56.85	46,486	24.04	25,024	12.94	11,928	6.17	193,370
1958	92,200	54.50	42,340	25.03	23,488	13.88	11,158	6.60	169,186
1959	113,768	50.33	58,908	26.06	42,412	18.76	10,960	4.85	226,048
1960	129,496	49.95	61,840	23.85	56,106	21.64	11,792	4.55	259,234
1961	141,189	49.43	79,027	27.66	53,470	18.72	11,975	4.19	285,661
1962	111,808	47.88	65,936	28.24	42,696	18.29	13,050	5.59	233,490
1963	102,792	39.42	79,076	30.32	64,483	24.73	14,423	5.53	260,774
1964	81,584	33.54	82,762	34.03	64,900	26.68	13,973	5.75	243,219
1965	109,887	34.33	100,689	31.46	96,618	30.19	12,857	4.02	320,051
1966	77,652	30.98	86,005	34.31	76,637	30.58	10,353	4.13	250,647
1967	85,716	32.84	100,064	38.34	59,887	22.94	15,352	5.88	261,019
1968	90,612	28.85	123,939	39.47	78,261	24.92	21,220	6.76	314,032
1969	107,040	30.20	141,958	40.06	82,729	23.34	22,664	6.40	354,391

Notes: SITC 1-digit sections are: 0, food and live animals; 1, beverages and tobacco; 2, crude materials; 3, mineral fuels, lubricants; 4, animal and vegetable oils; 5, chemicals; 6, manufactured goods; 7, Machinery and transport equipment; 8, Misc. manufactured articles; 9. Others.

Sources: Exports and imports by SITC classification
1956, United Nations, *Yearbook of International Trade Statistics, 1959.*
1957 through 1960, United Nations, *Yearbook of International Trade Statistics, 1961.*
1961, United Nations, *Yearbook of International Trade Statistics, 1964.*
1962 through 1963, United Nations, *Yearbook of International Trade Statistics, 1965.*
1964, United Nations, *Yearbook of International Trade Statistics, 1967.*
1965, United Nations, *Yearbook of International Trade Statistics, 1968.*
1966 through 1969, United Nations, *Yearbook of International Trade Statistics, 1969.*
1970, CBS, *External Trade Statistics,* December 1970.

Sources: Imports by end-use classification
1966 through 1969, Central Bureau of Statistics, *Economic Survey,* 1969, p. 37.
1964 through 1965, Central Bureau of Statistics, *Economic Survey,* 1968, pp. 125, 126.
1963, Central Bureau of Statistics, *Economic Survey,* 1966, p. 31.
1961 through 1962, Central Bureau of Statistics, *Economic Survey,* 1963, p. 43.
1956 through 1960, Central Bureau of Statistics, *Statistical Year Book,* 1963, p. 133.

Table A-4b
Ghana: geographic composition of trade, 1959–1969
(in thousands of new cedis and in percentages)

	Sterling area excluding African countries				European economic community			
	Exports		Imports		Exports		Imports	
Year	Values to	Percent of total to	Values from	Percent of total from	Values to	Percent of total to	Values from	Percent of total from
1956	68,462	39.53	96,249	54.13	33,000	32.56	33,400	18.79
1957	73,904	40.34	94,540	48.88	54,000	29.48	37,000	19.13
1958	84,648	40.46	84,721	50.07	69,400	33.17	32,200	19.03
1959	76,903	33.91	105,124	46.52	85,800	37.83	50,400	22.30
1960	78,988	34.05	103,824	40.05	81,478	35.12	66,254	25.56
1961	72,557	31.52	114,990	40.26	73,393	31.88	61,966	21.69
1962	78,585	34.16	89,482	38.33	64,342	27.97	52,174	22.35
1963	67,863	31.17	94,106	36.08	62,213	28.58	66,057	25.33
1964	58,814	25.65	77,394	31.82	67,414	29.40	55,924	22.99
1965	51,718	22.80	88,008	27.50	63,091	27.81	68,476	21.40
1966	53,065	27.73	75,244	29.95	42,060	21.98	53,178	21.17
1967	81,312	32.92	90,798	34.69	48,947	19.82	53,139	20.30
1968	108,879	31.83	102,060	32.50	88,266	25.81	63,894	20.35
1969	121,111	30.46	110,116	31.07	101,011	25.40	74,346	20.98

Table A-4b

	Dollar area				Centrally planned economies			
	Exports		Imports		Exports		Imports	
	Values to	Percent of total to	Values from	Percent of total from	Values to	Percent of total to	Values from	Percent of total from
1956	33,600	19.40	10,000	5.62	4,200	2.42	3,600	2.02
1957	30,800	16.81	15,000	7.76	12,400	6.77	5,400	2.79
1958	41,400	19.79	13,400	7.92	800	0.38	5,200	3.07
1959	44,800	19.75	20,200	8.94	4,800	2.12	7,600	3.36
`1960	36,874	15.90	21,490	8.29	16,774	7.23	•11,084	4.28
1961	56,782	24.66	31,407	10.99	10,940	4.75	15,614	5.47
1962	45,034	19.57	26,479	11.34	20,418	8.87	17,408	7.46
1963	36,754	16.88	22,853	8.76	29,830	13.70	28,597	10.96
1964	52,436	22.87	28,176	11.58	27,108	11.82	38,598	15.87
1965	42,107	18.56	33,758	10.55	48,264	21.27	84,158	26.30
1966	32,407	16.93	43,868	17.46	40,233	21.02	38,106	15.17
1967	44,444	17.99	47,907	18.31	37,058	15.00	21,834	8.34
1968	70,493	20.61	67,447	21.48	31,651	9.25	24,149	7.69
1969	82,134	20.65	71,803	20.26	28,804	7.24	31,209	8.81

	African countries				Japan			
	Exports		Imports		Exports		Imports	
Year	Values to	Percent of total to	Values from	Percent of total from	Values to	Percent of total to	Values from	Percent of total from
1956	4,778	2.76	11,382	6.40	–	–	18,000	10.12
1957	3,864	2.11	12,774	6.60	–	–	20,600	10.65
1958	5,250	2.51	12,728	7.52	–	–	13,600	8.04
1959	4,712	2.08	16,170	7.15	1,200	0.53	17,200	7.61
1960	8,144	3.51	17,762	6.85	1,790	0.77	21,674	8.36
1961	6,492	2.82	20,989	7.35	3,250	1.41	22,077	7.73
1962	8,110	3.53	15,642	6.70	4,930	2.14	15,481	6.63
1963	3,992	1.83	17,643	6.76	7,400	3.40	16,105	6.17
1964	4,626	2.02	22,760	9.36	8,172	3.56	13,034	5.36
1965	4,360	1.92	13,225	4.13	5,225	2.30	13,855	4.33
1966	4,041	2.11	10,723	4.27	9,388	4.91	13,348	5.31
1967	4,618	1.87	11,100	4.24	17,004	6.88	15,749	6.02
1968	3,744	1.09	11,974	3.81	23,108	6.76	17,332	5.52
1969	3,727	0.94	17,297	4.88	28,204	7.09	20,772	5.86

Table A-4b

	Others (including parcel post)				Totals	
	Exports		Imports		Exports	Imports
Year	Values to	Percent of total to	Values from	Percent of total from	Values	Values
1956	6,160	3.56	5,169	2.91	173,200	177,800
1957	8,232	4.49	8,086	4.18	183,200	193,400
1958	7,702	3.68	7,351	4.34	209,200	169,200
1959	8,585	3.78	9,306	4.12	226,800	226,000
1960	7,918	3.41	17,146	6.61	231,966	259,234
1961	6,807	2.96	18,607	6.51	230,221	285,649
1962	8,646	3.76	16,815	7.20	230,064	233,481
1963	9,655	4.43	15,457	5.93	217,708	260,819
1964	10,710	4.67	7,334	3.02	229,280	243,220
1965	12,116	5.34	18,571	5.80	226,881	320,051
1966	10,199	5.33	16,742	6.66	191,393	251,209
1967	13,611	5.51	21,180	8.09	246,994	261,707
1968	15,899	4.65	27,176	8.65	342,040	314,032
1969	32,667	8.21	28,848	8.14	397,658	354,391

Sources: 1966 through 1969, Central Bureau of Statistics, *Economic Survey,* 1969, Table 21, p. 46.
1965, Central Bureau of Statistics, *Economic Survey*, 1968, Table 21, p. 51.
1964, Central Bureau of Statistics, *Economic Survey*, 1967, Table 18, p. 41.
1961 through 1963, Central Bureau of Statistics, *Economic Survey*, 1965, Table 16, p. 39.
1960, Central Bureau of Statistics, *Economic Survey*, 1963, Table 17, p. 48.
1956 through 1959, Central Bureau of Statistics, *Statistical Year Book*, 1963, Tables 120, 121, and 122, pp. 120, 122, and 123.

Table A-5
Ghana: Ventral government accounts, 1957/58−1969
(in millions of new cedis)

	1957/58	1958/59	1959/60	1960/61
I. Current revenue				
(1) Income from property and entrepreneurship	6.712	8.598	7.670	13.968
(2) Taxes on production and expenditure	81.014	91.360	90.444	92.284
(3) Taxes on income and fines	16.012	16.138	14.866	17.836
(4) Grants	6.068	4.652	2.188	2.702
(5) Sales, fees and other items	10.346	13.074	13.900	17.410
Total current revenue	120.152	133.822	129.068	144.200
Less refund of revenue	0.104	0.126	0.118	0.336
Total net current revenue	120.048	133.696	128.950	143.864
II. Current expenditure				
(1) Consumption expenditure	54.660	63.152	68.638	90.140
(2) Interest on public debt	1.698	1.662	1.724	3.032
(3) Rent	0.168	0.532	0.440	0.644
(4) Subsidies	0.334	0.008	0.432	1.166
(5) Pensions	3.510	3.310	3.038	2.830
(6) Other transfers	18.036	22.612	26.320	36.178
Total current expenditure	78.406	91.276	100.592	143.868
III. Saving (=I−II)	41.640	42.420	28.358	9.878
IV. Capital receipts				
(1) Savings on current account	41.640	42.420	28.358	9.878
(2) Repayment of loans	0.182	0.196	0.190	0.372
(3) Capital taxes				
(4) Other capital receipts	4.652	4.802	2.984	4.286
(5) Capital transfers	0.072	−	11.204	22.254
(6) Borrowings	−	8.060	44.562	26.114
Total capital receipts	46.546	55.478	87.298	62.904
V. Capital disbursements				
(1) Capital expenditures	19.374	24.652	36.472	62.818
(2) Transfer payments	7.562	8.092	19.358	19.088
(3) Loans and advances	12.060	32.194	21.608	19.522
(4) Loan repayments	8.050	1.186	9.252	2.610
(5) Changes in reserves: (increase = +)	−0.502	−10.644	0.610	−41.134
Total capital disbursements	46.544	55.480	87.300	62.904

Notes: 1957/58 through 1960/61 are July-through-June fiscal years. 1960 through 1969 are calendap years.

Table A-5 (concluded)

1961	1962	1963	1964	1965	1966	1967	1968	1969
6.716	3.903	5.011	4.563	4.525	5.625	13.481	10.517	9.677
102.964	103.600	121.854	128.682	192.417	152.256	166.102	198.527	232.427
23.891	24.501	21.835	56.693	57.516	54.066	52.395	61.926	67.830
1.252	0.010	0.010	0.010	2.083	0.238	0.238	0.451	0.600
18.979	20.569	20.627	25.613	26.014	18.029	21.276	26.265	21.373
153.802	152.583	169.337	215.561	282.555	230.214	253.492	297.686	331.907
0.353	0.162	0.143	0.130	0.155	0.541	0.930	0.273	0.300
153.449	152.421	169.194	215.431	282.400	229.673	252.562	297.413	331.607
96.824	93.834	102.588	119.855	132.906	105.586	124.159	154.769	177.268
3.291	4.772	5.352	12.487	14.053	19.102	25.089	26.695	29.244
0.710	0.814	0.620	0.561	0.559	0.717	0.896	0.896	0.859
0.130	0.405	1.034	5.773	0.338	0.001	0.002	0.002	0.001
2.907	3.207	3.482	3.619	3.673	5.159	6.746	21.892	10.990
38.225	44.302	48.496	59.307	68.226	73.051	88.246	95.927	96.498
142.087	147.334	161.572	201.602	219.755	203.616	245.138	300.181	314.860
11.362	5.087	7.622	13.829	26.645	26.057	7.424	−2.768	16.776
11.362	5.087	7.622	13.829	26.645	26.057	7.424	−2.768	27.645
0.294	4.192	0.131	0.104	0.008	0.008	0.220	1.859	5.735
0.089	0.195	0.370	0.530	1.424	0.661	0.542	0.258	0.139
1.721	10.226	1.894	−6.014	6.717	9.807	18.253	24.186	2.346
19.692	0.024	0.010	37.240	−	−	−	−	−
36.019	78.986	132.565	89.008	103.700	137.307	56.529	99.392	77.993
69.177	98.710	142.592	134.697	138.494	173.840	82.968	122.927	113.858
69.862	76.698	69.118	83.020	101.305	46.561	41.582	48.639	44.879
20.923	23.955	35.598	44.924	40.666	18.199	27.017	18.701	11.324
38.479	−0.041	−8.480	−0.247	7.021	34.632	15.020	5.545	8.465
2.537	6.610	3.351	44.248	24.267	54.176	5.571	52.625	34.165
−62.625	−8.512	+43.004	−37.248	+1.235	+20.271	−6.222	−2.584	+4.154
69.176	98.710	142.591	134.697	174.494	173.839	82.968	122.926	102.987

Sources: 1961 through 1969, Central Bureau of Statistics, *Economic Survey,* 1969, Tables
IV, V, VI, VII, pp. 110-113.
1957/58 through 1960/61, Central Bureau of Statistics, *Economic Survey,* 1963,
Tables III, IV, V, VI, pp. 128-131.

APPENDIX B

TARIFF RATES AT SITC 1-DIGIT LEVEL

In Table II-1 of Chapter II we report our aggregate calculations of the effective exchange rates facing imports from 1955 through 1971, taking into account not only tariffs but also indirect taxes, surcharges, and other trade impediments operating on the price of imports. Full details of these effects for all years were not available at a disaggregated level of classification such as the SITC 1-digit sections. However, data on tariff collections were available on this disaggregated basis for the period 1955 through 1969. Because there is such a wide variation between sections, it is worth recording these details. Further, the conversion of the tariff rate into an effective exchange rate facilitates comparison between the pre-1967 and post-1967 situations. The data are contained in Table B-1.

Table B-1

Import tariff rates and effective exchange rates due to tariffs only by SITC 1-digit sections, 1955–1969
(tariff rates in percentages, effective exchange rates in new cedis per dollar)

Section	0 Food & L. anim.		1 Bev. & tob.		2 Crude mat.		3 Fuels & lubric.		4 Oils & fats	
Year	Tm	EERm	Tm	EERm	Tm	EERm	Tm	EERm	Tm	EERm
1955	2.1	0.73	141.1	1.72	1.1	0.72	42.8	1.02	—	0.71
1956	2.2	0.73	137.5	1.70	3.5	0.74	49.2	1.07	—	0.71
1957	2.1	0.73	122.3	1.59	3.8	0.74	45.3	1.04	—	0.71
1958	2.4	0.73	106.0	1.47	2.6	0.73	55.8	1.11	—	0.71
1959	2.3	0.73	99.3	1.42	3.8	0.74	61.3	1.15	—	0.71
1960	2.4	0.73	132.7	1.66	5.8	0.76	58.1	1.13	—	0.71
1961	8.3	0.77	138.4	1.70	23.0	0.88	91.8	1.37	0.4	0.72
1962	20.2	0.86	189.1	2.07	19.3	0.85	105.4	1.47	3.7	0.74
1963	30.2	0.93	218.7	2.28	29.2	0.92	120.6	1.58	13.9	0.81
1964	28.9	0.92	107.2	1.91	21.5	0.87	148.8	1.78	9.9	0.78
1965	36.2	0.97	66.4	1.19	71.2	1.22	52.2	1.09	11.0	0.79
1966	34.5	0.96	142.4	1.73	10.2	0.79	207.9	2.20	11.0	0.79
1967A	35.6	0.97	158.4	1.85	4.6	0.75	133.8	1.67	9.7	0.78
1967B	17.3	1.20	147.6	2.53	4.3	1.06	123.8	2.28	10.1	1.12
1968	12.3	1.15	80.2	1.84	3.9	1.06	92.0	1.96	10.2	1.12
1969	13.3	1.16	204.6	3.11	5.1	1.07	83.6	1.87	9.3	1.12

Notes: 1967A is January through June at the old official exchange rate (N₵ 0.714/dollar).
1967B is July through December at the new official exchange rate (N₵ 1.02/dollar).

Sources: CBS, *Quarterly Digest of Statistics*, 1956–1969 Issues (imports and import duties by section).

Table B-1. (concluded)

Section Year	5 Chemicals		6 Manufactures		7 Mach. & transp. E.		8 Misc. mfg.		9 NEC		Total	
	Tm	EERm	Tm	EERm	Tm	EERm	Tm	EERm	Tm	EERm	Tm	EERm
1955	17.0	0.84	9.9	0.79	2.1	0.73	16.0	0.83	15.8	0.83	17.1	0.84
1956	16.5	0.83	11.1	0.79	2.2	0.73	16.9	0.84	17.6	0.84	17.1	0.84
1957	15.8	0.83	15.0	0.82	2.5	0.73	19.3	0.85	18.2	0.84	17.5	0.84
1958	15.9	0.83	14.0	0.81	2.9	0.73	18.2	0.84	18.6	0.85	17.6	0.84
1959	14.1	0.82	13.3	0.81	2.3	0.73	18.2	0.84	17.5	0.84	15.4	0.82
1960	14.3	0.82	18.0	0.84	3.6	0.74	19.8	0.86	17.6	0.84	17.0	0.84
1961	16.1	0.83	22.4	0.87	5.4	0.75	23.8	0.88	19.0	0.85	21.5	0.87
1962	19.1	0.85	26.0	0.90	3.8	0.74	25.1	0.89	18.5	0.85	25.9	0.90
1963	19.8	0.86	25.0	0.89	4.1	0.74	26.7	0.90	16.1	0.83	26.8	0.91
1964	22.0	0.87	25.8	0.90	3.3	0.74	24.6	0.89	116.3	1.55	27.9	0.91
1965	24.7	0.89	37.1	0.98	3.4	0.74	40.4	1.00	43.4	1.02	26.5	0.90
1966	20.1	0.86	32.2	0.94	4.9	0.75	35.5	0.97	13.2	0.81	30.8	0.93
1967A	14.1	0.81	26.9	0.91	6.8	0.76	25.4	0.90	40.6	1.00	29.0	0.92
1967B	10.9	1.13	31.8	1.34	6.5	1.09	22.9	1.25	29.1	1.32	25.9	1.28
1968	8.3	1.10	24.0	1.27	6.2	1.08	23.9	1.26	85.3	1.89	20.1	1.23
1969	6.8	1.09	16.2	1.19	6.9	1.09	22.3	1.25	32.0	1.35	17.1	1.19

APPENDIX C

FORMULAS, DATA, AND METHODS FOR CALCULATING RATES OF PROTECTION

This Appendix is for the reader interested in the details of how we derived the formulas and handled the various data problems encountered in calculating the rates of protection reported in Chapter III.

1. Derivation of formulas

Given the usual relationship between the value of output (X_j), the value of material inputs $(\Sigma_i X_{ij})$, and value-added (V_j) at free-trade prices, we want to know the way in which trade distortions affect each of the elements:

$$X_j = V_j + \Sigma_i X_{ij} .$$

(C.1)

To simplify the analysis we will assume fixed physical coefficients of production.[1]

If the quota is the binding constraint on imports, the set of distortions results in an inflation of equation (C.1) in the following way:

$$X_j (1 + rb_j) (1 + qr_j) = \{V_j (1 + f_j) + \Sigma_i X_{ij} [(1 + rb_i)(1 + t_i) + r_i + l_i]\}(1 + sd_j)$$

where

(C.2)

qr = the rate of excess of domestic price over world price due to the quota restriction;

rb = the higher c.i.f. price charged importers due to the compulsory credit on imports, as a proportion of the c.i.f. free-trade price;

f = the effective rate of protection of value-added;

t = tariff rate on imports;

sd = indirect tax rate on domestic production;

---

1. For a specification of the usual set of assumptions, see J. Clark Leith, "Substitution and Supply Elasticities in Calculating the Effective Protective Rate," *op. cit.*

r = interest charge on compulsory credit on imports, as a proportion of the c.i.f. value;

l = import-licensing fee as a proportion of the c.i.f. value.

The inflation of (C.1) to yield (C.2) involves the following elements: The left-hand side is inflated first, due to the effect of the compulsory credit on imports whereby all importers must obtain a 180-day credit from the supplier. As a result, the c.i.f. cost of competing imports is increased by some amount over and above what it would be in the absence of this requirement. Part of this increased cost appears as a higher invoice price and hence is part of the base on which subsequent distortions build. We have labeled this portion the rate rb. The remaining part enters as an interest charge which is not part of the invoiced cost but is nevertheless a part of the cost of goods to the importers. We have used the rate r for this part when it appears. The second inflation of the left-hand side is due to the quota premium.

On the right-hand side of (C.2) we consider first the material input costs. Importable inputs are inflated due to the 180-day credit scheme (rb_i and r_i), input tariffs (t_i) and an import-licence fee (l_i). Manufacturers are exempt, from indirect taxes on inputs purchased for further processing; hence indirect taxes do not enter into the input cost structure. Second, the value-added is inflated by the residual, the effective rate of protection. Finally, the entire right-hand side is inflated by the domestic indirect taxes (sd).

Our data reflect the protected situation; hence for estimation purposes we must deflate the protected data relationship:

$$X'_j = V'_j + \Sigma_i X'_{ij} \tag{C.3}$$

where the primes indicate values at protected prices. The deflation of (C.3) proceeds in exactly the same way as the inflation of (C.1) to yield (C.2), with one exception. Our output data are at ex-factory prices exclusive of domestic indirect taxes. Hence the left-hand side of (C.3) is deflated not by qr_j, but by the rate of ex-factory mark-up over free-trade prices, for which we use the symbol q_j.[2] This also means that we do not deflate the entire right-hand side by the domestic indirect tax rate. The deflation of (C.3) then is:

$$\frac{X'_j}{(1 + rb_j)(1 + q_j)} = \frac{V'_j}{1 + f_j} + \Sigma_i \frac{X'_{ij}}{(1 + rb_i)(1 + t_i) + r_i + l_i}. \tag{C.4}$$

Solving for f_j, we obtain the effective rate of protection in the quota-constrained case, i.e., QR ERP$_j$:

2. Algebraically, $1 + q_j = (1 + qr_j)/(1 + sd_j)$, or: $q_j = (qr_j - sd_j)/(1 + sd_j)$.

$$\text{QR ERP}_j = \cfrac{V_j'}{\cfrac{X_j'}{(1 + rb_j)(1 + q_j)} - \Sigma_i \cfrac{X_{ij}'}{(1 + rb_i)(1 + t_i) + r_i + l_i}} - 1 \qquad \text{(C.5)}$$

Equation (C.5) applies when the quota is the binding constraint on imports. When it is not, the left-hand side of (C.4) is deflated by the tariffs and indirect taxes, yielding:

$$\frac{X_j'(1 + sd_j)}{(1 + rb_j)(1 + t_j)(1 + sm_j) + r_j + l_j} =$$

$$\frac{V_j'}{1 + f_j} + \Sigma_i \frac{X_{ij}'}{(1 + rb_i)(1 + t_i) + r_i + l_i} \qquad \text{(C.6)}$$

where

    sm = indirect tax rate on duty paid value of imports,
    sd = indirect tax rate on ex-factory value of domestic output.

The domestic indirect tax rate appears because $\overline{X_j'}$ is valued at ex-factory prices.

The difference between equations (C.4) and (C.6) lies solely on the left-hand side. This simplifies the test for whether or not the quota is binding. The quota is binding when the deflation of X_j' due to quotas exceeds the deflation due to tariffs and indirect taxes, i.e., when:

$$(1 + rb_j)(1 + q_j) > \frac{(1 + rb_j)(1 + t_j)(1 + sm_j) + r_j + l_j}{(1 + sd_j)}. \qquad \text{(C.7)}$$

When the inequality (C.7) does not hold, we simply substitute the right-hand side of (C.7) for the left-hand side in the deflation of X_j in (C.4) and (C.5).

Turning to the net rate of protection of output, in terms of the analysis above:

$$\text{NRP}_j = f_j \frac{V_j}{X_j}. \qquad \text{(C.8)}$$

Equation (C.8) can be converted to values at protected prices, utilizing the following relationships obtained from comparing (C.1) and (C.4).

$$X_j = X_j' / (1 + q_j)(1 + rb_j)$$
$$V_j = V_j' / (1 + f_j)$$
$$X_{ij} = X_{ij}' / [(1 + rb_i)(1 + t_i) + r_i + l_i]. \qquad \text{(C.9)}$$

Substituting from (C.9) into (C.8) for the case of QR's yields:

$$\text{QR NRP}_j = (\text{QR ERP}_j) \cdot \frac{V_j'}{(1 + \text{QR ERP}_j)} \cdot \frac{(1 + q_j)(1 + rb_j)}{X_j'} \cdot \qquad \text{(C.10)}$$

Calculation of the protection due to tariffs and indirect taxes is done by first determining the input and output values at free-trade prices, shown on the left-hand side of the relationships (C.9) and then applying the set of tariffs and indirect taxes to the world price data.[3]
Given X_j, X_{ij}, and V_j, we inflate the relationship (C.1) to obtain:

$$X_j \left[(1 + rb_j)(1 + t_j)(1 + sm_j) + r_j + l_j \right] =$$

$$\left\{ V_j (1 + f_j) + \Sigma_i \left[X_{ij}((1 + rb_i)(1 + t_i) + r_i + l_i) \right] \right\}(1 + sd_j) . \quad \text{(C.11)}$$

Solving for f_j yields the effective rate of protection due to tariffs and indirect taxes, TAR ERP$_j$:

$$\text{TAR ERP}_j =$$

$$\frac{[(1+rb_j)(1+t_j)(1+sm_j) + r_j + l_j]/(1+sd_j) - \Sigma_i a_{ij}[(1+rb_i)(1+t_i)+r_i+l_i]}{v_j} - 1$$

$$\text{(C.12)}$$

where $a_{ij} = X_{ij}/X_j$ and $v_j = V_j/X_j$. And utilizing the value of TAR ERP$_j$ obtained from (C.12), we can solve for the net rate of protection due to tariffs and indirect taxes, TAR NRP$_j$:

$$\text{TAR NRP}_j = \frac{(\text{TAR ERP}_j) V_j}{X_j} . \qquad \text{(C.13)}$$

Finally, to calculate the surcharge-inclusive rates of protection, we inflate

---

3. It is important to note that in general, consideration of any change in the protective structure must use world price input and output values. In the case of a reduction in protection such as is implied in the hypothetical comparison of protection due to tariffs with the actual protection due to QR's, use of the original protected data would understate the protection in the new situation. See J. Clark Leith,"Across-the-Board Nominal Tariff Changes and the Effective Rate of Protection," *op. cit.*, p. 983.

(C.1) in the same way as we obtained (C.11) with the addition of t^*, which is the rate of surcharge on the c.i.f. value:

$$X_j[(1 + rb_j)(1 + t_j + t_j^*)(1 + sm_j) + r_j]$$

$$= \{ V_j(1 + f_j) + \Sigma_i [X_{ij}((1 + rb_i)(1 + t_i + t_i^*) + r_i)] \}(1 + sd_j). \quad (C.14)$$

Solving for f_j, the effective rate of protection due to tariffs plus surcharges is:

TAR + SCHG ERP$_j$

$$= \frac{[(1 + rb_j)(1 + t_j + t_j^*)(1 + sm_j) + r_j]/(1 + sd_j) - \Sigma_i a_{ij}[(1 + rb_i)(1 + t_i + t_i^*) + r_i]}{v_j} - 1 .$$

$$(C.15)$$

The net rate of protection is simply:

$$\text{TAR} + \text{SCHG NRP}_j = \frac{(\text{TAR} + \text{SCHG ERP}_j) V_j}{X_j} . \quad (C.16)$$

2. Data sources and methods

(a) Input–output data

For each establishment identified by an industry and establishment code we had the following information extracted from the CBS Industrial Survey returns:

(a) Finished goods:
  (1) for each item, quantity and value produced, sold, stocks at beginning and stocks at end;
  (2) for total only, sales and excise taxes paid.
(b) Materials:
  (1) for each item, quantity and value purchased and consumed, stocks at beginning and stocks at end;
  (2) for imported items, quantity and value of each item purchased and total customs duties paid.
(c) Fuels: for each item, quantity and value purchased and consumed, stocks at beginning and stocks at end.
(d) Electricity: quantity and value purchased, generated, sold and consumed.

The data we received required some editing. We initially checked for completeness of each establishment's entries and were forced to omit a few. We also omitted a number of essentially non-traded domestic sectors, such as bakeries and printing. For the remaining establishments we checked:

(a) Addition of item values for total.

(b) Implied versus stated stock changes. This revealed a number of omissions in individual item entries, and emphasized provision (c) below.

(c) Inclusion of import duties in material values. Almost all establishments, contrary to CBS instructions, excluded import duties and transport charges from the factory-delivered values of materials purchased and consumed, but not from their stock figures. We added them in such cases.

(d) Inclusion of capital equipment in purchase of materials. Several establishments included major capital equipment purchases in their material purchases, in some cases yielding negative value-added at domestic prices. We deducted them.

(e) Major inputs omitted. A few establishments failed to include major inputs in their returns (e.g., one cocoa butter factory omitted cocoa beans). We omitted such establishments.

After the editing we were able to compute the output, input, and value-added data implied by the production and use relationships.[4] In addition, the sales and excise taxes paid enabled us to calculate the indirect tax rate on domestic production: we used the ratio of sales and excise taxes paid to sales.[5]

(b) Tariff and tax data

We had two possible types of sources for our tariff and tax data: the schedules and the amounts paid. Since our primary concern was with the actual rather than with some hypothetical protection, we opted for the duties and taxes paid as our best indicator of the actual tariff and tax-imposed price rises relevant for each product produced and used by an establishment.

(1) Protection of output. Each item of an establishment's output was matched with the appropriate SITC 6-digit item. There were a few exceptions to this rule. In some cases, output was not specified in sufficient detail to

4. We used production and input use rather than sales and input purchases to avoid problems of inventory changes.

5. The use of purchases and sales data for calculating the imported input tariffs and sales and excise tax rates involves a misstatement to the extent that the mix of material purchases differs from material use and the mix of product sales differs from the mix of production when the rates vary between items. However, because only totals were available, we had no alternative but to adopt this procedure.

permit exact matching. Hence we had to group two or more 6-digit items. These were

Product	SITC 6-digit groups
Distillery products	112-410, 112-420, 112-430, 112-440, 112-450
Pharmaceuticals	all 541
Furniture	821-019, 820-099
Shirts	841-101, 841-102, 841-103
Logs (export tax)	all 242
Timber (export tax)	all 243 .

For each competing item or group of items the tariff and sales tax rate was computed, using collections of tariffs and sales taxes from CBS, *Customs Duties Collections by Trade Classification,* 1968, unpublished; and imports from CBS, *External Trade Statistics,* December 1968. Given the tariff and sales tax on imports competing with each item of an establishment's output, we computed a weighted average combined tariff and sales-tax rate protecting the establishment's output, the weights being free-trade production proportions.

(2) Tariffs on inputs. Directly imported inputs are by far the most significant portion of importable inputs used by Ghanaian industries. This is because all manufacturers are granted major duty concessions on imports of inputs, and some are granted additional exemptions often to the extent of duty-free imports of inputs for the first several years of production. Hence the cost inflation due to input tariffs can vary between firms using identical inputs. For this reason we had to rely on reported duties paid on directly imported inputs to calculate the cost inflation due to input tariffs. The input tariff rate was calculated from the duties paid and import purchases data. In our subsequent calculations this was applied to use data.

(3) Other inputs. Electricity, fuels, and lubricants, in addition to materials, are part of the inputs. We assumed electricity to be valued at free-trade prices. Petroleum fuels and lubricants, however, are higher priced because of protection. The question is, by how much?

Ghana has a petroleum refinery that uses imported crude to produce propane gas, gasoline, kerosene, and various fuel and diesel oils. No lubricants are domestically produced. The refinery receives the imported crude from the Ghana Supply Commission, refines it for a fee, and returns the output to the Supply Commission, which sells to wholesalers. We have been unable to determine the extent to which the refining fee exceeds what it would be under free trade. Hence, as a minimum estimate of the tariff and tax rate on petroleum fuels and lubricants we computed the following ratio:

$$\frac{\text{duties and taxes on imported items} + \text{domestic taxes on domestic items}}{\text{c.i.f. values of imports} + \text{domestic production}} .$$

Data for the numerator were from CBS, *Customs Duties Collections by Trade Classification,* 1968, unpublished; the import values from CBS, *External Trade Statistics,* December 1968; and domestic production from CBS, *Industrial Statistics,* 1966-1968, August 1970. The result was an average excess of 87.137 percent over free-trade cost of petroleum fuels and lubricants.

Because petroleum fuels and lubricants constitute a relatively small proportion of the input costs of the establishments covered, we used the average figure as our input tariff on petroleum fuels and lubricants. We assumed non-petroleum fuels (mostly firewood) to be unaffected by the tariff and tax structure.

(4) Other trade impediments. The 1 percent import licence fee is included in the calculations for 1968, but is dropped from the 1970 calculations because it was abolished effective December 31, 1968. For the cost of the 180-day credit scheme we used two alternative assumptions of the average across-the-board costs (see Chapter II, section 2): 8 percent and 15 percent, which pretty well brackets the possible averages. This is made up of 3 percent interest charge and a 5 percent or 12 percent higher price. Only the 8 percent assumption is reported in the text. The 15 percent assumption made little difference in the ranking, so is not reported separately. The results, however, are available on request.

(5) Special cases: exports and input subsidies. An industry that exports all or part of its product does not, of course, receive any protection of its exported output or may even face an export tax. These cases involved gold mining, bauxite mining, fruit squashes, kente weaving, cocoa butter and sawmilling. The nominal tariff-protecting output thus was set equal to zero, or the appropriate negative rate in the case of an export tax, and the import-licence fee and 180-day credit cost were also set equal to zero. Of the commodities covered in our data, the export tax applies only to lumber and logs. The average export tax rate for these was computed from the collections data as noted above.

There is a case of an input subsidy relative to costs under free trade. The two cocoa butter factories (only one is included in our results) purchase cocoa beans at a price lower than the export price received by the Cocoa Marketing Board. The subsidy rate was computed by taking the difference between actual per-ton cost paid by the factory and the average export unit value of cocoa beans for 1968 (the former from our establishment data and the latter from the trade data) as a proportion of the export unit value. The net subsidy rate amounted to 7.854 percent, which was treated as a negative input tariff of that rate.

(c) Supplementary information

There are a few industries whose domestic production nearly meets domestic demand. In these cases our assumption that the international price plus tariffs and taxes is the minimum rise in the domestic price is open to some doubt. We have indicated those industries in which domestic production exceeds 90 percent of domestic demand. This was done at the SITC 6-digit level, using our industry data and the trade statistics plus tariff and sales tax data from the collections.

A further piece of supplementary information concerns those items produced domestically that are under price control. While we are skeptical of the effectiveness of the price control legislation as it concerns the final consumer, the manufacturer is in a relatively conspicuous position and is less able to evade than the small retailer. To the extent then that the control price is a binding constraint on the price the manufacturer receives, our results overstate his protection. We have indicated the industries where this may be the case, drawing on the price control legislation contained in "The Price Control (Maximum Prices) Order, 1967" (L.I. 100).

APPENDIX D

DERIVATION OF PRODUCTION AND INPUT USE RESPONSES TO INPUT SUBSIDIES

Given the production function as defined in the text:

$$X = A \ K^{\alpha} L^{\beta} M_F^{\partial} M_D^{\gamma} \tag{D.1}$$

we want to know what impact various subsidies might have on output and input use. We retain the assumptions made in the text: (a) the price of output is given to the producers, and (b) the prices of all inputs but one are given to the producers, and the remaining input is available only at increasing costs.[1] Equation (D.1) can readily yield a unit cost function:

$$p_x = \frac{p_k^{\alpha} \cdot p_l^{\beta} \cdot p_{mf}^{\partial} p_{md}^{\gamma}}{c} \tag{D.2}$$

where $c = C\alpha^{\alpha} \beta^{\beta} \delta^{\partial} \gamma^{\gamma}$, which is a constant, and the p's represent unit prices of outputs and inputs.

Keeping p_x constant, we now introduce *ad valorem* subsidies on the prices of capital and imported materials at the rates sub_k and sub_{mf}:

$$p_x c = [p_k(1 - sub_k)]^{\alpha} \cdot [p_l(1 + dp_l/p_l)]^{\beta} \cdot [p_{mf}(1 - sub_{mf})]^{\delta} \cdot p_{md}^{\gamma} . \tag{D.3}$$

Recalling that the constraint on expanding output is the price of the one input available at increasing costs, we want to solve for the proportionate change in its price permitted by the subsidies on the other inputs (but with the output price constant). This is done by setting all other prices equal to unity (because we are only interested in proportionate price changes). Assume for the present that labor is the constraining input.[2] Then:

1. The method used here follows closely the approach we developed elsewhere in dealing with tariffs. See J. Clark Leith, "The Effect of Tariffs on Production, Consumption, and Trade: A Revised Analysis," *op. cit.*
2. The analysis is readily adjusted to handle a different input as the constraining one, which we do below.

$$1 = (1 - \text{sub}_k)^\alpha \cdot (1 + dp_l/p_l)^\beta \cdot (1 - \text{sub}_{mf})^\delta \cdot 1^\gamma . \tag{D.4}$$

And solving for dp_l/p_l:

$$dp_l/p_l = [(1 - \text{sub}_k)^{\bar{\alpha}} \cdot (1 - \text{sub}_{mf})^\delta]^{-1/\beta} - 1 . \tag{D.5}$$

The next step is to find the expression for change in the use of labor. This is given by dp_l/p_l, together with the elasticity of supply of labor to the using industry (e_l):

$$\frac{dL}{L} = \frac{dp_l}{p_l} \cdot e_l . \tag{D.6}$$

We also want to know by how much output expands. Defining a_l as the quantity of labor used per unit of output in the initial situation:

$$X \equiv L/a_l. \tag{D.7}$$

With the introduction of subsidies:

$$X(1 + dX/X) = \frac{L(1 + dL/L)}{a_l(1 + da_l/a_l)} . \tag{D.8}$$

And because (D.7) holds, then:

$$\frac{dX}{X} = \frac{1 + dL/L}{1 + da_l/a_l} - 1 . \tag{D.9}$$

To solve (D.9), we already have dL/L from (D.6), but we need to know da_l/a_l. Since β is the share of labor payments:

$$a_l \equiv \beta \frac{p_x}{p_l} . \tag{D.10}$$

With the introduction of subsidies we obtain:

$$a_l(1 + da_l/a_l) = \beta \frac{p_x}{p_l(1 + dp_l/p_l)} \tag{D.11}$$

and solve for da_l/a_l to obtain:

$$\frac{da_l}{a_l} = \frac{1}{1 + dp_l/p_l} - 1 . \tag{D.12}$$

Substituting from (D.5):

$$\frac{da_l}{a_l} = \frac{1}{[(1 - \text{sub}_k)^\alpha \cdot (1 - \text{sub}_{mf})^\delta]^{-1/\beta}} - 1 . \tag{D.13}$$

We can now substitute the expressions for dL/L and da_l/a_l into (D.9) to obtain:

$$\frac{dX}{X} = [1 + (dp_l/p_l)e_l] \cdot (1 + dp_l/p_l) - 1 . \tag{D.14}$$

Finally, we want to know the changes in input use. Non-subsidized input use will expand in the same proportion as output, but use of subsidized inputs will expand relatively more. In the same way as we derived (D.14) we can use the relationships:

$$a_k \equiv \alpha \frac{p_x}{p_k} , \quad a_{mf} \equiv \delta \frac{p_x}{p_{mf}} \tag{D.15}$$

where the a's are quantities per unit of output, to obtain:

$$\frac{da_k}{a_k} = \frac{1}{1 - \text{sub}_k} - 1 \tag{D.16}$$

and:

$$\frac{da_{mf}}{a_{mf}} = \frac{1}{1 - \text{sub}_{mf}} - 1 .$$

Then, from expanding the relationships:

$$X = \frac{K}{a_k} , \quad X \equiv \frac{M_f}{a_{mf}} \tag{D.17}$$

and solving for the proportionate changes in the quantity of capital and imported materials, we obtain:

$$\frac{dK}{K} = \frac{[1 + (dp_l/p_l)e_l] \cdot (1 + dp_l/p_l)}{1 - \text{sub}_k} - 1 \tag{D.18}$$

$$\frac{dM_F}{M_F} = \frac{[1 + (dp_l/p_l)e_l] \cdot (1 + dp_l/p_l)}{1 - \text{sub}_{mf}} - 1 .$$

We now have expressions showing the expansion of output: equation (D.14) and the expansion of input uses: equations (D.6) and (D.18) in response to the introduction of subsidies where labor is the constraining input. If however the constraining input is domestic materials, the relevant equations are as follows — the relative change in the price of domestic materials is·

$$\frac{dp_{md}}{p_{md}} = [(1 - \text{sub}_k)^\alpha \cdot (1 - \text{sub}_{mf})^\delta]^{-1/\gamma} - 1 . \tag{D.5'}$$

The rates of expansion of input uses are:

$$\frac{dM_D}{M_D} = \frac{dp_{md}}{p_{md}} \cdot e_{md} \qquad\qquad (D.6')$$

and:

$$\frac{dK}{K} = \frac{[1 + (dp_{md}/p_{md})e_{md}] \cdot (1 + dp_{md}/p_{md})}{1 - sub_k} - 1 \qquad\qquad (D.18')$$

$$\frac{dM_F}{M_F} = \frac{[1 + dp_{md}/p_{md})e_{md}] \cdot (1 + dp_{md}/p_{md})}{1 - sub_{mf}} - 1 .$$

Finally, the proportionate expansion of output is:

$$\frac{dX}{X} = [1 + dp_{md}/p_{md})e_{md}] \cdot (1 + dp_{md}/p_{md}) - 1 . \qquad\qquad (D.14')$$

APPENDIX E

DERIVATION OF FORMULAS – RATE OF CHANGE IN NEW CEDIS PER DOLLAR OF TRADEABLES

For a given commodity there are two important local currency prices. First there is the new-cedi price paid or received by domestic residents who are the ultimate purchasers or producers of tradeable goods, P_d. Second, there is another new-cedi price, P_f, which is the price paid or received at the frontier, and is the value that is subsequently translated into foreign exchange: for imports it is the before-duty price, and for exports it is the after-export-tax price. In other words, P_f is the new-cedi price at the ocean-side door of the customs shed. In addition, the price P_f may be denominated in dollars as $P_\$$.

If the devaluation is fully transmitted to the domestic price P_d, the change in the dollar price must be reflected fully in the price P_d. Thus the following relationship must hold, where r is the N¢/$ exchange rate and the primes indicate the post-devaluation situation:

$$\frac{P'_\$}{P_\$} = \frac{P'_f/r'}{P_f/r} = \frac{P'_d}{P_d} . \tag{E.1}$$

If however the devaluation is not fully transmitted, we can translate (E.1) into a relationship indicating the extent to which devaluation is reflected in domestic prices: the proportionate change in the new-cedis-per-dollar price facing domestic residents. The magnitude of the proportionate domestic price change relative to the base of the change in the dollar price is:[1]

$$\frac{\Delta (P_d/P_\$)}{P_d/P_\$} = \frac{P'_d}{P_d} \cdot \frac{P_f}{P'_f} \cdot \frac{r'}{r} - 1 . \tag{E.2}$$

---

1. This follows from the definition of $P_d/P_\$$ as $P_d r/P_f$. Hence the proportionate change is:

$$\frac{\Delta (P_d/P_\$)}{P_d/P_\$} = \left[\frac{P'_d r'}{P'_f} - \frac{P_d r}{P_f} \right] \cdot \frac{P_f}{P_d r} = \frac{P'_d}{P_d} \cdot \frac{P_f}{P'_f} \cdot \frac{r'}{r} - 1.$$

In cases of infinitely elastic supply of imports or infinitely elastic demand for exports we can simplify (E.2). Since under this assumption $P_f'/P_f = r'/r$, the expression becomes:

$$\frac{\Delta (P_d/P_\$)}{P_d/P_\$} = \frac{P_d'}{P_d} - 1. \qquad (E.2')$$

Our measures of the impact of the devaluation can be obtained in terms of relationships (E.2) or (E.2$'$) as appropriate.

1. Exports

Here we are concerned with the extent of the change in the new-cedi price of exports received by domestic producers of export goods. There are a number of important points to note in the analysis of the Ghanaian case. First, the elasticity of demand facing some Ghanaian exports may be (and clearly is in the case of cocoa) less than infinity. Consequently relationship (E.2) rather than (E.2$'$) holds. Devaluation shifts the demand curve upwards, in terms of local currency, by the proportion of the devaluation. Because of the less than infinitely elastic demand (assuming some positive elasticity of supply), the national export price rises proportionately less than the devaluation. However, as long as the export-tax rate remains constant the proportionate change in the producers' price equals the proportionate change in the national export price. For there to be a difference there must be some mechanism whereby the export tax rate changes.

This leads us to a second complication. Not all export taxes are explicit *ad valorem* rates. Some are implicit taxes and others are specific. In the cases of all the commodities handled by the State Cocoa Marketing Board (CMB), the export tax is a residual: the producer price is fixed by the CMB without direct reference to the export price.[2]

(a) Cocoa

The case of cocoa involves both the issue of less than infinitely elastic demand and an implicit export tax. This is illustrated in Figure E.1. The pre-devaluation foreign demand in terms of new cedis is the curve D, and the domestic supply curve is the curve S. The producer price of P_d must be explicitly increased by the CMB if the devaluation is to have any effect on export volume: if it were kept at P_d there would be no expansion of the quantity supplied, and the export price in terms of new cedis could rise to $P_f'^*$. For the devaluation to be fully transmitted, the proportionate change in the

2. There is also an export tax paid by the CMB, but this simply affects the initial distribution of the total implicit tax between the government treasury and the CMB.

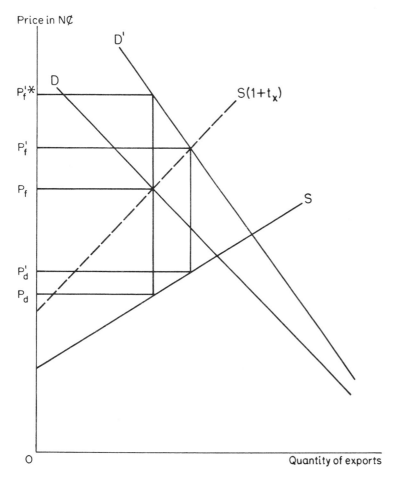

Fig. E.1. Devaluation and domestic market for exportables.

producer price [i.e. $(P'_d - P_d)/P_d$] must be equal to what the proportionate change in the foreign price would be if the export tax rate were to remain constant. To accomplish this graphically we draw an imaginary curve $S(1+t_x)$ above the supply curve S by the proportion of the existing tax rate $t_x(= P'_d, P'_f/OP_d)$. For the export-tax rate to remain constant, the producer price must rise to P'_d, yielding a foreign price P'_f. In other words, $(P'_d - P_d)/P_d$ must equal $(P'_f - P_f)/P_f$.

To determine the rate $(P'_f - P_f)/P_f$, given the rate devaluation and the demand and supply elasticities is the familiar incidence problem. We want to know $P_f' - P_f$ relative to $P_f'^* - P_f$, and both can be expressed *vis-à-vis* P_f. The solution for linear demand and supply curves is:

$$\frac{P_f' - P_f}{P_f} = \frac{dr}{r} \cdot \left[\frac{n}{n-e}\right] \tag{E.3}$$

where dr/r is the rate of devaluation and n and e are the demand and supply elasticities for Ghana.[3]

The actual magnitudes to be inserted in (E.3) are of course a problem. For the short-run (one to three years) some recent estimates of demand and supply elasticities yield $n = -0.58$ and $e = 0.17$ over the range relevant at the time of the devaluation.[4] Plugging these into (E.3):

$$\frac{P_f' - P_f}{P_f} = 0.4285 \left[\frac{-0.58}{-0.58 - 0.184}\right] = 0.325 .$$

In sum, to transmit the devaluation fully, the producer price would have to have been increased by about 33 percent, and this would have resulted in a new-cedi export price increase of the same percentage.[5]

(b) Timber

Another case of interest is timber, where the export taxes are specific.

3. The proof proceeds by noting:

$$\frac{P_f' - P_f}{P_f} = \frac{dr}{r} + \frac{dq}{q} \cdot \frac{1}{n}, \quad \text{where } dq/q \text{ is the proportionate change in the quantity}$$

demanded along the original demand curve. With some manipulation:

$$\frac{P_f' - P_f}{P_f}\left[1 - \frac{e}{n}\right] = \frac{dr}{r}, \text{ and hence: } \frac{P_f' - P_f}{P_f} = \frac{dr}{r} \cdot \frac{n}{n-e} .$$

4. M.J. Bateman, "Cocoa Study," *op. cit.,* finds that short-run supply elasticities are: for the Colony area (39 percent of output in 1966/67) $e = 0.1419$; and Ashanti/Brong-Ahafo area (60 percent of output in 1966/67) $e = 0.2146$. The average, weighted by 1966/67 output is: $e = 0.1840$. On the demand side his estimates of the elasticity facing Ghana depend on world price and market share. At a world price of 25 cents per pound and a market share of 29 percent, which approximates the situation for the 1966/67 crop year, interpolation yields a short run $n = -0.58$.

5. Note that we are considering only the question of the appropriate short-run response of the CMB in order to fully transmit the effect of the devaluation, given the short-run demand and supply elasticities for Ghana. The long-run issue of the appropriate producer price obviously requires a full specification of the objective function given the long-run demand and supply elasticities, both of which are considerably larger than in the short run. (See Chapter II, section 6.)

Here, in the absence of any change in the tax structure or specific charges,[6] the export tax rate would decline and prices paid domestic producers would rise proportionately more than the devaluation.

(c) Primary commodity exports

Finally, world prices of many of the primary commodity exports are constantly shifting. This can be thought of as movement of the demand curve facing Ghana. Hence as long as the export-tax rate is constant, the price facing domestic producers is a constant proportion of the dollar price, and the devaluation would be fully transmitted. But in making before-after comparisons as we do in the text, when export taxes are not explicit rates or are specific, the time period chosen for the before-after comparisons will, perhaps seriously, affect the results of our calculations. Nevertheless, whatever time period is under consideration, the appropriate comparison is between the change in the domestic price and the change in the export price.

2. Imports

The situation of early 1967 (most imports constrained by licences) is illustrated in Figure E.2. The curve ED is the excess demand for imports and P_f is the world price in terms of new cedis at the pre-devaluation exchange rate. Assuming an infinitely elastic supply of imports, and given an import licence valued at (OQ_1) (OP_f) new cedis, the quantity of imports is restricted to Q_1. When this quantity is placed on the domestic market for resale, it eventually fetches a price of OP_d. The price $P_f(1+t_m)$, where t_m is the *ad valorem* tariff rate on imports, is irrelevant in setting the domestic price level and hence in determining the level of imports. When devaluation occurs, assuming the dollar value of licences is kept constant, the c.i.f. value of the licences in terms of new cedis increases by the proportion of the devaluation to (OQ_1) (OP'_f), and the duty-paid price rises to $P'_f(1+t_m)$. Depending on the height of $P'_f(1+t_m)$ relative to P_d, the devaluation wipes out part or all of the premium attributable to the licence, and the price to domestic purchasers of imports rises not at all, or by less than the proportion of the devaluation. We have drawn Figure E.2 such that the licencee's premium is not entirely wiped out, and the price paid by ultimate purchasers is unchanged. (In terms of the foreign-exchange market, Figure V.1 in the text, this occurs when the postdevaluation price of foreign exchange is less than rm_0^*.) Of course, even when the licencee's premium is entirely eaten up by devaluation, the proportionate change in the domestic price will be less than

---

6. The tax is specific in local currency. And as long as foreign demand elasticity is (algebraically) less than zero, the local currency pre-tax price rises. Hence the tax rate declines.

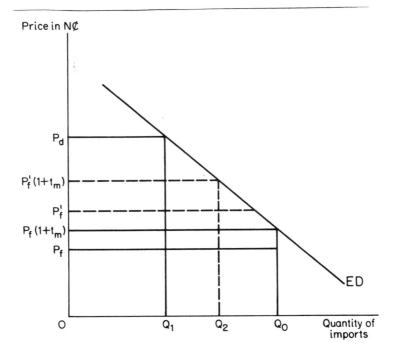

Fig. E.2. Devaluation and domestic market for importables.

the devaluation. In sum, it is the change in domestic price P_d that we want to measure as an indicator of the impact of devaluation on the licence-constrained situation of 1967.

APPENDIX F 1

DEFINITION OF CONCEPTS USED IN THE PROJECT

Exchange rates

(1) Nominal exchange rate: The official parity for a transaction. For countries maintaining a single exchange rate registered with the International Monetary Fund, the nominal exchange rate is the registered rate.

(2) Effective exchange rate (EER): The number of units of local currency actually paid or received for a one-dollar international transaction. Surcharges, tariffs, the implicit interest foregone on guarantee deposits, and any other charges against purchases of goods and services abroad are included, as are rebates, the value of import replenishment rights, and other incentives to earn foreign exchange for sales of goods and services abroad.

(3) Price-level-deflated nominal exchange rate: The nominal exchange rate deflated in relation to some base period by the price level index of the country.

(4) Price-level-deflated EER (PLD-EER): The EER deflated by the price level index of the country in question.

(5) Purchasing-powerparity adjusted exchange rate: The relevant (nominal or effective) exchange rate multiplied by the ratio of the foreign price level to the domestic prive level.

Devaluation

(1) Gross devaluation: The change in the parity registered with the IMF (or, synonymously in most cases, *de jure* devaluation).

(2) Net devaluation: The weighted average of changes in EER's by classes of transactions (or, synonymously in most cases, *de facto* devaluation).

(3) Real gross devaluation: The gross devaluation adjusted for the increase in the domestic price level over the relevant period.

(4) Real net devaluation: The net devaluation similarly adjusted.

Protection concepts

(1) Explicit tariff: The amount of tariff charged against the import of a good

as a percent of the import price (in local currency at the nominal exchange rate) of the good.

(2) Implicit tariff (or, synonymously, tariff equivalent): The ratio of the domestic price (net of normal distribution costs) minus the c.i.f. import price, to the c.i.f. import price in local currency.

(3) Premium: The windfall profit per dollar of imports accruing to the recipient of an import license. It is the difference between the domestic selling price (net of normal distribution costs) and the landed cost of the item (including tariffs and other charges). The premium is thus the difference between the implicit and the explicit tariff (including other charges) times the nominal exchange rate.

(4) Nominal tariff: The tariff — either explicit or implicit, as specified — on a commodity.

(5) Effective tariff: The explicit or implicit tariff on value-added as distinct from the nominal tariff on a commodity.

(6) Domestic resource cost: The value of domestic resources (evaluated at "shadow" or opportunity cost prices) employed in earning or saving a dollar of foreign exchange (in the value-added sense) when producing a good domestically.

APPENDIX F 2

DELINEATION OF PHASES USED IN TRACING
THE EVOLUTION OF EXCHANGE CONTROL REGIMES

To achieve comparability of analysis among different countries, each author of a country study was asked to identify the chronological development of his country's payments regime through the following phases. There was no presumption that a country would necessarily pass through all the phases in chronological sequence. Detailed description of the phases will be found in Bhagwati and Krueger, *Exchange Control, Liberalization, and Development: Expierence and Analysis* (publication forthcoming).

Phase I: During this period, quantitative restrictions on international transactions are imposed and then intensified. They generally are initiated in response to an unsustainable payments deficit and then, for a period, are intensified. During the period when reliance upon quantitative restrictions as a means of controlling the balance of payments is increasing, the country is said to be in Phase I.

Phase II: During this phase, quantitative restrictions are still intense, but various price measures are taken to offset some of the undesired results of the system. Heightened tariffs, surcharges on imports, rebates for exports, special tourist exchange rates, and other price interventions are used in this phase, but primary reliance is placed on quantitative restrictions.

Phase III: This phase is characterized by an attempt to systematize the changes which take place during Phase II. It generally starts with a formal exchange-rate change and may be accompanied by removal of some of the surcharges, etc., imposed during Phase II and reduced reliance upon quantitative restrictions. Phase III may be little more than a tidying-up operation (in which case the likelihood is that the country will re-enter Phase II), or it may signal the beginning of the removal of reliance upon quantitative restrictions.

Phase IV: If the changes in Phase III result in adjustments within the country so that liberalization can continue, the country is said to enter Phase IV. The necessary adjustments generally include increased foreign exchange earnings and gradual relaxation of quantitative restrictions. The latter relaxation may take the form of changes in the nature of quantitative restrictions or of increased foreign exchange allocations, and thus reduced premia, under the same administrative system.

Phase V: This is a period during which an exchange regime is fully liberal-ized. There is full convertibility on current account, and quantitative restric-tions are not employed as a means of regulating the *ex-ante* balance of pay-ments.

APPENDIX F 3

IMPORTANT GHANAIAN NAMES AND ABBREVIATIONS

Acheampong, Col. I.K. - Chairman of National Redemption Council, 1972–.

Afrifa, Brigadier A.A. - Member of National Liberation Council and Commissioner of Finance, later Chairman of National Liberation Council, 1966–1969.

Busia, K.A. - Prime Minister during entire period of elected Progress Party government, 1969–1972.

CBS - Central Bureau of Statistics.

CMB - State Cocoa Marketing Board.

CPP - Convention Peoples Party, founded and led by Nkrumah.

Danquah, J.B. - "Doyen" of Ghanaian politics, one of the early leaders of the independence movement.

Guggisberg, Sir F.G. - British Governor of the Gold Coast, 1919-1927.

Mensah, J.H. - Commissioner of Finance in the NLC government, and Minister of Finance in the Busia government, 1968–1972.

N¢ - New cedi, Ghanaian local currency unit. There have been a number of changes in the internal designation and scaling of the local currency unit, but to facilitate comparisons of values, throughout the period of this study we have converted all local currency values to N¢. These changes are entirely independent of changes in the foreign-exchange rate. Until July 1965 the local currency unit was the Ghana pound (£G), which was then replaced by the cedi (¢) at the rate £G 1.00 = ¢ 2.40. In February 1967 the cedi was replaced by the new cedi (N¢ at the rate ¢ 1.20 = N¢ 1.00, hence N¢ 2.00 = £G 1.00. In December 1971 the term "new" was dropped without a change in scaling: i.e., N¢ 1.00 = ¢ 1.00.

NLC - National Liberation Council, government from time of *coup* which overthrew Nkrumah to the inauguration of the Busia government, 1966–1969.

NRC - National Redemption Council, government from the time of *coup* which overthrew Busia government, 1972–.

Nkrumah, K. - Leader of Government Business, Prime Minister, and President of Ghana, 1951–1966.

PP - Progress Party, under leadership of Busia.

Valco - Volta Aluminum Company which established an aluminum smelter to use electricity from the Volta Dam project. Owned by Kaiser Aluminum (90 percent) and Reynolds Metals (10 percent).

VRA - Volta River Authority, the Ghanaian agency established to handle the entire Volta Dam project.

Bibliography

(1) Books, articles, and speeches

Acheampong, Col. I.K., Address to the nation, reproduced in the *Daily Graphic*, Accra, 18 January, 1972.

Acheampong, Col. I.K., Address to the nation, reproduced in the *Ghanaian Times*, 7 February, 1972.

Ady, P., "Supply Functions in Tropical Agriculture," *Bulletin of the Oxford Institute of Statistics*, Vol. 30, No. 2, May 1968.

Afrifa, Brigadier A.A., Devaluation announcement, reproduced in Bank of Ghana, *Report of the Board for the Financial Year Ended 30 June*, 1968.

Ahmad, Naseem, *Deficit Financing, Inflation and Capital Formation, The Ghanaian Experience 1960-1965*, Weltforum Verlag, Munich, 1970, p. 73.

Armah, Ayi Kwei, *Fragments*, Houghton Mifflin Co., Boston, 1969.

Bateman, M.J., "Supply Relations for Perennial Crops in Less Developed Areas," in C.R. Wharton, ed., *Subsistence Agriculture and Economic Development*, Aldine, Chicago, 1969.

Bateman, M.J., "Cocoa Study," IBRD, *Economic Report*, Vol. IV, mimeograph, Washington, D.C., March 1972.

Baumann, H.G., "Technological Change in Ghana's Economic Development," mimeograph, University of Western Ontario, January 1972.

Bhagwati, J.N., and A.O. Krueger, *Foreign Trade Regimes and Economic Development: Experience and Analysis*, forthcoming.

Birmingham, W., I. Neustadt, and E.N. Omaboe, eds., *A Study of Contemporary Ghana*, Vol. 1, *The Economy of Ghana*, Northwestern University Press, Evanston, 1966.

Blomqvist, A.G., and Walter Haessel, "The Price Elasticity of Demand for Ghana's Cocoa," *Economic Bulletin of Ghana*, Second Series, Vol. 2, No. 3, 1972.

Brown, Murray, *Theory and Measurement of Technical Change*, Cambridge University Press, Cambridge, 1966.

Brown, T.M., "Macroeconomic Data of Ghana," *Economic Bulletin of Ghana*, Second Series, Vol. 2, No. 1, 1972.

Busia, K.A., Address to the nation, reproduced in the *Ghanaian Times*, 28 December, 1971.

Cooper, R.N., "Currency Devaluation in Developing Countries," *Princeton Essays in International Finance*, No. 86, June 1971.

Corden, W.M., "The Structure of a Tariff System and the Effective Protective Rate," *Journal of Political Economy*, Vol. LXXIV, No. 3, June 1966, pp. 221-37.

Danquah, J.B., "The Akan Claim to Origin from Ghana," *West African Review*, Vol. XXVI, November and December 1955, pp. 963-70 and 1107-11.

Danquah Funeral Committee, *Danquah – An Immortal of Ghana*, Geo. Boakie Publ. Co., Accra, 1968.

Ewusi, Kodwo, "Notes on the Relative Distribution of Income in Developing Countries," *Review of Income and Wealth*, Series 17, No. 4, December 1971.

Frimpong-Ansah, J.H., "Stabilization and Development: Ghana's Experience," *Economic Bulletin of Ghana,* Second Series, Vol. 1, No. 1, 1970.

Grayson, L.E., "The Role of Suppliers' Credits in the Industrialization of Ghana," *Economic Development and Cultural Change,* Vol. 21, No. 3, April 1973.

Hicks, Norman L., "Debt Rescheduling and Economic Growth in Ghana," USAID Mission to Ghana, *Research Memorandum No. 8,* Accra, May 1969.

Johnson, H.G., "The Theory of Tariff Structure with Special Reference to World Trade and Development," *Trade and Development,* Institute Universitaire de Hautes Études Internationales, Geneva, 1965.

Kilby, Peter, *African Enterprise: The Nigerian Bread Industry,* Stanford University Press, Stanford, 1965.

Killick, Tony, "The Purposes and Consequences of Import Controls in Ghana," mimeograph, Accra, 1972.

Kontopiaat, "Commentary on the Devaluation," *Legon Observer,* Vol. 2, No. 19, 15 September, 1967.

Lawson, Rowena M., "Inflation in the Consumer Market in Ghana: Report of the Commission of Enquiry into Trade Malpractices in Ghana," *Economic Bulletin of Ghana,* No. 1, 1966, pp. 36-51.

Leith, J.C., "Export Concentration and Instability: The Case of Ghana," *Economic Bulletin of Ghana,* Second Series, Vol. 1, No. 1, 1971.

Leith, J.C., "The Competitive Performance of Ghanaian Exports in the Nkrumah Period," *Ghana Social Sciences Journal,* Vol. 1, No. 1, May 1971.

Leith, J.C., "Tariffs, Indirect Taxes and Protection," in H.G. Grubel and H.G. Johnson, eds., *Effective Tariff Protection,* GATT and Graduate Institute of International Studies, Geneva, 1971.

Leith, J.C., "The Effect of Tariffs on Production, Consumption and Trade: A Revised Analysis," *American Economic Review,* Vol. LXI, No. 1, March 1971.

Leith, J.C., "Substitution and Supply Elasticities in Calculating the Effective Protective Rate," *Quarterly Journal of Economics,* Vol. LXXXII, No. 4, November 1968.

Leith, J.C., "Across-the-Board Nominal Tariff Changes and the Effective Rate of Protection," *Economic Journal,* Vol. LXXVIII, No. 312, December 1968.

Mensah, J.H., Lecture delivered to the National Union of Students, Legon, 23 April, 1970.

Mundell, R.A., *International Economics,* Macmillan, New York, 1968.

Nathan Consortium for Sector Studies, *Ports Study: Transport,* 1970.

Nerlove, Marc, *Estimation and Identification of Cobb–Douglas Production Functions,* North-Holland, Amsterdam, 1965.

Newman, Peter, "Capacity Utilization and Growth," mimeograph, Accra, January 1970.

Nkrumah, Kwame, *Africa Must Unite,* first published 1963, new edition, International Publishers, New York, 1970.

Nkrumah, Kwame, *I Speak of Freedom,* Praeger, New York, 1961.

Omaboe, E.N., in W. Birmingham *et al.,* eds., *A Study of Contemporary Ghana,* Vol. I, *The Economy of Ghana,* Northwestern University Press, Evanston, 1966.

Omaboe, E.N., in *Legon Observer,* Vol. 2, 4 August, 1967, p. 16.

Progress Party, *Manifesto,* Accra, 1969.

Roemer, M., "Elasticities of Substitution in Ghanaian Industry," mimeograph, Accra, September 1971.

Roemer, M., "Relative Factor Prices in Ghana Manufacturing," *Economic Bulletin of Ghana,* Second Series, Vol. 1, No. 4, 1971.

Sharpston, M.J., "The Costs of Trade and Tariff Policy: The Case of Ghana," Cambridge University Department of Applied Economics, *Occasional Paper,* forthcoming.

Steel, W.F., "Import Substitution and Excess Capacity in Ghana," *Oxford Economic Papers,* New Series, Vol. 24, No. 2, July 1972, based on his unpublished Ph.D. thesis, M.I.T., 1970.
Stern, J.J., "Non-Cocoa Domestic Exports at Constant 1968/69 Prices, 1961—1970," mimeograph, Accra, March 1972.
Szereszewski, R., Chapter 4, in W. Birmingham *et al., The Economy of Ghana,* op. cit.
Tinbergen, J., *The Theory of Economic Policy,* North-Holland, Amsterdam, 1952.
Walters, A.A., *An Introduction to Econometrics,* Macmillan, New York, 1968.
Walters, Dorothy, *Report on the National Accounts of Ghana,* 1955—1961, mimeograph, CBS, Accra, 1962.

(2) Official publications

Agricultural Development Bank, *Organization and Functions,* Accra, 1968.
Bank of Ghana, *Notice to Banks,* irregular.
Bank of Ghana, *Quarterly Economic Bulletin,* quarterly.
Bank of Ghana, *Report of the Board for the Financial Year Ended 30 June,* annual.
Budget Statement, annual.
Capital Investments Board, *Annual Report and Accounts,* annual.
Central Bureau of Statistics, *Annual Report on External Trade of Ghana,* annual.
Central Bureau of Statistics, *Customs Duties Collections by Trade Classification, 1968,* unpublished.
Central Bureau of Statistics, *Economic Survey,* annual.
Central Bureau of Statistics, *External Trade Statistics,* monthly.
Central Bureau of Statistics, *Industrial Statistics,* biennial.
Central Bureau of Statistics, *Newsletter,* irregular.
Central Bureau of Statistics, *Quarterly Digest of Statistics,* quarterly.
Central Bureau of Statistics, *Statistical Year Book,* annual.
Cocoa Marketing Board, *Annual Report,* annual.
Cocoa Marketing Board, *Ghana Cocoa Marketing Board at Work,* Accra, 1968.
Commercial and Industrial Bulletin, weekly.
Customs and Excise Tariff, Accra, 1966.
Developments in the Ghanaian Economy between 1960 and 1968, Ghana Publishing Corporation, Accra, 1969.
Financial Statement, annual.
First Ghana Building Society, *Annual Report,* annual.
Ghana Commercial Bank, *Annual Report for the Year Ended 30th June,* annual.
Ghana Commercial Bank, *Monthly Economic Bulletin,* monthly.
Ghana's Economy and Aid Requirements in 1967, Accra, 1967.
Ghana's Economy and Aid Requirements January 1969—June 1970, Accra, March 1969.
International Monetary Fund, *Annual Report on Exchange Restrictions,* annual.
International Monetary Fund, *Balance of Payments Yearbook,* annual.
International Monetary Fund, *International Financial Statistics,* monthly and annual supplement.
Legislative Instrument 700, 2 July, 1971.
Manufacturing Industries Act, Act 356, 1971.
National Investment Bank, *Director's Report for the Year Ended 31 December,* annual.
National Liberation Council, *Decree 185,* 1967.
National Liberation Council, *Decree 325,* Gazetted 13 February, 1969.
Office of the Planning Commission, *Annual Plan for 1965,* Accra, 1965.
Report by the Auditor General on the Accounts of Ghana for the Period 1 January, 1965 to 30 June, 1966, Accra, March 1968.

Report of the Commission of Enquiry into Alleged Irregularities and Malpractices in Cennection with the Issue of Import Licences, Accra, February 1964.

Report of the Commission of Enquiry into Trade Malpractices in Ghana. Accra, January 1966.

Seven Year Development Plan, Accra, 1963, p. 93.

Two Year Development Plan: From Stabilization to Development for the Period Mid-1968 to Mid-1970, Accra, 1968.

United Nations, *Demographic Yearbook,* annual.

United Nations, *Yearbook of International Trade Statistics,* annual.

White Paper on the Report of the Commission of Inquiry into Alleged Irregularities and Malpractices in Connection with the Grant of Import Licences, W.P. No. 4/67, Accra, 1967.

Index